Chinese Law & Religion Monitor

中国法律与宗教观察

(07/01/2013—12/30/2013)　2013 年秋冬版

Chinese Law & Religion Monitor (07-12 / 2013)

December 2013 published by China Aid Association

1300 Pennsylvanian Ave. NW, Suite 700, Washington, DC 20004 www.ChinaAid.org

Tel: 202-213-0506

ISBN-13: 978-1493512294 ISBN-10: 1493512293

Printed in the United States of America

《中国法律与宗教观察》

对华援助协会出版　　www.ChinaAid.org

2013 年 07-12 月秋冬版

美国·华盛顿 ·1300 宾夕法尼亚大道，里根大厦 700 座

邮编：20004

本刊电话：202-2130506

ISBN-13: 978-1493512294 ISBN-10: 1493512293

美国境内出版印刷

中国法律与宗教观察

Chinese Law & Religion Monitor

(07/01-12/31/2013)

2013 年秋冬版

本期国际书号：

ISBN-13: 978-1493512294   ISBN-10: 1493512293

《中国法律与宗教观察》内含中国颁布、发行的涉及法律、政治、政府的政策文件、学术作品及其完整的英文译本。

本刊地址： 1300 Pennsylvanian Ave. NW

Suite 700

Washington, DC 20004

本刊电话： 202-2130506

总编辑： 傅希秋 牧师/博士（对华援助协会创办人兼会长，

俄克拉荷马卫斯理大学客座教授）

编辑： 单传航（中国家庭教会学者）

本刊编委会

傅希秋（对华援助协会主席-俄克拉荷马卫斯理大学客座教授）

大卫·艾克敏（David Aikman《时代周刊》前驻北京分社社长，Patrick Henry 学院历史系教授）

大卫•泰勒（对华援助协会首席法律顾问）

托尼•卡恩斯（《今日基督教杂志》资深记者）

斐斯•麦克唐纳（宗教与民主研究所）

黛博拉•斐克斯（国际人权政策顾问）

格兰姆•沃克（Patrick Henry 学院院长）

本刊编委会顾问委员

范亚峰： 中福圣山研究所所长　北京圣山教会负责人

迈克尔•赫尔维茨：哈德逊研究所

李柏光：北京共信律师事务所

李和平：北京高博隆华律师事务所

李劲松：北京忆通律师事务所

李苏滨：北京忆通律师事务所

滕彪：中国政法大学

林蔚：美国宾西法尼亚大学

王怡：成都大学

昝爱宗：自由记者和作家

张星水：北京京鼎律师事务所主任

总编按：

这是"对华援助协会"的最后一期《中国法律与宗教观察》。本期刊最初为季刊，后改为半年刊，共计发行了12期，始终致力于基于宗教和法律现象的理论创新，并将理论通过本协会的事业活动付诸于实践进行检验。这种科学的实证方法论与本协会秉持的基督教伦理相结合，对中国境内的宗教自由、法治和公民社会，不论是在思想概念上，还是在具体实践中，都起到了显著的推动作用。

本期2013年秋冬版的《中国法律与宗教观察》收录了4篇论文，主题是宗教自由与法律的关系以及两者相互作用而产生的社会文明效应，内容包括社会学角度的学术研究要点，基督教信仰-伦理对西方司法和自由市场的影响，对人类性本恶的基督教神学观是宪政原生原理，以及基督教信仰-伦理奠定了宪政并推动了人性自由且因此对社会文明的提升。

1、美国著名的华裔社会学家杨凤岗（普度大学）在《中国宗教自由的研究要点》中指出，中国宗教自由的课题研究富有潜力，但需要围绕概念、法规和公民社会这三个要点展开。在中国，基于无神论的宗教自由概念落后于宗教法规、党的政策，都严重干扰了宗教法规的实施，并导致与国际标准的差距。作为第三点，针对宗教团体和公民社会组织对宗教自由捍卫的研究，还严重匮乏。

2、中国著名宪政哲学家沈阳先生，在其《回应市场自由与社会公正的双重挑战：全球化中的基督信仰与西方法律传统》一文中论证说明道：启蒙时代，欧美兴起了各种以自由市场与宪政民主为批判对象的社会思潮与社会运动。一边是纳粹和斯大林模式兴起并挫败，一边是欧美社会福利主义兴起。在全球化浪潮中，东方国家整体上体现了相对英美原生宪政的特殊性。基督教及基督教会是否过时？基督教正义一元论是否仍旧适用？本文指出，基督教伦理及公共参与、系统而分层的司法正义，通过多个共同体间互动，规范了资本与劳工博弈，较好地实现市场自由与社会公正的平衡与节制。

3、生活在美国的著名中国家庭教会传道人、现为美国华人教会牧师的曼德（笔名；原名 Guo Baosheng）先生，在《基督教宪政与人性论》中指出，人性论——对人的道德本性和理性能力的判断，与宪政理论及实践息息相关。人在道德上的全然败坏、人自己获得救赎和达于完美的无能为力、人的理性和知识的有限性。总之一句话，人的"罪"的阐述，使基督教人性论超越其他宗教之人性论、自然而然地成为构建宪政理论的基础。本文从圣经文本、基督教教义神学和神学思想史三个角度，探讨基督教人性论对宪政观念的影响。在基督教教义神学中，人堕落后的全然败坏的本性、人获得救赎的神恩独作论强调了人性性恶论。就基督教神学思想史而言，无论是使徒保罗、奥古斯丁、阿奎那、马丁路德、约翰加尔文，都对人性恶及对其的监督制衡有精彩的神学阐述，深刻地影响了西方的伦理及政治思想史。

4、生活在美国的著名中国家庭教会学者单传航先生，在《文明的进程——基督教在中国的深化发展》一文中阐明，理想的社会文明生态当由四个板块组成，分别是神性信仰、伦理法典、宪政和人性自由。这种基督教文明模型说明了宪政不是无源之水，而是需要在信仰及其伦理的基础上才能正常运行，从而确保公民权利和人性自由。因此也可知，基督教文明是宪政和人权的原生环境。

综合而言，上述的 4 篇文章的中心论题是宗教（尤其是基督教）及其自由对宪政和社会文明的重要性。基督教会在中国的发展，包括官方许可的教会，特别是家庭教会的进一步成熟，必将广泛影响人们的信仰意识，产生社会进步思潮，从而推动中国政治生态、公民社会与法治的发展，并提升整体的社会文明。

正如有学者的研究指出，人类社会的腐败和强国的衰亡，如果不是因为外来干涉力量，总是始于内部社会的伦理道德腐败。基督教在西方缔造了辉煌的文明，但如今基督教所影响的伦理体系正受到前所未有的政治傲慢与民主偏见的挑战，并在欧美快速衰败，荒凉的事已经定了。

然而，中国社会正处于文明裂变并重组的时刻，基督教如春起之苗，又如大潮汹涌；这样的文明进程，岂能阻挡呢？不仅如此，令人惊奇的是，东正教伦理在俄罗斯通过教会的平台，已经在社会中复活，其文明的再度辉煌，指日可待。这样，一个人类历史文明的新纪元，其序幕正在徐徐揭开。

我们有幸目睹了这一罕见的历史现象。

总编：傅希秋 牧师/博士　对华援助协会创办人和会长

2013 年 12 月 31 日　　美国·德州·美德兰

中国宗教自由的研究要点

A RESEARCH AGENDA ON RELIGIOUS FREEDOM IN CHINA

杨凤岗

（原作刊登于英文刊物 THE REVIEW OF FAITH &
INTERNATIONAL AFFAIRS，2013 年 6 月 11 日）

　　中国的宗教自由问题，尽管不断出现在国际新闻、政府文件和非政府机构的报告中，但是尚未得到中外学者足够的研究。　在中国境内，许多学者看起来有些畏缩，境外的学者们在某种程度上也是如此。这是因为宗教自由的问题对于中国共产党当局来说，是过于敏感的政治话题，所以学者们用书面的方式讨论相关问题具有风险。一方面，在中国境内的学者们，普遍害怕有关宗教事务方面的写作会导致政治非难与代价。另一方面，中国境外的学者们有时候也担心，公开评论难以捉摸的中国宗教自由问题，可能会导致自己失去进入中国的机会。我相信，如果学者们能够配备合适的、理论性的和方法论的工具，中国的宗教自由可以成为一个富有潜在研究成果的话题。为了在这个领域中有所推进，当前需要解放思想。

　　首先，要遵循实事求是的原则。这是邓小平在 1970 年代后期所提倡的中国共产党政策的新原则，即在事实中寻找真理。学者们要致力于寻求事实，并发展解释事实的理论。寻求和解释事实，并不一定非要变得具有狭义的"政治"性质，即对抗性的或者是持有某种意识形态立场的。而广义的政治则是涉及到公共利益的事物，在这种含义上的政治性质则是每个人应有的责任。确实如此，按照正意分解，宗教自由的问题，在如今的世界里，是具有良知的公民所无法回避的问题。

再者，在宪政民主中，宗教自由可称为第一自由。也就是说，宗教自由先于其它自由，并且是作为其它自由的基础和源泉（参看Balmer, Grogerg 和 Mabry，2012 年）。我越来越相信，除非中国的精英们能够更好地理解并欣赏宗教自由，否则，中国的进一步民主化，即便是可能的，也将会是困难的。一方面，宗教自由的缺乏，妨碍着经济发展和社会秩序。从另一个方面来看，如果宗教自由先于其它自由到来，包括先于新闻出版和组织政党的自由，那么，在向民主的过渡中，就可能会少一些波动，多一些平稳 。

宗教自由的三个方面：认知观念、法律规章和公民社会

一些社会学家致力于发展宗教自由的理论，并进行跨国性的检验（Barker 2003; Richardson 2006; Grim 和 Finke 2011）。通过对中国和其它一些国家情况的综合考虑，我认为可以将与宗教自由相关的议题，在社会层面上分为三个主要的关注方面：认知观念、法律规章和公民社会。要想获得并保持宗教自由，这三个方面必须要整合协调起来；而这一点，在现实里的任何社会中，都是难以获得和保持的。

在西方，有一点是普遍的，即先有宗教自由观念，然后才成为由国家实施和受到民间组织及公民个人捍卫的法律。也就是说，在宗教自由法律的制定和实施之前，宗教自由的观念首先被公民们所接受，尤其是要被那些文化和政治精英们所接受。

在一些社会中，现代化进程是由外来的力量和挑战所触发的，因此公民们在接受宗教自由观念之前，成文的宗教自由法律从外在或国际团体照搬过来，或者是被强加过来。中国的情况就是这样的。尽管自中华人民共和国成立起，宪法中就包含了"宗教信仰自由"的条款，这项宪法权利却一直没有在实践中得到充分的实现。我认为，这主要是因为人们缺乏对宗教自由的一些基本理解和认知，尤

其是在政治和文化精英当中，同时，也是因为一个有意识捍卫宗教自由的公民社会尚待发育。

本文提出，需要在三个广阔的领域中，进行更多的实证性研究和理论性反思：变化中的**宗教法律规章**、中国精英和普通公民**对宗教自由的基本理解**、正在崛起的有助于更多自由的**公民社会**。在已有的论著中，有大量关于法律规章和政策的分析，这也许是因为成文的法律规章更容易直接拿来分析。然而，很少有对于公民们的宗教自由观念或与宗教自由相关的公民社会的分析研究。

对宗教自由的认知冲突和无神论种种

在今天的中国，政治和文化精英们并非完全不理解宗教自由的含义。事实上，在中国共产党的一些公开文件中，一些关于宗教自由的陈述是相当漂亮的。例如，中国共产党在 1982 年颁布的 19 号文件，标题是《关于我国社会主义时期宗教问题的基本观点和基本政策》，这个文件奠定了中国宗教政策的基石。文件中的其中一段是这样的：

> "宗教信仰自由，就是说：每个公民既有信仰宗教的自由，也有不信仰宗教的自由；有信仰这种宗教的自由，也有信仰那种宗教的自由；在同一宗教里面，有信仰这个教派的自由，也有信仰那个教派的自由；有过去不信教而现在信教的自由，也有过去信教而现在不信教的自由。"

这是一套关于宗教信仰自由的开明陈述，包括从一种宗教或宗派（Sect）皈依到另外一种宗教或宗派的自由。这与现代社会的基本理解以及联合国条约所反映的国际准则，具有相当的一致性，尽管在宗教实践和结社方面还缺乏清晰表述（Evans 2002）。

可是，紧接着这段开明陈述，这份中国共产党的政令却坚持说，共产党员必须是无神论者，应当坚持不懈地宣传无神论。换而言之，共产党员是被排斥在这项中国公民的宪法权利之外的，并且必须要坚守无神论。当然，如果共产党是一种人们可以自由选择参与或不参与的政治党派，这就不是问题了，因为公民可以加入或不加入这个党派。但事实上，由于共产党独掌政治权力，在中国几乎所有的社会单位和组织中，入党几乎成为任何人获得公职和领导职务机会的先决条件。任何有志于从事公职和进入领导岗位的人，几乎都别无选择，只能加入共产党，因此也就只得否定宗教，且宣布自己是无神论者。

在现实中，这种对共产党员坚持无神论的要求，几乎不可能执行。根据我们对 2007 年的《中国居民精神生活问卷调查》分析，其结果曾让中国学者和媒体震惊，大约有 84% 的共产党员和 85% 的公众，承认自己持有某些宗教性的信仰或者参与某些宗教性的实践。[1]

尽管无法将无神论信仰强加于共产党自己的成员，但这种无神论的意识形态却是共产党强制作为党国宗教政策的基础，针对所有中国公民。然而，不论当局如何辩解，这样的基础必然会颠覆 19 号文件中的那段有关宗教自由的开明陈述。共产党政策和宪法中的"宗教信仰自由"，与其无神论意识形态之间的冲突，是永久性的问题。这个问题不仅令普通公民和共产党员感到困惑，也让负责管理宗教事务的党国官员们，经常在这两条矛盾的原则之间，不置可否、首尾难顾、摇摆不定。

不仅如此，还存在着不同版本的无神论，分别是：战斗的无神论、启蒙的无神论、温和的无神论（杨凤岗 2011a）。中国官方的马克思主义意识形态的无神论认为，宗教的本质是人们的精神鸦片，

---

[1] 在北京的会议中我们公布了这些发现，许多在场的学者都表示惊讶。一些中国的记者们鼓起勇气在报纸和新闻杂志中对此进行了报道（Ning 2010; Zhu 2010）。同时，一位宗教研究学者评论说，即使是在剩余的 15-16% 的那些人当中，也不一定都是真实的无神论者。

并注定会最终消亡。尽管是采用同样的一套术语，不同版本的无神论是有所区别的，也就意味着对政策的不同导向。

启蒙的无神论认为，宗教是一种幻像或错误的意识，既是不科学的，也是落后的。因此，无神论的宣传有必要清除误导性的宗教观点。相比而言，战斗的无神论将宗教视为危险的鸦片和麻醉剂，是一种错误的政治意识形态，服务于剥削阶级和反革命分子的利益。因此，有必要用政治力量和手段来控制和消灭宗教（杨凤岗 2011a，第 46 页）。

不同版本的无神论对于中国的宗教自由的影响，是举足轻重的。尽管启蒙的无神论在 1982 年的 19 号文件中得到彰显，但是，战斗的无神论曾在"文化大革命"（1966-1976）中成为主导，并且通过共产党的组织机器——特别是通过为共产党员提干而提供阶段性培训的党校，已经持久固定下来。更重要的是，在负责宗教事务的党政官员中，转业军官所占的比例大，而他们对宗教的态度常常是粗暴而敌意的。鉴于战斗的无神论在中层和基层官员中的普遍存在，当听到一些地方官员压制宗教而中央官员却声称他们并没有许可这些违背政策的行为，就不令人感到奇怪了。由于启蒙的无神论和战斗的无神论在决策者和管理者当中同时并存，因此上述两种现象都是真实存在的。

换而言之，尽管基于启蒙的无神论的中央 19 号文件，已经赋予了相当的宗教自由，但是，由于负责宗教事务的中下级干部们倾向于坚持战斗的无神论，导致即使这种有限的自由也没有得到全部落实。在负责宗教事务的官员中，战斗的无神论和启蒙的无神论到底有多广泛呢？两者通过哪些方式影响政策的执行？要想回答这些问题，只能通过针对官员们的问卷、采访、观察和案例分析等进行实证性的研究。

在 2000 年，中共总书记江泽民在对统战部官员的一次讲话中，表达了对宗教认识的一种大胆的新观念。在强调无神论基调的同时，他提出，可能要在遥远的未来社会，阶级和国家按照所设想的那样消失之后，宗教才会消亡。基于这种观点，无神论的宣传和反宗教的运动，在当前是不必要的。这是一种很有意思的观念认知。然而，大部分的共产党理论家看起来是选择性地忽略了这个新提法，只有潘岳发表了一篇短文，题为《马克思主义的宗教观必须与时俱进》（2001），以响应江泽民的这次讲话。但是，马克思主义理论家们立刻群起而攻之，成功地将潘的观点消声。

然后在 2007 年，中央民族大学的一位宗教学者牟钟鉴，发表了一篇短文《中国社会主义者应当是温和的无神论者》。他在文中提倡说，温和的无神论者不信宗教，但是对宗教应当持理性的态度。这样的无神论者，不仅不应该参与反宗教的运动，还应该尊敬宗教信仰，持守现代社会中的文化多元观念，并保护人权。牟宣称这是马克思主义的正统宗教观。不幸的是，牟的温和无神论观念，遭到中共宣传系统的冻结。根据我从一些媒体编辑和学者那里了解得知，他们不再允许进一步公开讨论这一观点。

在 2002 年江泽民的任期结束之前，一些人希望在获得更多宗教自由方面有一些突破。例如，允许共产党员成为宗教信徒，正如允许商业雇主和资本家加入共产党一样。其中，后者在 2002 下半年的中共十六大中获得正式通过，但是前者却从未实现。由于战斗的无神论和启蒙的无神论在共产党理论家和干部当中的主导性，宗教政策难以有所突破，这是不可避免的。

自 1999 年，伴随着"镇压邪教"的运动，一系列的无神论宣传运动通过学校、共青团组织和媒体展开。作为"反邪教"运动的一部分，一份新的杂志《科学与无神论》在 2000 年创刊发行，成为战斗的无神论的喉舌和桥头堡。此外，中国社会科学院的马克思主义学院还建立了分支部门。这些宣传运动的影响不可低估。

通过我个人在中国不同地区的交流与观察得知，启蒙的无神论看起来在大学生、研究生和教授当中传播广泛，而战斗的无神论则在官员中比较普遍。要想验证这一评估，需要进行系统性的研究。我相信，在管理宗教事务的基层官员当中普遍存在的战斗的无神论，对于 1982 年 19 号文件的贯彻执行，起到了相当的牵制作用。因此，仅仅改变正式的法律规章，并不足以带来实质性的变化，还需要管理部门的负责人转变头脑。

宗教、迷信和邪教的区分

尽管中国的宪法和党的文件中确认了"宗教信仰自由"，中国当局却只承认五大宗教的合法地位，分别是佛教、道教、伊斯兰教、天主教和基督教。这种局限性来自于非常狭义的宗教概念，主要是基于坚持对"宗教与迷信"以及"宗教与邪教"的分类区别。由于声称迷信和邪教不属于宗教，因此他们就断言，宗教信仰自由并不适用于迷信和邪教信仰及其实践。

对宗教和迷信的区分，可以追溯到 19 世纪末和 20 世纪初。当时，在西方和日本列强的军事压力下，中国的精英们开始致力于中国的现代化（Goossaert, Palmer 2012; Nedostup 2010）。秉承这一现代主义者的传承，经过无神论意识形态的深化，中国共产党发动了一场又一场的运动，试图消灭迷信。1950 年代，所有没有被列入佛教或道教的传统民间信仰组织，都作为"反动会道门"而遭到禁止，而渗透到日常生活中的传统民间宗教信仰和活动，也被定为"封建迷信"。坚持这些信仰及其活动的人们，会受到公开的惩戒。即使在五大宗教当中，也经历了从内部对"封建迷信"和"反革命力量"的清除。[1]

在 1966 年，所谓的"文化大革命"，就是从"破除旧思想、旧文化、旧风俗、旧习惯"（破四旧）运动开始的。从"破四旧"扩展到破除所有宗教。红卫兵们响应毛的号召，洗劫了传统的建筑、

---

[1] 在政府认可的宗教中清除"迷信"的活动，至今仍然在进行（Blanchard 2013）。

烧毁了经书和古典书籍，打碎了古董文物。所有的宗教设施都被拆毁或关闭。在 1966 到 1979 年间的 13 年里，中国居民的任何宗教聚会都不合法。

1979 年，当邓小平开始领导中共将重点放在经济改革上，就解除了宗教禁绝。五大宗教的一些场所获得许可，重新开始宗教活动。但是，在正式的党国文件和陈述中，仍然重申了对宗教与迷信的区分（《人民日报》1979；Ya 1981）。[1] 在 1990 年代，党国的官方言论中，采纳了另外一个标签——"邪教"。这个标签，适用于传统的民间宗教派别和膜拜群体，从其它国家引入的新宗教运动，以及在中国出现的从基督教衍生出来的本土化宗派。1999 年，法轮功被政府认定为邪教，从此成为反邪教运动的主要打击对象。从那以后，其它一些主要的气功组织也被列为邪教（参看杨凤岗 2011a，114-118 页）。一些进口的新宗教运动包括"统一教"（Unification Church）、"上帝之子"（Children of God, The Family 又称"上帝的儿女"，"家庭"或"爱之家"）、"真佛宗"（True Buddha Sect），等等。一些新宗教，例如摩门教和巴哈伊教，虽然没有被正式定为邪教，但也同样遭到禁止。一些由基督教衍生出来的宗派仿佛是杂货包，其中包括基督教的异端例如"被立王"，"三班仆人"和"全能神"，同时也包括在某些教导和实践上极端、却被许多海外基督教视为正统的宗派，例如"全范围教会"和"华南教会"。目前被正式禁止的由基督教衍生的"邪教"有 16 个团体（参看杨凤岗 2011a，103-105 页）。

如今在中国，对于大部分人来说，包括精英分子和普通公民，看起来都接受了"宗教与迷信"以及"宗教与邪教"这两种区分，而对政府的镇压"邪教"或"迷信"，也没有什么异议。我认为，这不仅仅是人们对集权统治的默许，而且还说明党国之言论和认知

---

[1] 尽管如此，在今天，许多所谓的"迷信"信仰和活动，已经遍及全中国。根据报告，甚至超过一半的中层干部，都承认参与过某种形式的"迷信"（《科学时报》2007）。

观念已经被人们所接受而且内在化。这种不受质疑的认知观念，帮助维持了既有的有限宗教自由的现状。

在今天的中国，对于只许可五大宗教以及对某些宗教相对于其它宗教予以更严厉的限制，大部分人们对此看起来是并无异议。即使那些对现行宗教政策表达不满的人们，虽然他们呼吁修订政策，包括允许这个或那个的宗教合法化，但他们当中的大部分人，仍然认为一些限制是必要的，并且这些限制不需要对所有的宗教一视同仁。因此，我要再次强调，要想真正改变现状，仅仅对正式法律规章的轻度调整是不够的，还需要中国宗教事物相关人士的思想转变。

宗教法律规章：宪法和政令

西方的中国观察家以及在中国的法律学者，已经对中国正式的宗教法律规章进行了大量的分析。然而，很少有相关的研究，清楚地说明了中国法律规章的三种主要形式及其机制和份量：在中共文件和通告中表述的党的政策；人民代表大会通过的国家法律；中央、省级或地方政府或政府机关所制定颁布的行政条例。我们需要对这些政策、法律和条例的关系进行仔细的研究，因为它们的情况与民主社会中的法律规章是大不相同的。在中国，党的政策既是法律的基础又高于甚至凌驾于法律之上。"中华人民共和国的宪法是对党的政策的正式诠释（Potter 2003，324 页）。"全国人大对法律的修订过程复杂，但党的政策可以大笔一挥就调整了。行政条例本应该是对法律的落实细则，但在现实中却替代了法律本身，并且是为了执行党的政策。

许多针对中国法规的分析，都指出了 1982 年版《宪法》中宗教自由的有限性。该版《宪法》中的第 36 条：

> "中华人民共和国公民有宗教信仰自由。任何国家机关、社会团体和个人不得强制公民信仰宗教或者不信仰宗教，不得歧视信仰宗教的公民和不信仰宗教的公民。国家保护正常

的宗教活动。任何人不得利用宗教进行破坏社会秩序、损害公民身体健康、妨碍国家教育制度的活动。宗教团体和宗教事务不受外国势力的支配。"

重要的一点是，该宪法的第三十六条是关于"宗教信仰自由"，而不是"宗教自由"。一些中国的政治和文化精英们解释说，公民们可以在他们的头脑里自由信仰任何他们想要相信的，但是为了维持社会和谐的缘故，宗教活动和组织必须要受到限制（参看 Ye 1998，第 2-3 页）。从原则上来看，对宗教活动和组织进行某些限制，本身并不一定是对国际准则的违背，因为现代世界中的任何一个负责任的政府，都会制定一些宗教法规进行管理（Beaman 2003；Beyer 2003；Gill 2003）。第 36 条的问题在于，这里并没有定义什么才是"正常的宗教活动"，因此事实上就由宗教事务干部们来判定。由于不同地区有不同的诠释，那些持有战斗的无神论的基层干部们，就经常以此来对宗教活动进行严格限制。

宪法第 36 条的另外一个问题是，"法院在判决工作中，无法依靠或援引宪法的条款"（O'Brien 2010，第 376 页；同时参看 Kellogg 2009）。因为宪法不能直接在法院的案件中使用，所以违宪的案件就无法在法院中提起诉讼。这样的结果是，有关宗教自由的争端，只能由党政当局来解决，从而进一步令宪法对宗教信仰自由的保护打了折扣。

自 1980 年代，中共的一些高层领导人开始倡导逐渐加强法治，而不是任凭领导者个人意志的人治，因此，行政干部和宗教事务干部就开始呼吁制定宗教事务法（杨凤岗 2006；Ying 2006；Liu 2008）。然而，这样的努力并未产生结果，因为无法就一些基本的原则和概念达成共识，包括宗教的定义（哪些宗教应当被合法化）、正常的宗教活动（哪些活动应该获得许可）、宪法与中共政策的角色、全国人大与中共组织的角色、行政监督、政府支持的群众组织，以及周期性行政管理（O'Brien 2010）。宗教法没有制定出来，当局就采用了行政条例的手段。经过许多年对省级政府颁布的宗教"暂行条例"的试行，国务院终于颁布了综合性的《宗教事务条例》，并于 2005 年生效。

2005 年《宗教事务条例》的法规刚公布，卡尔森（Carlson）就发表了一篇分析论文，并附上了该条例全文的英语翻译。卡尔森提供了平衡的分析，指出"这项法规是一项进步，对于宗教团体与政府之间当如何通过申请和审批的过程进行交流，提供了更加清楚和更具有可预测性的依据"（第 758 页）。从另一方面来看，他也指出这份新条例中的严重缺陷：通过对宗教团体和场地进行登记注册的要求和对宗教人士、教义、活动的监督，通过对某些宗教团体的歧视，以及严厉而独断的惩罚手段，继续着国家对宗教的强势控制。

相形之下，Tong 在他的著作中（2010），首先承认了中国宗教政策的严重问题，然后又论证说 2005 年的宗教条例代表着在许多方面的重大进步：没有要求宗教组织拥护社会主义和共产党的领导；没有禁止基督徒在家里敬拜；承认了宗教团体的财产权利；增加了宗教团体的体制性自治；削减了国家干涉宗教事务的权力。他强调，这种进步之所以已经成为可能，是因为正统的共产主义意识形态已经让位，以及得益于党国所发动的系统性的政治和社会改革，旨在将国家与社会分离、保护人权和公民权利、依法治国。这是一种相对乐观的评估，认为此举是迈向更大宗教自由的结构性进步。

然而，通过研究自 2005 年以来的条例施行情况，荷马（Homer 2010，第 55 页）所看到的，只是 2005《条例》中的空洞许诺而已。

"未登记的(宗教)团体和他们的领袖，继续面对殴打、监禁、罚款和财物遭到破坏，以及其它经常性的可怕虐待。那些有足够勇气冒险来到政府办公室试图为他们的团体登记的领袖们，遭到回绝，有一些甚至因为登记前的宗教活动而被逮捕。事实上，许多代表家庭教会的律师们也被监禁，或者是因为'反政府的活动'而被吊销（律师）执照。"

也就是说，尽管 2005 年的宗教条例中包含了一些积极的潜力，但是却没有发挥出来。我再次指出，这种在贯彻落实方面的失败，当归咎于前面所探讨的认知观念的问题。

宗教法规：与国际准则相比较

在对宗教法规的研究中，有一个问题是：中国的宗教法规是否有所进步？如果将现行的政策与"文化大革命"（1966-1976）时期企图在整个社会中消灭宗教的政策相比，进步当然是显著的（Tong 2010）。如果与传统中国的帝王时期相比，中国现行的这些对宗教的限制，也是可以理解的（Qu 2011）。然而，当与中国也表示认可的国际法和国际准则进行对比，这些现存的法规明显是有亏欠的。

艾立克·克罗德纳（Eric Kolodner）在 1994 年发表的一篇文章中，回顾了有关宗教自由的国际人权体系，研究了中国省级的各样条例，并详细解释了中国当局是如何限制"宗教追随者的活动、敬拜的地点、新宗教场所的建造、对学生的宗教培训，以及宗教读物的发行。当局还限制宗教领袖的数量，禁止'迷信活动'，对违反者实施惩罚，建立政府部门专门负责宗教法规。"（Kolodner 1994，第 490 页）

在一篇研究文章中，包括对于最新的宗教条例的分析，作者依凡斯（Evans，2002）针对有关宗教自由的中国和国际的正式法律，进行了详细的分析。文章详尽地将中国宪法和其它正式法律，与联合国条约的具体内容进行对比，包括对《联合国宪章》产生的谈判过程和分歧、《世界人权宣言》、《公民权利和政治权利国际公约》，都进行了细致入微的探讨。作者认为，尽管中国政府针对有自残行为的邪教信徒或者掺杂民族政治的宗教，所进行的严格限制并非完全不合理，但是其打击力度，毫无疑问是过份的。这篇文章结论说（第 773-774 页）：

"尽管中国共产党不同时期的四部宪法都包含了对宗教和信仰自由的保护，但在现实中，宗教自由既没有得到以往中国政府的尊重，也没有得到现任北京当局的尊重……在国家控制宗教的领域里，中国违反了保护宗教自由的国际标准。中国已经宣称认可宗教自由的价值，正致力于其国际义务，平等对待所有的人，不论人们的宗教或信仰背景。然而，中国自己的记录表明，中国政府要做到言行一致，还有很长的路要走。"

在 2003 年，皮特曼·B·波特（Pitman B. Potter）在其文章中，对中国各种形式的宗教法规条例进行了全面综合性的分析，包括中共政策文件、宪法和相关法律、政府机关制定的条例、对不同宗教的不同待遇（同时参看 Cheng 2003）。波特认为，对宗教信仰和宗教实践的蓄意区分，事实上形成了一种挑战，不利于当局在维持政治控制的同时保持一种容忍的形象，以营建其合法性。他在结论中说："宗教管制法规一方面反应了党的政策允许对可接受的宗教活动赋予有限的自治，同时又试图压制对政治正统的挑战"（波特2003，第337页）。

近来，中国的一些法律学者们，开始共同致力于对正式宗教条例的研究分析。其中一个出色的例子是张千帆和朱应平的文章《中国的宗教信仰自由及其法律限制》（2011），两位作者分别是北京大学和华东政法大学的法学教授。在这篇发表于英语学术杂志中的文章中，两位作者对 2005 年的《宗教事务条例》进行了详细的批评，并总结说：

"总之，该条例设定了不少限制。在某些情况下，甚至是剥夺宪法第 36 条为公民提供的宗教信仰和实践自由，且没有提供足够的补救机制，来制衡宗教事务管理者们可能的权力滥用。"

这篇文章全面综合分析了《兵役法》、针对"邪教"的《刑法》部分、《民族区域自治法》、《消费者权益保护法》和《监狱法》中那些与宗教有关的问题。此外，作者还分析了一系列中国政府违反政教分离的案例，包括政府的系列干扰，针对宗教建筑的建设、宗教神学院或宗教学术、宗教职员的任命，以及宗教结社。文章的回顾与分析，很像是一份针对中共党国侵犯宗教自由的系统的起诉书。

在一篇重点分析有关邪教方面法律的文章中，作者朱国斌是一位在中国、香港和法国接受过高等教育并作为香港城市大学的教授，他的结论（2010，第500页）说，在现行的正式宗教法律中，有一些严重的问题：

> 首先，这种现行的法律系统，旨在规范、管理和控制宗教信仰及其活动。其次，对付非正常或非法宗教活动的法规和尺度过于严厉，有时候也是武断的。行政部门赋予了裁决权力，但是对于这重权力没有制衡，没有司法对于行政行为的控制。第三，政府采取的措施常常是过当的。最重要的是，对待边际案例或"非法"活动的制裁一般都是过于严厉，没有恩慈，没有容忍，以至于最终侵犯了信仰的权利以及其他的人身权利。

在上述两篇中国作者的文章中，有两点是值得注意的：首先，在现行的出版严格审查中，这些批评性的分析文章是不可能在中国国内发表的。其次，这样的文章在中国境外的学术杂志上发表，据我所知，这些作者并没有受到中国当局的惩罚，或者因此失去了入境中国进行研究的机会。这就说明了，在全球化的时代，是存在着相当程度的学术自由的，从而让中国境内外的学者们能够对中国的宗教自由进行严肃的研究，并在中国境外发表文章。

公民社会和宗教自由

在中国，公民社会与宗教自由之间的关系是复杂的，由地区性和民族性所导致的差异较大。一方面，"毫无疑问，在今天中国的两大重要少数民族——藏族和维吾尔族当中，人们在实践传统宗教的时候，受到了严重的限制……中国共产党对宗教与分裂主义之间的可能性联系高度紧张，于是就在西藏和新疆自治区，针对宪法所赋予的宗教信仰自由的权利，设置了许多限制"（Wellens 2009，第 434 页）。另一方面，对于在云南省的少数民族，"针对少数民族的宗教自由的整体形势，已经明显变得更加不同。可以这样认为，在某些情况下，少数民族在宗教实践方面的自由，要比他们的汉族邻居有更多的自由"（第 435 页）。一些民族性宗教，例如纳西族的东巴，得到地方政府的鼓励和支持，主要是为了旅游和经济的发展。确实如此，即使是"佛教和伊斯兰教，都能够踏上政府对少数民族（地区）旅游支持的节拍"，而且，地方政府支持重建了主要的寺院和清真寺（第 451 页）。更为重要的是，民族性宗教的复兴，已经坚固了这些民族的社会凝聚力和民族自豪感，因此也就让政府以保护的形式，让这些民族群体免受基督教传福音活动的影响。"在这个方面无条件的自由，一定会让这些本土宗教在不得不与全球化的'观点市场'竞争的时候，处于不利的状态（第 453 页）。"维伦斯（Wellens）在这里就宗教自由提出了一个重要的问题：如果保护少数民族的独特性是有价值的，或者是比保护宗教选择的自由更有价值，那么，政府对基督教和伊斯兰教的传教活动的限制，在中国和其它国家，就可以说是合理的。对于这个问题，需要仔细的研究和严肃的辩论。

关于在多数的汉族群体中的宗教，针对不同的宗教和中国不同地区的宗教生活已经有许多研究。例如，在现行宗教法规的管理下，在广东省一个客家村落的天主教，是怎样承受社会和政治压力而生存的（Lozada 2002）；在甘肃的一个偏远村庄，一个基督教会是怎样生存和复兴的（黄剑波和杨凤岗 2005）；在河北，是如何在一个已经遭遗弃几十年的古代佛教场所的废墟上重建一座佛寺，并兴旺成为在全国和国际范围内有影响的一个中心的（杨凤岗和魏德东2005）；一个在陕北的民间宗教庙宇，是怎样扩展成为多功能的社会中心的（Chau，2006）；以及在沿海城市温州的基督徒企业家，是如何与当局交涉，以扩大他们的社会空间进行宗教实践的（曹南来2011）。尽管这些研究并没有关注宗教自由本身，却对在当前社会和政治环境中宗教自由实践的不同程度，提供了丰富的描述和洞见性的分析。

对宗教和公民社会的研究，与宗教自由的议题有直接的关系，因为从概念上来讲，宗教自由是公民社会的组成部分。赵文词（Madsen 1998）作为这一领域的领先者，研究了正在崛起的中国公民社会中的天主教。一些近期的研究表明，一些明显的变化已经开始出现：家庭教会开始从避免讨论政治话题，转向积极地捍卫基督徒和其他人的宪法权利（洪朝辉 2012）。

通过分析网上出版物《爱筵》的内容，卫兰德（Wielander 2009）说明，一些家庭教会已经通过唤起权利意识而参与抗争，并致力于自由民主化。许多作者在《爱筵》中强调，"宗教信仰自由是上帝赋予的权利，也是中国宪法所保证的权利，所以没有任何级别低于全国人大的行政部门有权限制宗教自由（第 175 页）。"一些基督徒律师还受理了基督徒宗教自由权利受到侵犯的案例。"中国基督徒维权律师团"已经成立，其成员名单和联系方式也公布在《爱筵》上。这些成员都是这个国家里最著名的研究机构或大学中的宪法学者。因波登夫妇（Rana Siu Inboden 和 William Inboden 2009）也在《远东经济评论》（Far Eastern Economic Review）的报告中，提到基督徒律师的崛起和他们致力于宗教自由权利的工作。

情况确实如此，在 21 世纪的第一个十年里，宗教领域的一些新发展，令中国的公民社会活跃起来。例如，一些快速增长的大型城市教会的出现并走向公开化（杨凤岗 2011）。与此同时，基督徒企业家、教授、律师、记者、作家和艺术家在增加，他们组成团契或协会，并在公共领域谈论社会和政治问题。许多基督徒的书籍也得到出版（肯尼迪 2012），以及许多网上或印刷的基督徒杂志和刊物也纷纷发行。许多资料和数据也可以获得，从而有助于对宗教自由和公民社会在中国的发展进行更加实据性的研究。

结论

我提出了对一个社会中的宗教自由进行学术研究，必须关注三个尤其重要的方面：认知观念 、法律规章和公民社会。迄今为止，大部分针对中国宗教自由的学术关注点，主要是集中在正式的法规和中共的政策方面。宗教自由的认知观念研究是最近才得以开展的，因此尚需要通过问卷调查、访谈和内容分析，进行进一步的实证研究。研究最少的方面是，宗教团体和公民社会中的民间组织所进行的宗教自由的实践和捍卫，尽管许多针对宗教团体而进行的实证性研究，已经触及到了与宗教自由相关的话题。

许多议题都亟待研究。例如，对于不同类别的人们，尤其是文化和政治精英，在他们当中宗教和宗教自由的认知观念，可以通过问卷调查、访谈、对讲话和出版物内容的分析，来进行研究。官方许可的宗教团体、基督教家庭教会和天主教地下教会、藏传佛教徒、穆斯林少数民族、中国当局所称的那些邪教，在这些宗教团体当中，研究它们的宗教自由理念及其实践，应当是有趣的。同样，研究海外宗教团体、国际非政府组织和慈善机构、以及外国政府、国际组织等所采取的对话与制裁，对中国宗教自由所产生的实际影响，也应当是有趣的。

总而言之，如果学者们通过社会科学理论及方法，在其所分析过的事实中寻求真理，那么，中国的宗教自由就能够成为富有成效的研究话题。

参考资料

Balmer, Randall, Lee Grogerg, and Mark Mabry. 2012. *First Freedom: The fight for Religious Freedom*. American Fork, UT: Covenant Communications.

Barker, Eileen. 2003. "And the Wisdom to Know the Difference? Freedom, Control and the Sociology of Religion." *Sociology of Religion* 64 (3): 285–307.

Beaman, Lori G. 2003. "The Myth of Pluralism, Diversity and Vigor: The Constitutional Privilege of Protestantism in the United States and Canada." *Journal for the Scientific Study of Religion* 42 (3): 311–325.

Beyer, Peter. 2003. "Constitutional Privilege and Constituting Pluralism: Religious Freedom in National, Global, and Legal Context." *Journal for the Scientific Study of Religion* 42 (3): 333–340.

Blanchard, Ben. 2013. "China's 100 Million Religious Believers Must Banish Their 'Superstitions', says official." *The Independent*, April 21.

Cao, Nanlai. 2011. *Constructing China's Jerusalem: Christians, Power, and Place in Contemporary Wenzhou*. Stanford, CA: Stanford University Press.

Carlson, Eric R. 2005. "China's New Regulations on Religion: A Small Step, Not a Great Leap, Forward." *Brigham Young University Law Review* 2005 (3):747–797.

Chau, Adam Yuet. 2006. *Miraculous Response: Doing Popular Religion in Contemporary China*. Stanford, CA: Stanford University Press.

Cheng, May M. C. 2003. "House Church Movements and Religious Freedom in China." *China: An International Journal* 1 (1): 16–45.

Evans, Carolyn M. 2002. "Chinese Law and the International Protection of Religious Freedom." *Journal of Church and State* 44 (4): 749–774.

Gill, Anthony J. 2003. "Lost in the Supermarket: Comments on Beaman, Religious Pluralism, and What It Means to Be Free." *Journal for the Scientific Study of Religion* 42 (3): 327–332.

Goossaert, Vincent, and David A. Palmer. 2012. *The Religious Question in Modern China.* Chicago, IL: University of Chicago Press.

Grim, Brian J., and Roger Finke. 2011. *The Price of Freedom Denied: Religious Persecution and Conflict in the Twenty-First Century.* New York: Cambridge University Press.

Homer, Lauren B. 2010. "Registration of Chinese Protestant House Churches Under China's 2005 Regulation on Religious Affairs: Resolving the Implementation Impasse." *Journal of Church and State* 52 (1): 50–73.

Hong, Zhaohui. 2012. "Protecting and Striving for the Rights to Religious Freedom: Case Studies on the Protestant House Churches in China." *Journal of Third World Studies* 29 (1): 249–261.

Huang, Jianbo, and Fenggang Yang. 2005. "The Cross Faces the Loudspeakers: A Village Church Perseveres Under State Power." In *State, Market, and Religions in Chinese Societies,* edited by Fenggang Yang and Josphe Tamney, 41–62. Leiden: Brill Academic.

Inboden, Rana Siu, and William Inboden. 2009. "Faith and Law in China." *Far Eastern Economic Review,* September 4.

Kellogg, Thomas. 2009. "The Death of Constitutional Litigation in China?" *China Brief* 9 (7): 4–6.

Kennedy, John W. 2012. "Discipling the Dragon: Christian Publishing Finds Success in China." *Christianity Today,* January 20.

Kexue Shibao (Science Times). 2007. *"yiban yishang xianchuji gongwuyuan nan ju 'mixin'"* ["More than Half of Public Service Officials at the County or Above Levels Have Difficulties to Resist 'Superstitions'"]. Accessed May 11, 2007.

http://www.sciencetimes.com.cn/htmlnews/20075111193241656179151.html

Kolodner, Eric. 1994. "Religious Rights in China: A Comparison of International Human Rights Law and Chinese Domestic Legislation." *Human Rights Quarterly* 16 (3): 455–490.

Liu, Peng. 2008. "Zhongguo zongjiao fazhihuade lichen" ["The Course of Legalisation of China's Religions"]. In *Blue Book on China's Religions 2008*: 261-277, edited AQ7 by Jin Ze. Beijing: Social Science Documents Publishing House,

Lozada, Eriberto, Jr. 2002. *God Aboveground: Catholic Church, Postsocialist State, and Transnational Processes in a Chinese Village.* Stanford, CA: Stanford University Press.

Madsen, Richard. 1998. *China's Catholics: Tragedy and Hope in an Emerging Civil Society.* Berkeley, CA: University of California Press.

Nedostup, Rebecca. 2010. *Superstitious Regimes: Religion and the Politics of Chinese Modernity.* Cambridge, MA: Harvard University Asia Center.

Ning, Er. 2010. "Magic Thrives when Religion is depreciated: Chinese Beliefs and the Reconstruction of Ethics and Morality." *Nanfang Metropolis News* (Guangzhou), August 8.

O'Brien, Roderick. 2010. "Two Chinese Commentators on the Slow Progress towards a Law on Religions." *China: An International Journal* 8 (2): 374–385.

Potter, Pitman B. 2003. "Belief in Control: Regulation of Religion in China." *The China Quarterly* 174(2): 317–37.

Qu, Hong. 2011. "Religious Policy in the People's Republic of China: An Alternative Perspective." *Journal of Contemporary China* 20 (70): 433–448.

Renmin ribao (People's Daily). 1979. "Zongjiao he fengjian mixin" ["Religion and Feudal Superstition"], March 15.

Richardson, James T. 2006. "The Sociology of Religious Freedom: A Structural and Socio-Legal Analysis." *Sociology of Religion* 67 (3): 271–294.

Tong, James W. 2010. "The New Religious Policy in China: Catching up with Systemic Reforms." *Asian Survey* 50 (5): 859–887.

Wellens, Koen. 2009. "Negotiable Rights? China's Ethnic Minorities and the Right to Freedom of Religion." *International Journal on Minority and Group Rights* 16: 433–454.

Wielander, Gerda. 2009. "Protestant and Online: The Case of Aiyan." *The China Quarterly* 197 (1): 165–182.

Ya, Hanzhang. 1981. "Carry Out the Policy of Freedom of Religious Belief and Oppose Feudal Superstitious Activities." *Guangming ribao* (Guangming Daily),April 20.

Yang, Fenggang. 2010. "Quantifying Religions in China." Paper presented at the seventh annual conference for the social scientific study of religion in China, Beijing, July 26–27.

Yang, Fenggang. 2011a. *Religion in China: Survival and Revival under Communist Rule*. New York: Oxford University Press.

Yang, Fenggang. 2011b. "Chinese House Church Goes to Public." Sightings, an online magazine published by Marty Martin Center for Advance Study of Religion at University of Chicago, May 12.

Yang, Fenggang, and Dedong Wei. 2005. "The Bailin Buddhist Temple: Thriving Under Communism." In *State, Market, and Religions in Chinese Societies*, edited by Fenggang Yang and Joseph Tamney, 63–87. Leiden: Brill Academic.

Yang, Junfeng. 2006. "Guowuyuan 'zongjiaoshi tiaoli' shuping [An Evaluation of the State Council 'Religious Affairs Regulations']." In *Blue Book on China'sLegal System 2005*, edited by Li Lin et al. Beijing: Social Science Documents Publishing House.

Ye, Xiaowen. 1998. "Zongjiao yu pufa – Zongjiao gongzuo pufa duben xu" ["Religion and the Propagation of Legal Knowledge"] (Preface). In *Zongjiao gongzuo pufa duben* [A Reader in the Promotion of Legal Knowledge in Religious Affairs Work]:1-15, edited by Policy and Regulation Department of the State Council Religious Affairs Bureau. Beijing: Religious Culture Press.

Ying, Fuk-Tsang. 2006. "New Wine in Old Wineskins: An Appraisal of Religious Legislation in China and the Regulations on Religious Affairs of 2005."*Religion, State & Society* 34 (4): 347–373.

Yue, Pan. 2001. "Marxist View of Religion Must Advance with the Times." *Newspaper of Shenzhen Special Zone*, December 16.

Zhang, Qianfan and Yingping Zhu. 2011. "Religious Freedom and Its Legal Restrictions in China." *Brigham Young University Law Review* 2011 (3):783–818.

Zhongjian, Mou. 2007. "The Chinese Socialists Ought to be Mild Atheists." *China Ethnic News*, January 16, p. 6.

Zhou, Hualei. 2010. "Chinese Believing Gods." *China News Weekly* (Beijing), August 30.

Zhu, Guobin. 2010. "Prosecuting 'Evil Cults:' A Critical Examination of Law Regarding Freedom of Religious Belief in Mainland China." *Human Rights Quarterly* 32 (3): 471–501.

回应市场自由与社会公正的双重挑战：

全球化中的基督信仰与西方法律传统

作者：沈阳

（文载《正义一元论：从民情到法政》，武汉大学出版社 2012 年版，第 193-235 页）

近代社会兴起了各种以利伯维尔场制度与宪政民主制度为批判对象的社会改良与革命运动。围绕着这个主题，几乎所有思想家都参与了一场持续数世纪的大讨论和大辩论：涉及了利伯维尔场理论的利弊、社会公正是否可能、自由与公正的哲学关系，以及人类目前已经实行的各种制度能否、如何有限避免已经出现的那些现象，形成了不同的社会理论（自由主义、社会主义和保守主义），经济制度则有计划经济和市场经济之分；市场经济又可分为凯恩斯学派、芝加哥学派、奥地利学派、供给学派与货币学派，等等。

有教堂的'开放社会''"与"基督教—法政系"这种复合型结构的分析范式，曾经以英美立宪时期的政治发展为例，尝试揭示"开放社会"从个体价值、小共同体到政治国家的运行逻辑。这个解说范式，是否仍旧适用于这些国家的经济生活？如果适用，经济生活中各个社会主体又是如何互动的，这种互动关系又是如何构建出了今天的市场文明？针对上述思考，本文试图指出，"开放社会"的公共精神、基督教的市场伦理、以普通法为主的司法正义，通过市场共同体与其他共同体的互动，以多维而体现为正义一元论的方式规范了资本与劳工的博弈，能够相对较好地实现市场经济与社会公正的平衡。

一、小共同体体系与资本主义发展：

法学家对社会学家的一段学术批评

如果说马克思致力于批判西方传统和现代性发展，韦伯则在另外一个意义上对西方传统进行了勤奋的捍卫。虽然韦伯的学术研究中，很少直接批判马克思主义，可我们却很容易在韦伯思想中发现马克思主义这一靶子。韦伯最知名的贡献体现在宗教社会学和政治社会学学术里。与"宗教是人民的鸦片[1]"的论断相反，韦伯在《新教伦理与资本主义精神》中指出某些禁欲的新教教派（尤其是加尔文教派），基督教义逐渐演变为争取理性的经济获利，以此表达他们受到耶稣基督的祝福。韦伯还主张，受到这种理性教义基础扶助的资本主义很快便会发展得越来越庞大，并且与原先的宗教产生矛盾，到最后宗教便会无可避免地被抛弃。因此，韦伯所关注的与其说是成熟的资本主义精神，不如说是转型时代的（即近代的）资本主义精神。除了《新教伦理与资本主义精神》之外，韦伯还著有《中国的宗教：儒教与道教》、《印度的宗教：印度教与佛教的社会学》、《古犹太教》，对此进行了较为全面的论证。

韦伯的政治社会学研究也延续了这样的观点。在《政治作为一种职业》这一演讲里，韦伯将国家定义为"拥有合法使用暴力的垄断地位"的实体[2]。韦伯还认为，一个政治家不能被视为是"真正道德的基督徒"，也不可能如同"山上宝训"里所叙的那样高尚无私。现实政治中既没有这样的圣人型政治家，又不可能为这样的政治家提供活动空间。一个政治家应该采纳的伦理是道德与政治目标的权衡（Proportion）、负责任的伦理(Responsibility)、对他的职业拥有强烈的情感(Passion)，同时学会将自己的情绪好恶与实际目标区

1（德）马克思：《黑格尔法哲学批判·导言》，1843—1844 年，《马克思恩格斯选集》第 1 卷，人民出版社 1995 年版，第 2 页。

2（德）马克斯·韦伯：《论经济与社会中的法律》，张乃根译，中国大百科全书出版社 1998 年版，第 43 页。

隔开来(Distance)。由此，韦伯提出了三种正式的政治支配和权威的形式：魅力型支配（家族和宗教）、传统权威（宗主、父权、封建制度）以及官僚型支配（现代的法律和国家、官僚）[1]。通过了权威的三种合法性划分，韦伯将政治从神坛上拉下来，体现了其走向了世俗化的基督教精神。

由此，韦伯为基督新教辩护。"在我看来，常被人们信奉的关于经济在某种意义上是因果关系链条中终点的历史唯物主义的观点，作为科学的命题是彻底总结了"[2]，西方法制史学者伯尔曼这样评价韦伯，"虽然他随后作为社会学家，尤其是政治和宗教社会学学家取得了名望，但他的社会学理论总是借重于法律史，他最重要的著作有一本是法律学。比较之下，马克思虽然也（先韦伯60年）在法律方面取得了第一个学位，并在深受德国最伟大的法学家卡尔·弗雷德里克·萨维尼影响的柏林大学研究法律，但他不仅背版了萨维尼探讨法律的历史方法，而且彻底反对法律史和法学。"[3] 如果承认伯尔曼对马克思的批评中所说的是事实，并且承认马克思的核心关切不在司法正义而在其他方面这一显明事实，我们便不难理解，缘何马克思作为一个跨学科的百科全书型思想家具有如此鲜明的局限性；也就明白追求人类的自由解放这一套显性道德和愿望道德迟迟难以发展为体现法政文明的隐性道德和义务道德，从而发

---

1 本段总结于：（德）马克斯·韦伯：《论经济与社会中的法律》。

2 Proceedings of the First Conference of German Sociologis-ts,1910,quoted in Max Weber, Economy and Society,ed.Guenther Roth and Claus Wittich(New York,1968),I,lxiv.转引自：（美）哈罗德·J.伯尔曼：《法律与革命——西方法律传统的形成》第 535 页，贺卫方、高鸿钧、张志铭、夏勇译，法律出版社 2008 年版。

3（美）哈罗德·J.伯尔曼：《法律与革命——西方法律传统的形成》，贺卫方、高鸿钧、张志铭、夏勇译，法律出版社 2008 年版，第 538 页。关于马克思的这一部分：see Donald R.Kelley,"The Metaphysics of Law:An Essay on the Very Young Marx,"American Historical Review,83(April 1978),350-367.

展为体现制度—程序正义的正义一元论体系。比较下来，韦伯显然优秀了很多：在韦伯的思考与研究中，法律与正义始终是人类挥之不去的文明要素，且必须转化为制度文明。

然而，由于未能在自己的思考体系中明确指出，深受加尔文思想影响的基督教新教伦理的世俗化成果，与其所主张的核心价值，究竟是多元的正义观还是基督教正义一元论在不同秩序时空中的两种不同表现，作为世俗主义者和现实主义者，韦伯就与马克思殊途同归。在伯尔曼这位法学家看来，"韦伯也认为西方的法律是资产阶级的法律、资本主义的法律，或用韦伯特殊的术语讲，是官僚政治的法律、形式合理的法律。"[1] 这样，"韦伯最终把观念和法律归源于政治，而把政治归源于统治和强制。在韦伯看来，神授能力、传统和合理性是为更有效地实行强制的政治权威提供合法性的主要源泉"。[2] 与具有浓厚超越主义精神和理想主义色彩的加尔文主义（基督教正义一元论是其主张之一）相比，韦伯的这套综合了信仰-经济-政治的分析范式，实际上更显明了路德宗的现实主义和国家主义品质。

就这样，韦伯展开了一场大跨越，从新教精神的一个肯定者和推崇者，发展为了一个在民族国家的政治秩序的倡言者，开始了其政治思想的逐步走向多元论的历程。霍布斯所言的"利维坦"是人权保障的带刀护卫，本身就存在自由与强制之间的绝对困境，能够联结这二者的只有落实在法律中的正义。对"祛魅化"和政治的技术理性在社会学意义上的肯定，使得韦伯不可避免地表现出了进化主义倾向。韦伯反对基于社会进化论的马克思主义唯物史观，却又拒绝委身于加尔文式的以基督救恩为中心的圣经史观（即上帝护理史观）。在世俗主义（缺乏基督教的末世盼望情结）之下，一旦确

1《法律与革命——西方法律传统的形成》，第 539 页。

2 同上，第 540 页。

立了为现代性辩护和参与为中心的价值观，韦伯必然被接近自然神论的启蒙主义所裹挟。韦伯明显超前于德国同时代的学者。早在"一战"结束前，这位"魏玛宪法之父"，便结合当时德国的国情对议会制进行了深入的研究。

韦伯认为德国社会缺乏"有组织的民主"或"代议制民主"，却有丰富的非民主煽动家和群众暴乱传统。他进一步指出，民选的国家元首与民选的议会之间必然会发生冲突，即"大众民主"与"代议制民主"之间的不兼容性。不过，议会至少可以稳定权力关系，使总统权力地位有受控性，保留民治的法律手段来反抗总统，改进官僚体系的有序方法，当总统失去大众信任时用和平手段消灭恺撒式的独裁者。[1] 然而，在韦伯的支持下，宪法第48条赋予总统"公众秩序与安全受到严重骚扰或威胁"时可以"采取任何必需的政策"。第48条作为紧急法令，但在1933年前它常常被用来在没有议会的批准下通过法案，故此令纳粹党更容易完成一体化，例如以第48条为基础通过了国会纵火法令。

如果不对学术或者思想简单地寄予自由民主这样的政治转型期望，本来是相对安全的。这就涉及对启蒙运动及其道德决断的评价问题。相对各种蒙昧状态，启蒙运动的进步意义自不待言。比韦伯更早的康德这样定义启蒙："就是人类摆脱自我招致的不成熟。不成熟就是不经过别人引导就不能运用自己的理智。如果不成熟的原因不是在于缺乏理智，而在于不经别人的引导就缺乏运用理智的决心与勇气，那么这种不成熟就是自我招致的。""自由"指的是，"亦即在所有问题上都公开利用一个人的理性的自由"，"理性的公共使用就是任何人作为一个学者在阅读整个世界的公众面前对理性的运用"，"这样一个契约，为了一劳永逸地阻止人类想一切进一步的启蒙而缔结，即使竟然得到最高的权力、得到国会、得到

---

1 Max Weber,Parlament und Regierung im neugeordneten Deutschland,in Max Weber Gesamtausgabe,Band 15,Hrsg.von Horst Baier…,1984 J.C.B.Mohr（Paul Siebeck）Tübingen,S.538ff.

最庄严的和平条约的确认，却完全是空洞无效的"，"断然拒绝启蒙，那就无论对本人，尤其是对于后代，都可以说是侵犯且践踏了人类的神圣权利"，"我已经把启蒙的要点，亦即人类对自我施加的不成熟状态的挣脱，主要放在宗教问题上……在宗教问题上的不成熟不仅是最有害的而且是最无耻的"。[1]

然而，类似叙述的吊诡之处也可能被忽视：启蒙也许能够作用于社会现实，并且改变社会结构，但是这种转变，究竟是因启蒙这种道德决断被改变，还是基于其他因素，对此人们无法定量分析，也就是难以用精确的自然科学意义上的统计方法予以准确说明。"耶和华不像人看人，人是看外貌。耶和华是看内心"（《撒母耳记上》16:7）。这种对人的"成熟"程度、"理性"程度的判断，由于缺乏明确的标准而致的不确定性的认识，几乎是人类文明的基础知识。正是基于这个古老的信念，当对人的内心对诸如促进法政这样的功能寄予太大的期望，并且论证启蒙的至高无上的地位时，启蒙的严重问题就凸显了。韦伯作为一个宗教社会学家，当他对基督宗教的这种世俗性、理性化色彩（并不是挪亚之约所承诺的"万事互相效力"这样的神圣护理）对德国进步寄予更大的期望之时，由于最后寄予了道德决断（几乎完全存侥幸心理，这既是一种英雄史观，又是一种机遇史观，类似中国人所说的"圣王创世"、"天命靡常"），就犯了同样的错误。

这里涉及关于博弈论的基础知识。有个基本预设，就是资源的绝对稀缺，人的理性的绝对有限、欲望的绝对无限（如果有限，那是自我审查和自我节制的结果），信息的绝对不对称。因此，人类社会到处存在着超出人们想象的"两难困境"。"启蒙"或者宗教对人的道德心智的提高，作为知识拓展和培养信息获取能力的一种方式，的确能够减少"两难困境"之中的非理性成分，帮助人们创

1（德）康德：《对这个问题的一个回答：什么是启蒙？》，见（美）詹姆斯·施密特编，徐向东、卢华萍译：《启蒙运动与现代性——18 世纪与 20 世纪的对话》，上海人民出版社，2005 年版。

造并维护"纳什均衡"和"合作博弈"的理性局面。然而，这仅仅是一种可能。不仅如此，人类由于自身的绝对有限，在转型期间，在新旧政权交替之间，常常被迫陷于某种丛林战争。这个时候的"两难困境"，并不仅仅是囚徒A与囚徒B之间的博弈，事实上是更多主体参加的、更为广泛的博弈。例如，"一战"之后的德国，既有国内的宗教与民族矛盾、不同政治势力之间的矛盾，还有本国与更多国家之间的矛盾，以及本国面临的经济危机（涉及人与自然之间的矛盾）；如果是社会个体，还有他与周围人之间的矛盾，与自身小共同体之间的矛盾。可以说，迄今几乎所有成功的转型，就是类似的多种博弈互相交织的博弈的"合作解"。

换而言之，韦伯所犯的，乃是反对基督信仰的启蒙运动形成以来自由主义启蒙系在关于道德决断与政治转型之间本身并无正相关关系的经典疏忽。其本质乃是人类英雄主义。正是在《政治家的职业和使命》、《政治作为一种职业》这样的道德决断精神的指引下，韦伯对第一次世界大战和当时帝国扩张的看法，随着战局的每况愈下而改变。在1918年，作为德国休战委员会的一名成员，韦伯前往凡尔赛会议代表德国谈判。后来又参与了魏玛共和国宪法的起草委员会。魏玛德国实行议会民主制。国会内小党林立，每个小党都占有一定的议席，这些政党秉持不同的政治观点，由于外在环境的千变万化（如恶劣的经济局面、严峻的边疆危机、国内频繁的工人革命运动、战败国的外交危机），几乎难以取得有效的共识，导致国内很难形成稳定而强大的政府。例如，1930年3月底，社民党的赫曼•穆勒（Hermann Müller）领导下的魏玛最后一届多数政府，仅仅因为一场关于整顿失业保险的一场争论，就破裂了。正是出于对战乱的恐惧，当时韦伯支持在宪法中加入授权紧急戒严的"第48号条款"。

我们暂时搁置对韦伯学说和魏玛宪政的种种基于特定问题意识的议论，而是对比英国、美国立宪时期的民情和制度成因加以分析。针对韦伯病症，伯尔曼指出："应把法律看作物质基础的一部分还是意识形态的上层建筑的一部分。对这个问题的回答是：在西方，法律既是前者的一部分又是后者的一部分——也就是说西方法律表明这种两分法本身是错误的。……法律实质上既是（both）物质的又是（and）意识形态的这一事实是与以下事实相联系的：法律既是（both）从整个社会的结构和习惯自下而上发展而来，又是（and）从社会中的统治者们的政策和价值中自上而下移动。法律有助于这两者的整合。因此，至少在理论上讲，被马克思看作革命动因的社会—经济条件与政治—道德的意识形态之间所存在的冲突，可以通过法律解决。"[1] 然而，法律究竟在何种层面上与一个国家的政治文化、哲学与信仰互动起来？这是比较政治学和比较法学的一个重要课题。因此必须在英美和以德法为代表的欧陆之间，寻找出社会结构和民俗民情的差异。

正是在丰厚的新教民情和小共同体基础之上，在一种广泛而深刻的正义一元论共识之下，也就是说，正是具备——从小共同体的社会结构到正义一元论的观念结构——的双重基础，英美这样的国家才顺利地而不至于更持久动荡地转型。并不是说这些国家没有道德决断，英国历史上克伦威尔的清教徒革命和它的斗争对象，就一直试图进行道德决断。美国历史上的潘恩和杰斐逊，也可以确定是道德决断的典型。杰斐逊这位《弗吉尼亚宗教自由法案》和《独立宣言》的起草者反复指出，"自由之花必须时时用爱国者和暴君的血来浇灌"，"但愿每隔二十年来一次这样的叛乱"[2]。《常识》之后，潘恩也有类似的感言。对类似的叙述，中国人一定非常熟悉。毛泽东就曾经说过，为了防止官僚专制，"文化大革命"七八年应该再来一次。官僚专制的确令人反感，为此底层社会必须动员起来，直接辅助革命战争，以促进人的尊严？依据杰斐逊的逻辑，倘若没

---

1 《法律与革命——西方法律传统的形成》，第 545—546 页。

2 （美）梅利尔·D·彼得森编：《杰斐逊集》，刘祚昌、刘红风译，北京三联出版社 1993 年，第 1021 页。

有超越性的临在，美国不是要周期性陷于革命和"维稳"交替的丛林战争，最终形成西方式的"血酬定律"（这一定律为中国历史学者吴思发现）？

二、劳工阶层抗争与资本的文明化：

公正评价各种社会主义思潮及运动

社会主义从理论走向抗争，从抗争走向建制，改变了人类发展的进程。批判马克思学说，尤其成为20世纪西方政治哲学的重大使命。伯林在他的《马克思传》1963年版的序言中，高度评价波普尔的《开放社会及其敌人》。在波普尔看来，马克思许多重要的预言已经被历史证伪了；作为一种历史决定论，马克思主义必将导致对社会实践做出整体的和长远的计划安排。对社会主义批判最系统且影响最大的当属哈耶克。可以根据系列著作的书名总结哈耶克学说：社会主义在知识论上"致命的自负"，违反"自由秩序原理"，破坏"个人主义和经济秩序"，从而产生专制极权，导致"通往奴役之路"。

然而，这个世界的确不是只有苏联东欧和一些亚洲国家的斯大林模式。某种以社会公正为宗旨的思潮与理想（不是罗尔斯那种以公平正义为导向的自由主义思潮，而是各种社会主义思潮，如民主社会主义和社会民主主义思潮），以及由此发展而来的社会主义政党所领导的社会主义运动，也不是必然导致专制极权。以北欧的瑞典为例。"一战"前夕，从马克思主义的支持者里分离出来了民主社会主义。社会民主主义者与民主社会主义者有共同的国际组织：社会党国际。俄国革命后，"社会民主主义"成了非革命路线的社会主义者专有的称呼。现代的民主社会主义强调通过立法过程以改革资本主义体制，使其更公平和人性化。

社会民主主义和民主社会主义的共同组织为社会党国际。社会党国际认为民主社会主义为代议民主制的一种模式，能够解决在一般自由民主制里所产生的问题。社会党国际强调："民主"不只是个人的自由，也同时包含免于被歧视和被控制了生产工具的资本家滥用政治权力的自由；"平等和社会正义"不只是在法律前人人平等，也包含在经济和文化上的平等，同时也要给予身心残障和其他社会条件不佳的人平等机会；最后，要团结起来同情那些遭受不公正和不平等待遇的人。实行民主社会主义的典范国家是瑞典。高税率下，瑞典经济仍然具有相对于另外一些国家的活力；经济结构也相当健全，从独资公司到跨国公司，同时保持世界上最高的平均寿命、低失业率、低通货膨胀、低国债、低婴儿死亡率和低生活费用，拥有较高的经济增长。事实上，英国工党、澳大利亚工党、法国社会党、奥地利社会民主党、比利时社会党、德国社会民主党、荷兰工党、挪威工党的执政，都没有如哈耶克的社会与经济理论所描述的：改变了这些老牌市场经济国家的宪政体制，进而通往奴役之路。

一种观念自洽的宪政理论，不应该在这个思想体系中，就"正义"赋予除了"正义"之外的其他核心价值，如平等、民主、自由、权利、族群利益。如果视这些价值为正义本身的标准，那么正义就难免走向多元化。焦点在于，如果正义及其实现方式多元化，在一个以弱肉强食为特征的竞争型社会里，弱者就会被迫卷入到一个对他来说最不公正的体系中，这样这种世俗"正义"就不是相对正义，而是相对不正义。

公民具有免于匮乏的自由，资本与市场的自由不能以制造这种恐慌为途径实现资本的意义。资本与市场的参与者，不是正当性的来源。资本和市场都是基于特定的个人诉求来参与特定的社会分工的，并且遵循优胜劣汰、弱肉强食的逻辑。当然不是说这种逻辑必然是非正义的。而是说，市场逻辑必须限定在特定领域；一旦超出这种领域，就有可能承担起自身不能承担的功能。充分的市场竞争，不受政府限制的利伯维尔场，被法治制度全力呵护的资本逻辑，由于资源本身的有限性，以及哈耶克所强调的知识和理性的有限性，决定了再充分的市场竞争环境，都不可能满足人类的多种需要。经济自由,很多时候,甚至满足不了经济自由自己的目标。这种现象,被称为"市场失灵"。当然可以用"政府失灵"来论证"市场失灵"的可接受。但是这种可接受性,在一个并不仅仅有政府、市场与企业家、劳工阶层这些利益主体的开放性体系中,是必须被认真讨论的。

尤其是在各种将人力简单作为劳动力资源的劳动密集型企业里,产业资本对人的全面而无孔不入的奴役,更是导致了"人的异化"。产业资本让技术工人与资本家更缺乏联系,让工人更少社会性与公共性。"当一个手艺人始终只制作一种产品时,他的手艺当然会十分熟练。但是,他同时会丧失用其精神全面指导工作的能力。他虽然越来越熟练,但也越来越不动脑筋。可以说,随着他作为一个工人在技术上的进步,他作为一个人在本质上却日益下降。……旧时代的地方贵族,都在法律上或自己认为在习俗上,对自己的下属负有救济和减轻他们的困苦的义务。但是,现代的实业贵族,把他们所使用的人变穷和变蠢以后,在遇到经济危机的时候便把他们推出工厂的大门,让社会去救济他们。"[1] 具体说来,没有周末的休息,工人就失去了去教堂礼拜的权利,于是产业资本威胁到了宗教小共同体。由于工人公共交往的减少,又产生了其他各种社会问题,如维权能力等公共表达能力的降低。

基于各种考虑,在社会多维结构自有规律的推动下,成熟的"开放社会"对产业资本进行了认真而全方位的限制。长期为社会主义所批判的"垄断"就是如此。今天,即使在美国这样一个比英国更加强调"小政府"和"守夜人政府"的国家,早在被列宁称为垄断开始成为资本主义之特征的垄断资本主义(即帝国主义)时代,也即1890年,美国国会就制定出了第一部授权联邦政府控制、干预经济的法案,也即至今仍在这个普通法国度中执行的《谢尔曼法》(全

1(法)托克维尔:《论美国的民主》,董国良译,商务印书馆 1988 年版,第 687—794 页。

称为*An Act to Protect Trade and Commerce against Unlawful Restraints and Monopolies*，中译为《保护贸易和商业不受非法限制与垄断之害法》）。该法规定：凡以托拉斯形式订立契约、实行合并或阴谋限制贸易的行为，均属违法；违反该法的个人或组织，将受到民事的或刑事的制裁。20世纪以来，各种干预市场的方式大行其道，西方社会也没有走向专制极权。对劳工权利在社会福利层面的有限度的倾斜，人类社会接着发生的一个重大事实是，第二次世界大战之后，西方社会完全不再爆发大规模的暴力革命运动。与斯大林模式的日益破产相比，宪政民主政体显示了强大的生命力。

然而，也正是在这个民族国家化的现代体系之下，在那些基督教色彩鲜明的法治社会，当资产者和资本家认识到自身在祖国的不能为所欲为时，产业资本和工人异化的情况必然发生变化。明确地说，开始转移到"殖民地和半殖民地"国家；用20世纪中后叶的话来说，转移到了"第三世界"。由此形成了鲍曼所说的"全球精英的在外地主模式"。通过这种模式，资本家阶层甩离了他们自己面对的工人，比如底特律，而使用在外地主的方法，通过跨国企业和订单生产模式，变成流动的、轻灵的、随时可以抛弃的现代性。

对各种常常被称作"后现代"的社会批判理论，哈耶克主义的信奉者似乎可以以哲学家的气质来反驳，哈耶克的问题意识就在于他担心，类似民主社会主义的价值主张成为一个社会所有人都认可、而且所有人都必须认可的价值规范，上升为国家的政治主张、政体精神和法律体系。然而，这样一种危险也许存在，但是，也仅仅是一种"也许"，并非是一种"必然"。一种政治主张成为极权国家体系，是有非常复杂的社会条件的，必须在戴维·伊斯顿所说的"政治生活的系统分析"中揭示出来。以前述所列举的以社会主义价值为目标的社会党运动为例，由于以司法正义为核心的宪政民主政体早已建立，各种工党和社会党的执政，并没有在事实上导致这些国家放弃了宪政民主的制度安排；正义一元论体系的长期存在，由此而进行的公民教育功能，则进一步让这些信奉马克思主义的工人阶级政党，最终放弃了暴力革命的夺取政权方式和科学社会主义的政治理想。这个事实本身足以证明，马克思主义、民主社会主义，也是人类宪政文明的重要参与者。

由社会民主党（社会民主主义政党、工党或是民主社会主义政党）所组成的社会党国际深刻影响了人类的历史进程。社会党人曾经领导了下列影响重大的社会运动：1889年成立的第二国际在1889年宣告5月1日为国际劳动节，1910年宣告3月8日是国际妇女节等。第二国际破裂后，其成员以国际社会主义委员会为名继续运作。1923年，工党及社会党国际成立。"二战"结束后，欧洲地区受纳粹压迫的社会民主主义与民主社会主义政党成立了社会党国际。当葡萄牙与西班牙于1974年及1975年正从独裁转为民主政体时，社会党国际热情支援两国的社会民主党的组织重建。截至2007年6月，社会党国际有各类成员党和组织约161个，是当今世界上最大的国际性政党组织。活动于欧洲议会的欧洲社会党，为社会党国际的联盟组织之一。社会党国际的成员政党曾经至少在如下西方发达国家执政：澳大利亚、奥地利、比利时、德国、意大利、荷兰、葡萄牙、西班牙、瑞士、英国、法国、瑞典、以色列、希腊、丹麦、加拿大、挪威。相对于上台执政者，社会党国际成员为非执政者、咨询政党、观察政党的身份的国家同样足以列出一个巨大的表格。苏东剧变后，社会党国际的成员至少曾经在保加利亚、黑山、爱沙尼亚、匈牙利、立陶宛、蒙古、斯洛伐克、乌克兰、捷克等原共产党执政的国家中执政。

我们可以回到伯尔曼这位法制史作家对韦伯的批判来理解否定工人抗争的经济自由主义的局限性。经济自由主义视市场自由与资本自由为人类正义的天然尺度，事实上是将一个在基督信仰中被视为人之"罪"性载体的资本与市场，当成共同体合法性的来源。在基督教正义一元论体系看来，经济自由主义是试图在人间建成利伯维尔场乌托邦的社会理论和价值努力。如果视基督为人类正义的来源，视基督宗教为信仰标准，那么经济自由主义就是显而易见的异教了。这一"异教"的核心教义在于，它将人类正义的落实使命赋予了远远不能承担此一使命的，以追求利润和人类不平等为导向的市场与资本。

自由主义（包括经济自由主义、政治自由主义、文化自由主义和各种其他形式的自由主义）塑造了意识形态想象：宪政国家的执政党必须是特定形式的民主党、自由党或者自由民主党、宪政民主党；这种政党必须将大写的"自由民主"写在自己的党名党章里。倘若承认英国的柏林和波普尔、中国的胡适和其他"健全的个人主义者"所鼓吹的政治理论为科学真理，我们就永远无法理解为何"二战"后的联邦德国能够形成根基相对牢固、大众非常认同的宪政民主秩序：不是经典自由主义意义上的那种自由党和民主党，而是民主社会主义政党和基督教民主主义的政党在轮流执政。具体说来，是联邦德国的社会民主党和基督教民主同盟、拜恩基督教社会联盟在内的轮流执政。这种政党政治结构的形成，与德国的民情具有决定性联系：新教和天主教各有大约2600万信徒（新教主要分布在北部和东部，大部分新教徒属于基督新教路德教派，即德国福音教会）；天主教主要在南部和西部；另有90万东正教徒（主要来自希腊和塞尔维亚）；330万人信奉伊斯兰教（大部分来自土耳其，包括土耳其人和库尔德族人）；约23万佛教徒和9万印度教徒，多为华人、印度人与其他亚洲人；12万的犹太人，几乎全数信奉犹太教。

下列举例应该有助于我们理解北欧国家的宪法政治。1814年颁布的挪威宪法被认为是当时最民主的宪法，却具有系列条款。关于宗教与政治，宪法第一条规定"挪威王国是自由、独立和不可分割的国家。其政体是世袭君主立宪政体"，第二条规定"全体国民均有自由信奉宗教的权利。福音派基督教路德教为国教。信奉基督教路德教的国民应当培养其子女信奉基督教路德教"，第三条、第四条规定"行政权属于国王。国王必须信奉福音派基督教路德教，并维护基督教路德教"，第九条规定"达到成年的国王执政时，应立即向挪威议会作如下宣誓：'朕保证并宣誓：朕将遵照挪威王国的宪法和法律治理国政，愿无所不知的全能的上帝真诚帮助我。'如果议会当时正处于闭会期间，国王应向内阁作书面宣誓，并应在此后举行的议会第一次会议上作正式宣誓"，第十二条规定"在内阁成员中，信奉国教者应占过半数"。另外一个北欧国家瑞典的宪法文件则有五部：1809年的《政府组织法》，1810年的《王位继承法》，起源与1766年、制定于1810年（1949年经过了大的修改）的《出版自由法》，1809年的《议会法》，1991年的《表达自由法》。其中《王位继承法》第四条规定，"根据政府组织法第二条'国王应永远信奉纯正福音派基督教'的明文规定，亦即为奥格斯堡信仰声明书出及1593年乌普萨拉会议决议的未修改的文本所采纳并说明的规定，应在王国境内培养与教育王室的王子皈依上述信仰。凡不皈依上述信仰的王室成员，一律取消其王位继承权。"

吸取纳粹上台的教训，更加广泛地接受自由民主为价值观，天主教世界在教宗领导下，进行了历史上罕见的宗教改革，基督教民主主义兴起。后来，持基督教民主主义立场的政党组成了基督教民主主义和人民政党国际（Christian Democrat and People's Parties International）这一国际性政党组织，是仅亚于社会党国际的第二大国际性政党组织。欧洲的基督教民主主义政党还有地区性的组织欧洲人民党，组成了欧洲议会里最大政党组织。法国民主联盟加入了欧洲民主党，采取更拥护欧盟的立场。拉美的基督教民主主义政党，较之欧洲的同类型政党，更加倾向左翼的价值观。与社会党国际一样，基督教民主主义也是特定意识形态的多样性混合体，因此能结合了自由派、保守派、社会主义者等在内的各种观点，突出强调以超越性道德和基督教教义作为其广泛的架构。

正是基于这些因素，基督教正义一元论所强调的神人关系、神的主权、人的罪性、善与正义的"政教分立"被忽视了。"基督教—法政系"理论赋予了工人抗争以及各种小共同体（如劳动者抗争体、法律人共同体、学术共同体、传统宗教共同体、区域政府体系）参与和促进法治文明这一世俗正义的落实者的合法性与正当性，从而以法学家的精神重申了公民权利。经济自由主义却以市场自由与资本自由为道德准则，否定了传统小共同体和劳工阶层集体抗争的道义性和权利性。由此，以正义多元论为表现的经济自由主义应该感谢西方的基督教及其法政传统，是这一传统挽救了它的自由主义名声。明确地说，不是简单的资本主义民主和其他主义的民主，而是宪政民主。对那些尚未建成宪政制度的发展中国家来说，一般意义上缺乏司法正义要求的哈耶克主义者，则是社会不公正在事实上的缔造者。这里的经济学家，越是反对"民粹主义"，就越体现出专制色彩。

三、自主交叉性小共同体与公正的可落实：

市场共同体与其他共同体的互动

对宪政民主运行中诸多状态的清晰定义，较为合适者，即为进行描述性阐释。我们可以以几起在人类历史上具有重大转型意义的事件及其文献来展开相对详细的举例式论证。英国玛丽一世（Mary I）1553年即位后，因残酷迫害宗教改革家，烧死新教徒达300多人，而获得了"血腥玛丽"的称谓。1603年，詹姆斯一世掀起了对清教徒的又一轮迫害。于是1620年9月，搭乘"五月花号"的100位清教徒在前往北美新大陆的大海上订立了《五月花号公约》。公约载明他们愿意在新大陆建立小区，服从其中的法律。

条约签订时，全船一共有乘客102名，其中分离派教徒35名，其余为工匠、渔民、贫苦农民及14名契约奴，带领者为牧师布莱斯特。这些人很难说是优秀的经济学家，或者是企业家，或者是改革派，或者是到处写论文批判"民粹主义"的国立机构研究员或教授。"恩赐原有分别，圣灵却是一位。职事也有分别，主却是一位。功用也有分别，上帝却是一位。这一切都是这位圣灵所运行，随己意分给各人的。"（《哥林多前书》12：4—6）这样一个小共同体，有来源于各种小共同体的成员，如工场、农场、教会。这个共同体的核心体是教会，多种小共同体在教会这个核心体中有自己的参与和特定形象。这些互动性参与的公民签订了一个新的捍卫个人自由、限制未来共同体的政治契约。

如果说《五月花号公约》的签订者为流亡在英国海外的异议人士，数百年前的英国《大宪章》的斗争，则带有体制性色彩，参与者是来自各种小共同体的领袖和代表人物。订立大宪章的主因是英王约翰及各地的封建贵族对王室权力出现意见分歧。1215年6月10日，英格兰的封建贵族在伦敦聚集，挟持英格兰国王约翰。约翰被迫赞成贵族提出的"男爵法案"（Articles of the Barons）。同年6月15日，约翰在兰尼美德（Runnymede）为法案盖上王室的盖章，贵族在4日后重申效忠约翰。最后王室秘书将国王与贵族间的协议正式登录，即成为最初的大宪章，并将副本抄送至各地，由指定的王室官员及主教保存。大宪章中，最为重要的条文是第六十一条，即所谓"安全法"。该条规定，由25名贵族组成的委员会有权随时召开会议，具有否决国王命令的权力，并且可以使用武力，占据国王的城堡和财产。这是出自中世纪时期的法律程序，加之于国王却是史无前例。

由此，一个话题产生：既然国王恶毒，在双方已经失去信任的情况下，凭什么一方要妥协，而不是将作恶的一方彻底"消灭"？对这个问题的回答，从人类有限的历史来看，必须寻找一种超越于斗争双方、顺理成章地重申臣民权利、又在权利被重申之后节制公民反抗情绪的机制。对此，今天的一些道德家立即会想到加强公民素质和修养建设，然而这个说法也的确太富有想象精神了。事实是，在这个特别重视传统的国家，传统伦理——尤其是基督教信仰——起到了基础性作用。《大宪章》由序言和63条组成。序言体现了宗教性色彩：

> 按照天主的恩宠（By the grace of God），英格兰的
> 王、爱尔兰之主、诺曼底及阿奎潭之男爵，安州之伯爵，
> 吾，约韩，向总主教、主教、修道院院长、伯爵、男爵、

大法官、森林官、县长、代理家、奴仆以及其他所有代表
和从属者请安。

你们应知道，由于我们关心天主以及自己、我们祖先
及后裔的灵魂之得救，为了显主荣、圣教会之进步以及我
们王国内之治政，我们确定以下各条件如我们可敬的父老
所建议，即坎特伯雷总主教，英格兰首席主教与圣罗马教
会的枢机主教斯德范……

很快大宪章就进入了可司法化的立法阶段。其重要内容有："永
远保障英格兰教会的自由，使她享有充分地权利及自由"，如"自
由选举"；"未成年的继承人之土地，监护者不应由土地夺取任何
物品，除非是合理的财产、合理的关税、合理的服务，同时不应破
坏或浪费人（如释放仆役）或财产"；"除非得我们王国参议会之
共识，在我们王国内不得要求免服兵役税或贡助，例外只有为赎还
我们本人，为王长子之封爵士仪式与王长女的一次嫁礼"；"伦敦
城市应享有其昔日的自由和税关，无论在陆地或水面上；而且我们
命令且赏赐所有其他城、市、镇和港口的自由和税关"；"普通法
庭不随我们的朝廷走动，应于固定之地点行之"，有独立于国王的
司法权；"若所谓'王家法庭命令'之法律书，使得一位自由人失
去其自己法庭之权利，将不许出此书"；"任何自由人不得被捉拿、
拘囚、剥夺产业，放逐或受任何损害。除非受同等人之合法判决及
本地法律所允许，我们亦不会自己充当军队或派军攻击他"。最后，
第63条规定，"因此我们愿意以及强力命令英格兰教会应享有自由，
以及我们王国内之人民，在良好、和平、自由、安静的气氛内，享
有及保存前上所述的一切自由、权利和特许，完全与完整的，为自
己及其继承人"，也即在必要的时候使用武力强迫包括国内的一切
人来尊重全国君王和臣民的自由。[1]

---

1 《大宪章今译》，雷敦穌译，台湾辅仁大学若望保禄二世和平研究中心
2002 年，和平丛书 26，ISSN 1606-4976。

现代多元论者极有可能非常反感《大宪章》对国王或臣民违背宪章的惩罚性条款。不过在某些政治哲学中混乱不堪的、在这些思潮中争论不休的道理在法理学中却是一个基本常识：那就是任何一个契约和作为社会契约的法律和宪法必须附带强制性保证。换而言之，契约内在文字的逻辑前后一致性、契约执行的强制性正是正义一元论的体现。《大宪章》从前面的信仰性宣告，如何顺理成章地过渡到后面的可司法化的立法性条款，是宪法学的重要命题。其成功探讨，对我们探讨某些意识形态化色彩的传统国家如何过渡到司法中立和程序正义的宪法政治具有重要的启迪意义。

实践证明，能够制约政治斗争双方，迫使彼此在力量均衡时很快顺理成章尊重现状，就必须让斗争双方成为"明白人"。其意义在于，要让斗争双方意识到自己是行为上的有限者，也要认识到自己是道德上的有限者，并不具有任何"替天行道"的特权与能力，进而在耶稣的十字架之爱中饶恕那些曾经逼迫自己的弟兄姊妹。由此，力量均衡的双方很快就会订立契约，通过对彼此的制约，达成对彼此的保护：制约性条款，我们称呼为义务；保护性条款，我们称呼为权利；连结二者的是来源于神的正义，必须落实为人间的成文法，发展为宪法性文件。为了归正政治性抗争中的"血气"，大宪章第62条合理地阐释了基督教的宽恕精神：

由我们和我们人民，无论神职人员或否，争吵起所造成的一切争执、仇恨和报怨，我们要彻底宽恕大家，而且，此争吵引起的所有罪由我们在位的第十六年复活节到恢复和平之时间内，我们尽所能全部宽恕。为此，我们使坎特伯雷总主教斯德范，都柏林总主教亨利，上述之主教以及大使潘德福，收专利证函说明此保证与上述之一切特许。

然而，光有单一性小共同体，仍然不足以实质上捍卫小共同体的持久利益，尤其是让公民试图用脚投票，以迁徙自由来摆脱特定小共同体对个人自由之压迫。由于内在的正义精神之失去、结构的走向等级化，小共同体难免腐败堕落，成为压迫个人的平台。崇拜单一小共同体无异于崇拜寡头铁律。一种文明的社会体系，必须拒绝任何形式的个人崇拜、群体崇拜和小共同体崇拜。个体如果要更加细节地、全面性地兼顾社会各个利益群体的价值观与具体诉求，势必相对熟悉其他小共同体的价值观和具体诉求，对他人的思维方式和生活方式相对了解。这里实际是说，有能力作为宪政民主制度之基础的小共同体必须有来自于各个小共同体的成员，其来源、所跨的职业和地域越广越好。《五月花号公约》和《自由大宪章》的签署者，就是如此。耶稣基督的有形教会之交互参与状态，本文称之为"自主交叉性小共同体"。

正是在这个基础上，社会福利制度之构建，在美国这样一个强调自由和小政府的国家，可以并行不悖地存在着，并未导致美国走向专制极权。哈耶克作为一个经济学家，由于相对缺乏宗教社会学知识，产生了一个巨大的思考盲点。新教倾向明显的美国，以基督教色彩鲜明的美国共和党为例。这个党特别重视经济的放任自由主义，却是文化的保守主义呼吁者。这样一个奇怪的价值安排，事实上是主张基督教会和社区，而不是政府更多承担社会福利与社区慈善的功能。这样，政府仍是小政府，社会却并未缺少爱与慈善。公益与基督教传统密不可分。在基督教世界，财富在法律意义上是私人所有的；但在信仰层面上，超过生活需要的财富就是社会的。慈善是基督教及其教会的传统之一。世界上最主要的福利国家，几乎都是基督教国家。天主教行善者特蕾莎修女终身为穷人服务，于1979年被授予了诺贝尔和平奖。虽然世俗公司以追求利润为己任，但慈善之心仍会进入企业和社会。慈善与公益本身是世界各大宗教的普世价值，只是基督教相对较好地将慈善与法治结合起来。在美国，遗产税制度和慈善基金管理制度已经相当完善。一方面，美国的遗产税、赠予税实行高额累进制，当遗产在300万美元以上时，税率高达55%，而且遗产受益人还必须先缴纳遗产税，后继承遗产。法律规定向慈善机构捐款的捐款者享有扣除相应数额税收的待遇，包括免税、所得税豁免和捐赠减税，以激励人们捐赠。21世纪初，美国税率逐步在下降，但慈善捐款仍在上升。作为贫富差距较大的国家，美国也因此是很少有大规模阶级矛盾的国家。这个局面，使得美国政府不必过多承担欧洲福利国家的负担，而有能力承担维护世界和平的责任，包括领导世界反法西斯战争那样的艰巨使命。可以想象，如果宪政的美国单有经济自由主义，而没有以基督信仰为母体的共同富裕精神，没有普通法传统，劳资斗争将会迅速兴起且难以遏制。

需要强调的是，在基督信仰看来，人在现世任何意义上的付出，并不具有任何相对于他人的道德意义上的优势。慈善被认为是一种信仰下的社会责任，并不在任何意义上完成慈善家（或者是企业家）以高于他人（尤其是经济地位远远弱于他们的工人阶级和中产阶级）的道德优势的合法性论证。这里的逻辑很简单：付出的多少往往仅仅与不同的社会主体对社会资源的占有的多少有关。且不论企业家的经营机制是否为合法合理，即使完全取之有道，也并不赋予他们这种"因慈善称义"的权利。今天我们根据人类竞争的相关理解不难知道，这种"因慈善称义"的做法，必然将导致劳资之争中天然地倾向为财富占有者阶层辩护，从而加剧社会不平等，形成社会竞争的"马太效应"。在这种逻辑下，一切看似"爱"的"慈善"，最终都可能被操作为一种控制和压迫社会机制。反之，"因信称义"（Righteousness by Faith，Justified by Faith）的慈善机制及其世俗化的各种慈善观念与相关机制，有力地缓解了西方雇佣劳动制下的劳资矛盾。

北欧国家仍然能建成并维系宪政民主政体。路德宗之成为国教，使北欧世界的基督福音传播，呈现了与美国截然不同的特点。路德宗有助于民主社会主义运动的发展。路德宗与社会主义具有价值观上的亲缘关系。其中介就是作为国教的基督教路德宗。决定了路德宗政教关系观的则是路德宗作为基督新教一个教派的神学理解。和民主社会主义具有巨大的同构性，如果说基督教民主主义有什么不合适之处，这种不合适在于，它们将对底层民众的救济责任，托付给了国家（政府）。这种民主主义价值观（实际上是某种变体的国家主义价值观）天真地以为，政府的民主化和福利化取向，特定道德觉悟的主体的政府参与能够让政府承担起更大的责任，由此系统拒绝了"小政府""守夜人政府"的治理模式。基督教民主主义和民主社会主义，可以说是西方版本的"好人政府"。

本来，在圣灵的感召和《圣经》的要求下，出于福音之目的，教会承担起了社会慈善的功能。对教会来说，慈善是通往救赎的"便车"（的确有不信者"搭便车"，但也有不信者因此接近教会和基督徒，从此走上了救赎之路；更何况这本身就体现了耶稣基督对弱者的关怀——因而是很值得提倡的），却不是因而可以让慈善者"因行为称义"、可以代替救赎本身的机制。教会的慈善，讲述的是关于耶稣基督的"道路、真理、生命"的经典故事，因而是一个拒绝神圣化政府却能够升级政体精神和政治文化的机制。

对比党政大楼，基督教会才是真正的委身场所。基督教民主主义和民主社会主义，将基督耶稣的教会置于了与公益慈善毫无关联的社会结构体系中，其结果必然是社会进一步地世俗化和多元化，让国家（政府）承担起超出它能力的沉甸甸的道德义务。鉴于人在本性上的罪性，权力在本质上的扩张性和全面控制、走向暴政的本能，当国家治理上的财政危机和司空见惯的国家主权危机激起了民族主义激情，曾经的强有力的分权与制衡机制便非常容易失效，民族国家主权范围内的多中心秩序就岌岌可危，此时必然是"通往奴役之路"。魏玛宪政的挫败与纳粹德国的兴起多少就基于此逻辑。

换而言之，与韦伯一样，基督教民主主义犯有人本道德决断的错误，尤其是将道德决断放置于类似国家政权运作这样对人的试探必然超出人自身能力的层面之上。正如主祷文所倾诉的："我们在天上的父，愿人都尊你的名为圣。愿你的国降临，愿你的旨意行在地上，如同行在天上。我们日用的饮食，今日赐给我们。免我们的债，如同我们免了人的债。不叫我们遇见试探，救我们脱离凶恶，因为国度，权柄，荣耀，全是你的，直到永远，阿门。"（《马太

《福音》6:9—13）政治性的试探，对非基督徒来说无可避免，对基督徒来说同样如此。

四、何种法律体系最适合于市场经济体系：

信仰法治正义一元论的政治原则

谈及法律传统，就得提到"法律体系"这个概念。法律体系是比较法学中用来对各种法律进行划分的概念，意指具有相同或相近的传统、原则、制度和特征等要素的一类法律制度的总和。一个法律体系通常涵盖了若干个国家或地区，但有时一国的不同地方也会采用不同的法律体系。法律体系并没有绝对的划分标准。根据研究的需要，在同一法系下可以划分不同的亚类型，例如英国法和美国法就是普通法系中两个不同的亚类型。一般都认为，英美法系和欧陆法系是当今世界最重要、最有影响的两大法律体系。不过，这两大法律体系也越来越有交流与融合之处。

英美法系，又称普通法系。包括英国，所有现在或以前曾经是英国的殖民地（属土、英联邦国家），例如加拿大、澳大利亚、新西兰、新加坡、马来西亚、印度、巴基斯坦，均采用普通法系。公元1066年，英王威廉一世征服英格兰后，普通法系开始在12及13世纪成型。王室为加强司法审判权，便派出法官巡回各地审判案件。王国境内有很多法律问题，没有成文的法律规范，法官只好根据当地的民俗、习惯、道德观念和一般常理来作出判决，最重要的自然是《圣经》教义。这些判例日积月累，加之法官习惯上都会尊重和跟随以前法官（尤其是较高级法庭的法官）判案的原则，历经数百年，这些判例便形成了适用于全国的法律。印刷术普及之后，更多律师将许多重要的判例记录下来，印刷出版。每当新手接案件时，律师都会翻查相关判例作为依据，法官也会详细地加以解释、分析他的审案和判案理由。大约到了15世纪，这种无须经过立法机关立法而被法官所"发现"而成的"法律"慢慢确立。所以普通法又叫不成文法。普通法系非常重视社会习俗，由于道德理解的多样性，以及几千年民族习俗超出想象的多变性，强调"以人为本"的中国很难诞生普通法系。

衡平法也是源自英格兰的法律体系之一。大部分法院均以普通法审理案件。然而，由于普通法十分注重程序，很多案件单单因为不符合相关程序——如过了起诉期限而得不到公正审判——于是大不列颠大法官另设一法院，以相对宽松的程序来处理案件。和普通法比较，衡平法较为重视实质正义，较少拘泥于程序正义原则。普通法和衡平法的案件曾经必须由不同法庭处理。同一件案件，普通法法庭上败诉后，原告就可以将案件申请由衡平法法庭来审理。这种司法不统一，带来了巨大的麻烦。为此，英国通过Judicature Acts（1873—1875年），决定合并普通法和衡平法的法庭。衡平法凌驾于普通法之上，两者有矛盾时以衡平法为准。就此而言，衡平法体现出尊重民意的司法民主性之特点。

大陆法系，主要由欧洲大陆的国家及其他受上列国家影响的国家采用。主要历史渊源是古罗马帝国的法律。中世纪时，罗马法在欧洲大陆再度受到重视。18世纪，欧洲大陆的许多国家纷纷颁布了许多法典，尝试列出各种法律分支的细节规范。区别于普通法系，大陆法系也叫成文法、欧陆法系、罗马法系。大陆法系也有自己的优点（如法律条文的确定性），因此，普通法系开始逐步吸纳大陆法系的形式和优点，发展为混合法系。有一些地区，由于历史传承，同时带有普通法系和欧陆法系的一些特色，例如英国的苏格兰、美国的路易斯安那州、加拿大的魁北克省和南非。路易斯安那曾是法属殖民地，加入美利坚合众国后，为了司法统一和保障人权，刑事类案件逐步采取普通法系。作为当今唯一的超主权、超国界且有直接法律效力的欧盟法庭，就不得不长期面对和认真调和普通法和欧陆法的这一组矛盾。

普通法系重视案例和判例，相对不重视成文法。这既是机遇，又是挑战。机遇是赋予了法律人更大的主动权，挑战就是可能对法律人赋予超出他们本身德性和能力的功能。为了制约和节制法律人，必须确立一种制度，确保判案的严肃性、传承性和有效性；如果法官尽随己意，法律便不能成形。普通法系下的法院均自我规定：下级法庭必须遵从上级法庭以往的判例；同级法官虽然审判独立，但如没有很好的理由，必须互相思考，支持更加具有"说服力"的案例。法院的判词，本身就是国家法律的一部分。普通法系对法官素质的要求，与对私人执业律师的要素，正好一致，因此任命法官时多数会从私人执业多年的成功律师中选任。相反，大陆法系的国家认为法官主要职能是解释和运用法规，对法官素质相对放低了要求，也不再更多寄希望于法律人的"经验"和"德性"。可以说普通法系下的法官和律师，相对于大陆法系的法律人，几乎就是天然的"法学家"。因此，托克维尔在《论美国的民主》里，盛赞美国的法律人为"法学家"，具有"法学家精神"。这就是普通法系下法律人共同体的意义。可以说，没有基于神圣信仰的法律人共同体，就没有普通法系的有效运转和良性运行，也就没有多中心秩序及其一元性正义在政治社会领域的坚守与改善。

一般来说，在现代化的转型过程中，普通法国家远较大陆法系的国家社会稳定。迄今，普通法系的两个主要国家英国和美国，是世界上第一波的民主化国家。这两个国家虽曾爆发多种形式的内战，但是一直没有发生过那种大规模的政体性倒退现象。相反，实行大陆法系的国家，无论是德国、法国、日本还是俄国、葡萄牙、西班牙，都曾经一度复辟传统的专制制度。这些国家形成大陆法系的目的，最初都在于维持专制制度，加强中央权力，而不是促进自由民主。例如法国的拿破仑时期、德国的俾斯麦时期、日本的明治维新时期、中国的晚清民国时期。大陆法系国家转型之后所以仍然维系大陆法系，基本原因更多在于它们历史上实行的也是大陆法系，体现出制度转型的路径依赖。

相对普通法系，大陆法系更加依赖于立法者相对于其他人员的"先知先觉"。不过，正如我们都知道的基于生命体的有限性和人类普遍的罪性，立法者的智识和预见能力终究是有限的。我们很难想象有多少人有能力成功预见数百年之后的事情。人的生命就在几十年间，国家和民族、法律与制度的确立却不能满足于短短的历史瞬间。因而，从习俗、传统中发现法律，远远要优胜于立法者的造法。商品经济发展之后，市场信息千变万化，更是超出了立法者的预见能力，这样普通法系就体现出了针对大陆法系的优越性。长期以来，在远洋航行和进出口贸易等方面，国际社会普遍实行以普通法为主的制度。尤其是现代金融的兴起，文明迄今的几大金融中心的产生，更是体现了普通法的优越性。现代金融涉及如此巨大的财富，又是如此之专业，更加需要一个强有力的法治保障，这就意味着一个国家的法律体系必须随时能对这个国家的金融发展作出变化。普通法显然更加具有此种适应性。

公平正义是现代金融和证券市场的基础与核心原则；为了落实这个原则，促进金融与证券交易的健康发展，在普通法国家，金融业和证券业实行"证券监管的有罪推定"原则。1720年，由于缺乏监管的股市，机构投资者操纵股价，内幕交易横行，最终导致英国股市崩盘；1929年美国证券市场崩溃原因之一，也在于投资者的内幕交易。为此，美国政府成立了证券交易委员会（Securities and Exchange Commission）。与此同时，为了有效实施监管，规避内幕交易给证券市场带来的损害，美国政府推出了对于证券交易者的"有罪推定"。由于资本基于正义逻辑所受到的节制，迄今为止的国际金融中心，都诞生在普通法系国家和地区，如纽约、伦敦、中国香港和新加坡。同样以节制资本为目的的《谢尔曼法》也是美国这个普通法系国家促进正义的原则；该法奠定了反垄断法的坚实基础，至今仍然是美国反垄断的基本准则，却对什么是垄断行为，什么是限制贸易活动，没作出明确解释，为司法解释留下了广泛的空间，而且这种司法解释要受到经济背景的深刻影响。

更为重要的是，普通法的成功，与其说是普通法系的成功，不如说是这些国家的基督教传统和小共同体法治传统的成功。实行普通法系的国家，在民情基础和政治文化中与那些实行大陆法系的国家，往往很不一样。不过，即使同为普通法系，民情不一样也会导致法制规范的失效和法治建设的难以成功。托克维尔在《旧制度与大革命》中尖锐批评他的祖国，却在《论美国的民主》里盛赞美国。人们普遍将两种发展模式归结为采取不同的法律体系。然而，"墨西哥所处的地理位置，其有利性不亚于美国，而且墨西哥还采用了与美国相同的法律，但墨西哥没有促使自己建立民主政府的民情。"[1]

英美国家实行普通法系对其经济发展的促进给了我们远远超出司法制度变革的启发。制度与程序的"可操作"，前提是制度与程序的确定性、易于理解性和无法取巧性。必然不是针对超越性的多元论和怀疑论的彷徨。缺乏决断的人生是不存在的，缺乏决断的法治是一种梦幻。为此，一种成功的司法制度，它至少包含着诸多层次的一元性。

首先是法社会学意义上的：一个国家必须选择相对适应自己民情民风的政治制度和司法制度。这样一种一致性，有利于这个社会形成坚定的法治文化。最好莫过于这个国家的各种小共同体都是以法治正义为导向的。强大的政府很多时候是对法治的威胁，这里的小共同体还能为普通人提供尽可能的福利，以减少这个社会由于贫富差距而产生的对全能政府的需求与依赖。

第二点，司法正义应该成为这个国家主权决断的底线，绝不允许存在超出法律允许的政治权力之运行，如以立法和行政代替司法的决断。立法必须体现出普遍的爱，司法则必须以独立与公正的方式体现普世正义的原则。

第三点，这个国家的法律条款之间，必须具有内在的一致性，不能在形式逻辑上互相矛盾，或者形成多样性标准，以致守法者无

1（法）托克维尔：《论美国的民主》，董国良译，商务印书馆 1988 年版，第 357 页。

所适从，为了生存被迫知法犯法，执法者依据丛林法则为所欲为。如果法律随着人事的变化而任意变化，或者被选择性执法，弱势群体势必被纳入到对他最不利的法律解释中去。法制史上著名的"造法失败的八种可能"即讨论这个基本原理。

第四点，这个国家的司法运行规则必须具有确定性和一致性，除了对特定强势主体（如政府及其官员、强大的经济集团）等实行有节制的有罪推定，对广大公民，尤其是弱势群体实行无罪推定原则，最终确立起一种充分保障普通人，尤其是弱势个体的自由权利的程序正义原则。

上述四个层次的基督信仰与西方法律传统的一致性与层次性，由于启蒙运动和东方文化对西方的影响，在如今经济全球一体化、强大经济体文明日益多样化的时代，俨然日益失去其文明理解与国家治理的伟大意义。结果是，今天世界被视为密不可分的"地球村"，政治上、文化上、司法上，尤其是核心价值观上，世界远远未达到"地球村"的欣赏者所能达到的那种程度。即使都将"人权保障"列为国家基本宗旨，世界各国的人权标准仍然是不一样的。由此导致的结果是，信仰价值观与市场选择之间曾经那么密不可分的关系，由于"西学东渐"，日益看似风马牛不相及。

现存主要政体、法律体系、宗教选择、福利制度（社会党执政状况）、国际金融地位一览表（略）

然而，如果我们承认本页的这个表格所描述的政治社会学现象为事实，就应当承认：凡是社会党国际成员党曾执政的国家，其宗教背景几乎都是天主教的、新教的安立甘宗和路德宗，这些国家至少同时都有强大的基督教民主主义政党的活动，实际上二者轮流执政；一旦这些国家失去了其保守党的参与和制衡，哈耶克的担心马上就会因为其哈耶克的"反对社会主义"而成为事实。此外，我们也会承认：政府、企业和社会三方互动才是文明的常态，才能确保个人自由与社会自治的空间不受侵犯。国家掌握暴力，经济掌握财富，社会往往是羸弱的。只有以传统价值为纽带的小共同体才能坚持不懈地超越于世俗化的维权中司空见惯的利益原则来维护社会自治。只有让国家和市场相互制衡，以社会自身的力量（例如集体抗争）来维持国家、市场和社会的相对平衡，才有可能建成一个宪政民主的法治社会。

市场经济、社会公正、司法正义与基督教传统，看上去风马牛不相及。然而，由基督教正义一元论所延伸出的"节制资本"的法理学结论，直指经济自由主义的僭政本质，加之对法正义的制度落实，促成普通法系国家产生出国际金融中心，从而成全经济的全球化和一体化。基督教正义一元论所试图归纳的"正义"在多个层次的"一元性"，在法理学、政治社会学、政治科学上直指价值多元论的僭政本质。基督教会对社会公正与公共福利的参与，无论在路德宗立国的国家还是在加尔文改革宗影响深远的社区，都是有效节制劳资矛盾、避免"通往奴役之路"的坚定基础。对比制度崇拜情结深厚的世俗正义一元论版本，基督信仰及西方法律传统这种"基督教正义一元论"范式深刻地体现出了其之于宪法政治的伟大意义。

（完）

基督教宪政与人性论

曼德

（BAOSHENG GUO）

简介及导言：人性论——对人的道德本性和理性能力的判断，与宪政理论及实践息息相关。人在道德上的全然败坏、人自己获得救赎和达于完美的无能为力、人的理性和知识的有限性，总之一句话，人的"罪"（Sin）的阐述，使基督教人性论超越其他宗教之人性论、自然而然地成为构建宪政理论的基础。本文从圣经文本、基督教教义神学和神学思想史三个角度，探讨基督教人性论对宪政观念的影响。《圣经》文本中的领袖、英雄们，都带着根深蒂固的罪性，他们自己，也常带着沉重的罪恶意识。在基督教教义神学中，人堕落后的全然败坏的本性、人获得救赎的神恩独作论强调了人性性恶论。就基督教神学思想史而言，无论是使徒保罗、奥古斯丁、阿奎那、马丁路德、约翰加尔文，都对人性恶及对其的监督制衡有精彩的神学阐述，深刻地影响了西方的伦理及政治思想史。

政治是人类社会才有的现象，政治也是处理人与人关系的各种活动、知识和制度安排，政治的基础在人。正如英国政治学者格雷厄姆·沃拉斯在《政治中的人性》中所说的："对一个一、二百年前的政治思想家来说，现在唯一缺少的一种研究方式，是按照政治与人性的关系来研究政治。过去时代的思想家，从柏拉图、边沁到米尔，都对人性有独到的看法，并把那些看法作为思考政治的基础"（注 1）。政治学说的不同归根到底在于对于人性的看法，尤其是对人的道德本性的判断和对人的理性能力的评估上。人性恶抑或善？

人性靠人自己能够达到至善吗？人的理性是有限的还是无限的？人类社会的所有事情没有理性解决不了的吗？人们都期望国家统战者或统治集团是全善全智全能的，但是如何使统治者的绝对属性得到持续保障呢？对这些问题的不同回答构成了不同政治学说大厦的基石。

与人性论有关的一些政治现象是显而易见的：认为人性本善、人可以通过自己的道德修养而非制度制衡就可以成为"完人"和"圣王"的学说是绝对不会导出宪政的，这种学说的唯一结局就是国家元首或领导集团不受限制的"王道""王政""专政"；而认为所有人人性本恶，尤其是有权力者更容易趋向恶，并且人性之恶靠人自己的道德努力无法根除的学说，自然会导出对有权力者的限制、约束和制度制衡。

而就人的理性而言，一种理性可以解决一切社会问题、理性可以把握人类历史的绝对规律,也即卡尔.波普 (Karl popper)批判的历史决定论（Historicism）（注2）和理性可以建构最完美社会的学说，也即哈耶克（F.A.Hayek）所说的"建构理性主义"（constructive rationalism），无疑构成计划经济、共产主义社会的思维起点，这些对人性中理性的高估无疑与宪政理念是背道而驰的。而如哈耶克一样认为人只拥有有限理性（Bounded Rationality）、如康德等认为"物自体不可知"、有限的人类的无法把握无限、绝对、终极的知识的观念，肯定不会使人、尤其是统治者狂妄自大、计划一切，而使人更多的具有谦卑和顺服法律的品格。正如《圣经》箴言 1:7："敬畏耶和华是知识的开端"，在永恒的真理（神）前面，人类只有敬畏的份。政治首脑和集团任何的僭妄、自命为神的举动，必然导致专政和专制。

可见，人性论——对人的道德本性和理性能力的判断，与宪政理论及实践息息相关。人在道德上的全然败坏、人自己获得救赎和达于完美的无能为力、人的理性和知识的有限性，总之一句话，人的"罪"（Sin）的阐述，使基督教人性论超越其他宗教之人性论、自然而然地成为构建宪政理论的基础。而自由主义者们的"有限理性""人的局限""幽暗意识"（注 3）无非是对基督教中罪的概念的学术性阐述而已。

基督教对人的道德本性的看法不是简单的性恶论，整体上将人性分为三个阶段，起初被创造的人是善和完美的，但后来由于与神隔离而陷入罪中。耶稣救赎、信耶稣后的信徒被称为义（义 Righteousness 或 Justice，就是无罪的意思），但也只是被动地被神称为无罪（Justice，被神判为、称为无罪之人和义人），实质上还有罪性。第三阶段就是信徒死后升天或耶稣基督再来时，才能全然成圣、达于至善。这三个阶段中，最初和将来都不是当下的，而当下阶段、现实和历史中的人都是有罪的。

与此相关，基督教对人的理性能力也非常悲观，历史和现实中的人在神眼里都是"瞎子""聋子""你们听是要听见，却不明白；看是要看见，却不晓得"（马太福音 13：14），人类的知识也不过是"世间的小学"（歌罗西书 2:8），而人通过知识把握绝对真理、认识神的努力，如同建造"巴别塔"（即通天塔，创世记 11 章）一样是徒劳无益、注定流产的，正如新约哥林多前书 1:21：世人凭自己的智慧，既不认识神，神就乐意用人所当作愚拙的道理，拯救那些信的人。这就是神的智慧了。

除非神主动给人启示（Reveal）神的话（《圣经》）、神主动道成肉身启示神（约翰福音 1:18），否则人认识不了神——那绝对的真、善、美。启示是绝对客体对主体的主动展现，而认识是作为主体的人去把握绝对客体。后者是徒劳的，唯有启示才有可能使人类接触到绝对。

与中国法家韩非、李斯和马基雅维利的性恶论相比，基督教的性恶论更加周全。因为前二者更多地强调的是臣民的性恶，而对于君主，"目的证明手段正确"，似乎都是伟大、光荣、正确的。马基雅维利在《君主论》中指出："当遵守信义反而对自己不利的时候，或者原来使自己作出诺言的理由现在不复存在的时候，一位英明的统治者绝不能够、也不应当遵守信义。假如人们全都是善良的话，这条箴言就不合适了。但因为人们是恶劣的，而且对你并不是守信不渝的，因此你也同样地无需对他们守信"（注4）。

可见，马基雅维利们是选择性的性恶论，是君王性善、百姓性恶论，如此绝不会导出宪政来，反而直接导致专制暴政。而《圣经》罗马书 3:10-12：就如经上所记，"没有义人、连一个也没有。没有明白的、没有寻求神的。都是偏离正路、一同变为无用。没有行善的、连一个也没有。"不仅臣民，而且君王、皇帝、主教、教皇等等都是罪人、都不是义人。"有权必腐、极权极腐"（英国天主教徒阿克顿勋爵语），基督教人性论成为限制有权者权力的理论基础。

不仅如此，跟任何政治学说和宗教相比（儒家、佛教等都对人的罪有涉及），基督教对人的罪、人的性恶和人的理性有限性的阐述发挥到了人类语言的极致、强调到了无与伦比的程度，人的罪是基督教教义神学的基点，它也为人类宪政理论提供了最早也是最有力的注脚。比如，中国知识界仰慕称道的 1688 年光荣革命确立的"君主立宪"政体，其人性论基础，恰恰是在早于光荣革命近 40 年的清教徒教义信条《威斯敏斯特信条》中预备的：1642 年英国内战爆发，代表国教的国王查理一世的军队和代表新教（即基督教，Protestantism）的清教徒军队进行了数年战争，最后以 1649 年查理一世上断头台为标志战争结束。在战争后期，清教徒占多数的国会议员们，在威斯敏斯特大教堂召开会议，制定神学信条，以为新的政体奠定思想根基。与会人士有 121 位牧师，30 位议院的议员，及 8 位列席的苏格兰代表。1646 年 12 月完成了威斯敏斯特信条。该信条提供给议会和全体国民，无疑成为英国宪政的神学基础，为英国的君主立宪、三权分立、代议制等宪政安排提供了人性论、契约论的理论前提。例如：

《威斯敏斯特信条》第六章（论人的堕落、罪恶和刑罚）第二条：因此罪使他们从原始之义，并与神的交往上堕落了，于是死在罪中，并且灵魂和身体的一切才能与各部分都完全玷污了；第四条：由于本源的腐败，我们完全不愿意行善、不能行善，并且被改造成为一切良善的反面，又全心倾向一切邪恶的事情，便不断行恶犯错。第五条：这种人性的腐败，也留存在重生的人身上，直到今生的终结。虽然籍着基督，这腐败已被赦免和治死，但它本身和由它发动的活动都是真确的罪恶；

第十九章（论神的律法）第六条：又因令他们发现他们的本性、内心和生活上有罪的败坏，当他们按律法检查自己的时候，就越发知道罪，为罪而谦卑，以致憎恶罪，同时更明确认识自己需要基督和他完全的顺服（注5）。

不仅人人有罪，而且就是被耶稣基督救赎的人，仍然存留"人性的腐败"，仍然需要律法来检查自己。《威斯敏斯德信条》中的人性论深刻地影响了英国教会界、政治界，它颁布后即对英国政体发生影响，直到光荣革命正式确立了君主立宪体制。

下面我们从圣经文本、基督教教义神学和神学思想史三个角度，来看基督教人性论对宪政观念的影响：

与中国的历史经典不同，圣经中的人物除了耶稣外，都没有完美的、都有瑕疵，如摩西、大卫、彼得、保罗等等。这是因为圣经的重点在神而不是人，赞美的是神而不是人，以人的败坏突出神的荣耀。而中国的典籍重点在人，一个个圣贤、明君大都伟大、光荣、正确，史书大都没有记载他们的污点，因为史家要树立作为人之楷模的偶像。圣经中人的罪恶和败坏随从可见、从头到尾，让人触目惊心。

圣经一开篇，就是人类始祖亚当和夏娃违背上帝旨意、偷吃禁果、犯罪堕落（创世记3章）。他们的两个儿子，人类的第二代就因为献祭的事情自相残杀（创世记4章），挪亚的时代，人心大坏，

"世界在神面前败坏，地上满了强暴。神观看世界，见是败坏了；凡有血气的人，在地上都败坏了行为"（创世记 6:11-12）。经过大洪水洗礼后，不守安分的人类又开始建造通天塔，"为要传扬我们的名"（创世记 11:4）。被神立为多国之君的亚伯拉罕也为了自身的安全，撒谎说自己的妻子是妹妹（创世记 12 章）。

领导犹太人出埃及的伟大领袖摩西，几近完美，但也因不听神的指导，击打磐石，而被罚在有生之年不能进入迦南美地（民数记 20 章）。至于以色列最伟大、光荣、正确的君王大卫，在功成名就、平定天下之后，却淫人妻、杀人夫，这些罪行一个不漏都写在圣经上（撒母耳记下 11 章）。大卫之后的以色列君王和人民更加悖逆，民众敬拜偶像、淫乱污秽，政府贪污腐败、践踏公义，最后导致国家分裂、被外敌亡国多次。这就是圣经旧约所刻画的人性，充满了罪恶、急需神的救赎；而旧约中的君王、政治领袖们，也没有一个是全知全能全善的圣人，都是罪人，都需要制度、法律（十诫）和上帝的约束和制衡。

在圣经新约中，犹太人充满罪恶，以致于先知施洗约翰发出了："天国近来，你们应当悔改"的呼吁（马太福音 3:2）。新约中的两个最值得人敬仰的圣徒彼得、保罗，是人中的楷模，彼得还被天主教定为第一代教皇，但圣经也毫不留情地记载了他们的缺陷。彼得在耶稣基督上被钉十字架之际三次没有承认自己是耶稣的门徒，这是撒谎（约翰福音 18 章），后来在初代教会时代为了照顾耶路撒冷教会的元老，彼得又一次的装假（加拉太书 2:13）。作为最富有智慧和能力的圣徒保罗，却一直自称自己是"罪人中的罪魁"（提摩太前书 1:15），并说自己"有一根刺加在我肉体上"（哥林多后书 12:7），成为他身上的难以根除的瑕疵。

总之，圣经文本中的领袖、英雄们，都带着根深蒂固的罪性，他们自己，也常带着沉重的罪恶意识，而阅读圣经的一代一代基督徒、西方人，都被这种罪恶意识所感染，本能地知道自己需要不断悔改认罪、世上没有完人、有权有势者的罪性更需要监督制衡。这就构成的宪政而非王政、专政的人性论基础。

在基督教教义神学中，人的本性和人的救赎的教义最与基督教宪政理论相关，这两部分是我们阐述的重点。人堕落后的全然败坏的本性、人获得救赎的神恩独作论（这是与儒家、佛教凭己力成圣、成佛有本质区别、也与犹太教等凭人的宗教行为得救有本质区别），更加强调了人性性恶论，从而更加拉近了基督教与宪政的关系。

圣经认为人是由上帝用泥土和灵来创造。"耶和华神用地上的尘土造人，将生气吹在他鼻孔里，他就成了有灵的活人"（创世记2:7）尘土的部分构成人的肉体，"都是出于尘土，也都归于尘土"（传道书 3:20），肉体也成为人容易被魔鬼（妄想成为神的天使、堕落后成为魔鬼）诱惑的地方。最初美善的人性由于魔鬼的诱惑开始背叛上帝，被神惩罚后与永恒的真善美——神——从此隔离起来，陷入罪中不能自拔。这就是亚当所犯的原罪，正如罗马书 6:23：罪的工价乃是死。由于亚当是人类的代表，代表犯的原罪，被代表的人类世代都要承担，因此"人人都有一死，死后且有审判"（希伯来书 9:27）。也因此正直的品行变为歪曲（创世记 4:5,8），纯洁变为污秽（创世记 19:31,38），知识变为无知（创世记 11:4），人似乎完全失去了神的形象（创世记 6:5.11-12）。

罪——道德上的堕落、知识上的有限和浅薄、自己寻求救赎上的无能为力构成了人的本质特色。圣经上说："人心比万物都诡诈，坏到极处；谁能识透呢？"（耶利米书 17：9）。"我是在罪孽里生的，在我母亲怀胎的时候就有了罪"（诗篇 51:5）。这就是现实中的人性。无论皇帝、君王、总统、总书记概莫能外。就是被耶稣基督救赎了的基督徒，也只是蒙恩的罪人、也披上了耶稣基督给的"义袍"而已，实质上还有罪性的存在。信徒由于肉体的存在，身体尚未得赎（罗马书 7:23-24：但我觉得肢体中另有个律、和我心中的律交战、把我掳去叫我附从那肢体中犯罪的律。我真是苦啊，谁能救我脱离这取死的身体呢），所以这种罪性也在基督徒身上。基督徒也要被制约、被监督。

由于对人道德败坏和知识有限的强调，使基督教救赎论——人如何获得永生、如何与至真至善至美的上帝合一、如何除掉罪孽与神同在或者"天人合一"——是典型的神恩独作论。神恩独作，就是人在救恩上无丝毫作用，人得救（即与神同在），完完全全是神单方面的功劳。人靠自己的良知、善行、知识、律法、苦修甚至人一己的信心（而非圣灵感动和信的对象是耶稣）获得救恩的道路，被彻底堵死了；人在自己得救上没有哪怕是 0.001%的功劳，人的得救完全是神 100%的单方付出。以弗所书 2:8-9：你们得救是本乎恩、也因着信、这并不是出于自己、乃是神所赐的。也不是出于行为、免得有人自夸。

加拉太书 2:16：既知道人称义不是因行律法，乃是因信耶稣基督，连我们也信了基督耶稣，使我们因信基督称义，不因行律法称义。因为凡有血气的、没有一人因行律法称义。律法是人的行为，否定了律法在得救上的功用，也就是否定了人的功用。救赎论上的如此教导，唯一指向就是再一次的强调人的有限、无力和道德之败坏，也再一次的强调神的恩典的唯一和可贵。这就是基督教救恩论中最有魅力和穿透力的"预定论" Predestination，我们会在下文中进一步阐述。

与救赎上的神恩独作论形成强烈区别的是中国的传统哲学和信仰，以及马克思主义。它们虽涉及人的恶，但也只是蜻蜓点水，而且不是所有人都有罪，总是有部分人有成圣、成佛、成为历史主宰的潜在可能性。

儒家相信人凭自己完全可以成圣，因为人性本善，只不过被世俗玷污，只要通过人的修身养性、学识、静观等方法，就可以除去玷污，直接成圣。这就是所谓的"人之初、性本善"，孟子更说："人人皆可以为尧舜"，"人之趋善，如水之就下也"，孟子认为人有天生的"善端"，本此"善端"，便可成德、成圣。（注6）可见儒家对人向善、尤其是君王有善的可能性的判断跟基督教性恶论确有天壤之别。

儒家的荀子在"性"论上主张性恶论，但在心论上主张圣王论，所谓："途之人可以为禹"，在《荀子不苟篇》中道："诚心守仁则形，形则神，神则能化矣；诚心行义则理，理则明，明则能变矣，变化代兴，谓之天德。""天地生君子，君子理天地.君子者，天地之参也，万物之总也，民之父母也"。可见，君子通过"诚心守仁"等伦理方法，即可成为参天地万物的圣王也即神了。

这种人的自信或者人的狂妄在后期儒家中也表现出来，如理学大师朱熹提出了完整的"修齐治平""内圣外王"之道，将基于人的善性的得救、永恒、天人合一之路系统化。心学大师王阳明认为："心即理，心外无物"，将宇宙的本体最后归结为自己的人心或意识，这已经是极端化的以人为本体了。而另一大师陆九渊认为的；"宇宙即是吾心，吾心就是宇宙"，"仰首攀南斗，翻身倚北辰，举头天外望，无我这般人！"将以人为中心和人的狂妄达到一个最极致的地步。

佛家的主流思想，也是高举人、确信人并非全然败坏而是有成佛的潜质，人完全可以通过自己的努力——修行、顿悟、禅定、苦修、行善、咒语、法事等成为佛。大乘佛教强调佛性和法身，与涅槃等同，二者是植根于个人内在的心性，也即人有内在成佛的潜能，透过"发"心，人可以发挥此潜能，体现佛性，证成佛身.正如佛经上写道："众生皆有佛性，我即是佛，佛即是我"，"佛在我心，净心自悟，见性成佛"。禅宗六祖慧能运用儒家理念使佛教中国化。正如慧能所说的："一念若悟，众生是佛。""菩提本无树，明镜亦非台。本来无一物，何处惹尘埃"。这段慧能的佛诗之所以为他赢得了禅宗史上的地位，是因为它把人的性善、人即是神、人通过自己可以成为神发挥到极致。

马克思主义的人性论是非常乐观的，它相信凭着人的理性能力人可以把握历史及宇宙的规律，它宣告人类历史必然是社会主义代替资本主义，而资本主义社会的被压迫者无产阶级将是人类历史和新天新地的缔造者，无产阶级已经发现了宇宙及人类历史的规律（辩证唯物主义与历史唯物主义），发现了资本主义社会要灭亡的结局（政治经济学），也发现了进入人类自由王国的途径（科学社会主义），无产阶级将要主宰人类历史，拯救人类进入"新天天地"——共产主义社会。无产阶级被神圣化，成为了人类的弥撒亚、救世主。马克思主义在中国的代表毛泽东曾说："服从神何不服从己，己即神也，己以外尚有所谓神乎？""十亿神州尽尧舜"，这些无一不表露出人要成为神的狂妄。马克思主义对中国的流毒就是人的神化、个别领袖的上帝化、某个阶级及其先锋队的弥赛亚化。

综上所述，与其他异教不同，基督教在人的救赎论（与天人合一、立地成佛等类似）上对人的作用彻底否定，限制了人的至善、人的狂妄、人的无法无天，这为人类正确的政治安排及制度打下了坚实的人性论基础。宪政而非专政在基督教文化占主流地区成为理所当然、自然而然的制度选择。

就基督教神学思想史而言，无论是使徒保罗、奥古斯丁、阿奎那、马丁路德、约翰加尔文，都对人性恶及对其的监督制衡有精彩的神学阐述，深刻地影响了西方的伦理及政治思想史。尤其是加尔文主义的五要义，与宪政价值观有着密切的联系。

新约中使徒保罗在圣灵感动下所写篇目占很大部分，保罗神学的一个主题就是反律法主义。简单而言，律法主义就是靠人的宗教行为和教条而得救。保罗指出得救仅仅在于"因信称义"（罗马书1：17），在于上帝创世之先的预定拣选（罗马书9:11），而根本不在于安息日、割礼、饮食等犹太教规（加拉太书2:16），也不在于人的善行，因为人的善行、功德在神眼里不过是破烂的衣服（以赛亚书64: 6：所有的义都像污秽的衣服）。这种把神的恩典的极致化强调、把人性之败坏和无能的极致化强调，导致了基督教从犹太教中彻底地分离出来，并开始影响欧洲的社会文化。

当基督教在西方文化开始占主流之际，伟大的神学家奥古斯丁对人性之恶和对君王之制衡有众多精彩的论述。奥古斯丁延续保罗神学中对上帝主权和人的败坏和无能的强调，他坚决主张：人的本性已经因亚当的堕落彻底败坏到一个地步，完全不可能靠自己来遵守律法或接受福音；罪人必须要有神的恩典才能够相信以致得救，而神的恩典只赐给那些神在创世以前就预定要得永生的人。信心这个动作不"来自罪人的自由意志"，而是出于神的恩典，而且这恩典只赐给蒙拣选的人。（注 7）奥古斯丁在其《上帝之城：驳异教徒》中指出："两个最初的人的罪改变了人的自然，让我们看到和感到那么大的腐败，这使人遭受死亡，让他们遭受相互冲突的情感的搅扰和变动。他们已经不再有犯罪之前的特质了，虽然仍然住在灵魂性的身体中"（注 8）。

由于人性的邪恶导致由人组成的社会国家的败坏和扭曲，如果不是人类始祖的堕落，国家完全不必要。"人不管理人，但管理牲畜。因此，上帝首先确立的义人是放牧牲畜的牧人，而非人王。这样，上帝就确立了，如何安排被造物的秩序，如何按罪人的品行宽免他们"（注 9）。可见，国家不过是上帝为了对付人性邪恶而不得不设置的工具。由于地上国家的败坏和扭曲，它在地位上完全低于天上的国家——上帝之城。而这个上帝之城，在地上的代表就是教会。奥古斯丁将大公教会（Catholic Church）的地位前所未有地抬高，使其开始制约地上的世俗政权。作为基督徒个人，也就具有了双重身份，既是教徒又是臣民，既然上帝之国高于地上之国，那么教徒身份也就高于臣民身份，对上帝的虔敬和服从是绝对优先的，而对帝王的效忠和服从则是次要的。

奥古斯丁在其名著《上帝之城：驳异教徒》中上帝之城和地上之城的二分法，也开始导致了西方历史上教权对政权、教皇对国王、信徒对臣民、信仰自由与政治压迫之间的二元对立与抗衡，这无疑为西方的宪政民主提供了相互制衡的二元性社会结构。

中世纪神学的集大成者托马斯•阿奎那坚持了性恶论，并认为人类社会由于罪性无法避免陷入在集权统治中，统治者如果是顺服上帝的明君是最好的，但遇到违背上帝的暴君，也完全有可能。"人们逃避暴君，像逃避凶恶的野兽一样；听任一个暴君摆布，也同听任一只野兽摆布没有什么分别。"（注10）。当遇到暴君的时候，就应该向上帝求助。阿奎那认为："当没有希望靠人的阻力来反抗暴政时，就必须求助于王之王的上帝，即所有那些在苦难之时向其呼吁的人们的救助者。这是因为他有力量使一个暴君的铁石心肠变为柔和："王的心在耶和华手中，好像垄沟的水，随意流转。"（箴言21:1）（注11）同时，民众也有不服从的权利。"因为这个暴君既然不能尽到社会统治者的智者，那就是咎由自取，因而他的臣民就不再受他们对他所作的誓约的拘束。"（注12）

宗教改革运动的发起者和领袖马丁路德之所以重申"因信称义"教义，是因为天主教在中世纪后期无视人的性恶、有限性，高抬人的宗教行为，以善行、功德甚至赎罪券来得救。"因信称义"的强调，实际上强调了人在救赎中的无能为力，强调了神的独一作用。路德认为："除了历史上的十字架、所宣讲的福音，以及在罪人心里的信心，并没有任何东西对于救恩是有必要的。并且也没有任何补赎行为，可以加增救恩的任何层面。基督徒所得到的义是属于基督的，因此是属于'外来'和'归给'的义"。（注13）在这里，路德通过唯独信心消除了律法主义，告诉人们，唯独因为信心和上帝的恩典，神赦免罪人，并把基督的义归算在罪人头上。

在路德的唯独恩典理论中，他强调救恩乃是神怜悯的白白恩赐，人类对于救恩完全无能为力。路德把任何不依靠超自然恩典与信心的恩赐，而想要透过人类理性和行为发现神的方法，称为"荣耀神学"。荣耀神学是以人类的善、理性为中心的神学，它高估人类的力量和能力，是一切理性主义、人本主义的源头。而路德的十架神学宣告，人类完全依赖神，并且除了神的自我启示之外，没有能力了解任何关于神的事情。从荣耀神学到十架神学的转变，实际上重申了基督教彻底的道德性恶论和理性有限论。

作为一个基督教神学思想体系的加尔文主义（Calvinism），是法国著名宗教改革家、神学家约翰加尔文及其忠实的追随者们许多主张的统称。神学家巴刻所认为的："如果要归纳加尔文主义，五要点是最有价值的工具。"（注 14）加尔文主义五要点（TULIP）是：

1.人的全然败坏（Total depravity）或完全无能力（Total inability），人类由于亚当的堕落而无法以自己的能力作任何灵性上的善事。

2.上帝对人的无条件的拣选（Unconditional election）上帝对于罪人拣选是无条件的，他的拣选并非因为人在伦理道德上的优点，也非他预见了人将发生的信心。

3.有限的代赎（Limited atonement）基督钉十字架只是为那些预先蒙选之人，不是为世上所有的人。

4.不可抗拒的恩典（Irresistible grace）人类不可能拒绝上帝的救恩，上帝拯救人的恩典不可能因为人的原因而被阻挠，不能被人拒绝。

5.圣徒蒙保守（Perseverence of the saints）已经得到的救恩不会再次丧失掉，上帝必能保守蒙拣选者。

这五点教义的英文首字字母恰好是 Tulip，即"郁金香"。Tulip将人的罪作为逻辑的起点，将神的主权作为逻辑的终点，非常之严谨缜密。只要宣告并认信人全然败坏的基本认知，其他的论点就迎刃而解、不断呈现出来了。五要点所体现出来的加尔文救恩论是彻底的神恩独作说，这种彻底化使人的全然败坏的观念深入人心，依靠人的理性、道德、意志、修行、各种宗教仪式等一切的一切于救恩都毫无用处；而个人的条件对于是否被拣选也毫无关系，得救的唯一根源在上帝自行其是的主权之中。

加尔文主义对世界近现代历史影响巨大，但并非中国知识界所熟悉。在韦伯的旷世经典《新教伦理与资本主义精神》开篇就有这样一段话："在十六、十七世纪最发达的国家中，如尼德兰、英国和法国，正是加尔文主义这一信仰引起了这两个世纪中重大的政治斗争和文化斗争"。而加尔文主义这一信仰指的就是预定论（注15）。的确，神学上的不同最后引起了政治观、经济观及其实践的不同。我们看到，预定论 Tulip 教义使人彻底认识到人类的有限和罪恶，使人们在关于教会、政府等制度设计时无不以"无赖"假设为前提，各种制度安排来防范、监督人尤其是有权力、有地位的人的无赖本性。这为平等自由的教会制度和宪政、法治奠定了根基。三权分立、多党竞争、新闻监督等民主体制基本制度无不以此理论为基础。加尔文主义影响所及，深刻地改变人们的思想观念、国家的政治制度。伟大的神学家、布道家司布真（Charles H. Spurgeon）深情地说："我以加尔文主义为信仰的标准，便看到在这古道上到处都是我的弟兄；放眼望去，成千上万的人与我有相同的信仰，认定这是神的教会应有的信念。"（注16）。

行文最后，我们从圣经文本、基督教教义神学和神学思想史三个角度梳理了基督教的人性论及其对宪政观念的影响。我们应该感到，没有那一个宗教信仰或思想体系，如基督教般强调人的罪——道德的败坏、理性的有限、自己救赎自己的不可能；也没有哪一个教义，把人的罪作为神学体系、社会洞察的逻辑起点。如此的人性论必然导致社会实践中的权力制衡、监督和限制观念。

我们整个中国人都有必要明白：人不是神，人也不可能通过人的一切努力成为神。人自身存在着多种的罪性和有限性，人尤其是有权位者必须要受到足够的监督和制约；而且人的罪性靠自我的道德修养是根除不了的，必须靠悔改和信靠真正的上帝方能改变，所以人必须敬畏上帝、顺服法治、制约罪恶、千方百计在经济、政治领域用制度制衡人的罪性。这无疑构成了宪政理论的人性论基础。

参考资料：

注 1：见《政治中的人性》〔英〕格雷厄姆•沃拉斯 商务印书馆 朱曾汶译 1995 出版 汉译世界学术名著丛书

注 2：见《历史决定论的贫困》原作名: The Poverty of Historicism 卡尔.波普 华夏出版社 译者: 杜汝楫 / 邱仁宗 1987 版 二十世纪文库

注 3：见《幽暗意识与民主传统》 作者: 张灏 新星出版社 2006 出版

注 4：见《君主论》马基雅维里著，潘汉典译，商务印书馆 1985 年版

注 5：见《历代教会教条精选》 赵中辉等译 基督教改革宗翻译社 1993 年版

注 6：见《幽暗意识与民主传统》 作者: 张灏 新星出版社 2006 出版

注 7：见台北基督教改革宗翻译社《加尔文主义五要点》第 20 页

注 8：见《上帝之城：驳异教徒》中，207 页，吴飞译 上海三联书店 2008 年版

注 9：见《上帝之城：驳异教徒》下，150 页，吴飞译 上海三联书店 2008 年版

注 10：见《阿奎那政治著作选》，52、53 页马清槐译；商务印书馆 1982 年版

注 11：见《人性恶与自由宪政》一文

注 12：见《阿奎那政治著作选》 59、60 页马清槐译；商务印书馆 1982 年版

注 13：见《基督教神学思想史》 422 页 北京大学出版社

注 14：见《加尔文主义五要点》第 34 页 台北基督教改革宗翻译社

注 15：见马克斯韦伯《新教伦理与资本主义精神》网络电子版

注 16：见《加尔文主义五要点》第 15 页 台北基督教改革宗翻译社

文明的进程——基督教在中国的深化发展

单传航

（原刊于"中国基督教理学协会网站"）

人类历史可以视为是上帝不断教育人类并逐步提升人类文明的过程。这种文明一旦形成，就如阳光和春雨，成为普世恩典，上帝的子民和世人都能享用。上帝教育人类的方法和内容，都记录在《圣经》里，也反映在犹太-基督教文明史中。

耶稣基督的教会和基督教在中国发展到今天，急需进入**信仰深化**的成熟稳固阶段。信仰的深化，就是指教会和基督徒需要将《圣经》的直接真理和延伸应用真理知识，在个人、家庭、教会和社会中，深刻广泛地实践出来。这样的结果之一，就是影响更新社会文明。

对于基督徒个人，这种信仰的深化，主要表现在有意识地对心理模式进行更新。对于教会，主要表现在开始有意识地影响更新社会文化。只有这样，基督徒个人和基督的教会才能长大成熟，成为山上之城和社会之光，并不可避免地缔造出**中国环境里的基督教文明体系**。然后，通过这种新文明的结构为载体，对内继续抢救灵魂、更新人心和社会公德，对外进行跨文化的宣教，拓展上帝的国度，影响其它民族的文明，荣耀主耶稣基督的圣名。

基督徒和教会在中国社会中有意识地建设基督教文明，这是世界基督教史和中国历史中令人兴奋和极其壮丽的新篇章。

一、《旧约》和犹太文明

文明是什么？我认为，简单地说，文明是人类主动脱离邪恶、愚昧和诅咒而接近真理并获得自由的程度，即伦理道德、客观知识和哲学思想不断提高并接近上帝期盼的过程。因此，文明不是静态的，而是可以不断成长的个人、家庭和社会的生命，类似于一种艺术。文明始于人的心灵，达于人的头脑，显于人的言行。

最理想的社会文明形态应该包括**两部分文化要素：以《圣经》为基础的信仰神性文化和以理性逻辑哲学思维模式为基础的人性文化**。前者是上帝对人类心灵的启示性教育，后者是人类头脑创造力的责任。两者之间的联合运作，形成最有活力而有发展前途的文明生态。这样的文明是人类区别于动物的重要特征，是人类拥有上帝形象的美好标志。

根据《圣经·旧约》记载的初期人类和以色列犹太人的文明发展过程和文明内涵，可以深刻理解和学习理想文明形态的形成原理和**四大组成板块：《圣经》神性信仰（神权）——伦理法典（人权）——宪政（管理）——人性自由（文艺）**。

1、人类初期的文明

《圣经》中记载了人类文明的起源。根据《创世记》可知，上帝用 5 天的时间创造了天地万物，然后在第 6 天创造了人类，并赋予人类创造文明的能力和责任。下面的这两段经文包含了丰富的真理信息：文明是人类的事务，是以家庭和社会为机体；上帝非常重视人类的文明程度，因此不断提供教育进行帮助。

"上帝说：我们要照着我们的形象、按着我们的样式造人，使他们管理海里的鱼、空中的鸟、地上的牲畜，和全地，并地上所爬的一切昆虫。上帝就照着自己的形象造人，乃是照着他的形象造男造女。上帝就赐福给他们，又对他们说：要生养众多，遍满地面，治理这地，也要管理海里的鱼、空中的鸟，和地上各样行动的活物。"
——创世记 1：26-28

"耶和华上帝用地上的尘土造人，将生气吹在他鼻孔里，他就成了有灵的活人，名叫亚当。耶和华上帝将那人安置在伊甸园，使他修理，看守。耶和华上帝吩咐他说：园中各样树上的果子，你可以随意吃，只是分别善恶树上的果子，你不可吃，因为你吃的日子必定死！耶和华上帝说：那人独居不好，我要为他造一个配偶帮助他。耶和华上帝用土所造成的野地各样走兽和空中各样飞鸟都带到那人面前，看他叫什么。那人怎样叫各样的活物，那就是它的名字。那人便给一切牲畜和空中飞鸟、野地走兽都起了名；只是那人没有遇见配偶帮助他。耶和华上帝使他沉睡，他就睡了；于是取下他的一条肋骨，又把肉合起来。耶和华上帝就用那人身上所取的肋骨造成一个女人，领他到那人跟前。那人说：这是我骨中的骨，肉中的肉，可以称它为女人，因为它是从男人身上取出来的。因此，人要离开父母，与妻子连合，二人成为一体。当时夫妻二人赤身露体，并不羞耻。"——创世记 2：7-25

根据上述经文可知，**第一、人类具有上帝的形象，并且是有灵的活人，这是人类区别于动物的本质特征。**那么，"上帝的形象"和"有灵"在人类身上，具体表现是什么？这是一个困难的神学问题，因为是属于启示性真理范畴，如果没有来自上帝的具体启示，就超出了人类思维的界限。我认为，上帝的形象，本身就是人类的文明标志，是文明的原生形态符号。此外，人类的创造性能力是上帝形象的表现之一。创造不是指制造物质性的东西，因为人手造出来的物品，无非是对上帝创造物的模仿。人类能创造文明，这是最接近于"无中生有"的创造性，属于上帝的形象之一。文明始于上帝赋予人的灵，并通过人性展示出来。

第二、管理和命名，是人类创造文明的第一步。管理是政治和法治，命名是文学和艺术。管理和文学艺术是文明的硬指标。文明程度越高，文艺（美学）就越发达，治理和管理水平也就越高超。文明能满足人们的心理和精神，这是人类被上帝创造时所赋予的需求。管理的职责，是上帝所赋予的权柄，主要是通过头脑来运作。动物无法形成社会，只有人类能够，主要是因为管理和命名的能力。社会不是简单的群居和利益共同体，而是复杂的人际关系在伦理和法律的框架下，通过权柄所实施的管理和命名的责任而形成的。如果观察人们的说话，就会发现大多数的言语是评判性的，诸如，"是什么，不是什么"、"应该怎样，不应该怎样"，等等，是出于管理和命名的意识。

第三、神性法律与伦理是文明的基石。上帝让亚当管理伊甸园，同时命令说："园中各样树上的果子，你可以随意吃，只是分别善恶树上的果子，你不可吃，因为你吃的日子必定死！"上帝的命令是伦理，也是律法——其意图是，限制人类管理的权柄，不致任意妄为，因为人类并不是被管理对象的主宰。然而，亚当和夏娃违背上帝的命令吃了禁果，就不仅滥用了管理的权力，还导致魔鬼撒旦成功将罪性传播给人类，毁坏了伊甸园里上帝所启动的人类最初的文明。这种原始的文明是如此纯洁和高级，以至于上帝能够与人类同在，面对面的谈话。之后，上帝将亚当和夏娃流放到一种低级的文明中。这种低层次文明进一步被罪污染，就变得如此荒蛮，以至于亚当的长子该隐谋杀了亲弟弟亚伯。

根据上帝的伦理和法律进行自我约束，是人类文明的高级形态的必要前提。文明中的自由是伦理和律法框架中的安全范畴，是真理所赋予的平安和释放。越是文明发达的社会，人们的自我约束性就越强，就越容易遵守法律和伦理道德。亚当夏娃就是没有重视自我约束，或者是自我约束的力度不够，导致了一失足成千古恨。上帝在《创世记》第3章中对亚当夏娃犯罪的宣判，其中"苦楚"、"终身劳苦"、"汗流满面"的关键字，说明了堕落后的人类文明的本质是没有盼望的。接着，"耶和华上帝为亚当和他妻子用皮子做衣服给他们穿"，标志着上帝对人类进行文明教育的功课开始了，如同父母对叛逆子女的教育，出于恒久忍耐的爱。

第四、婚姻、家庭和子女。家庭是社会的基本单元。上帝说："那人独居不好，我要为他造一个配偶帮助他。"于是，上帝设立了第一次婚姻，第一对夫妻和第一个家庭。家庭是社会的基本单元，两个家庭就可以组成一个社会。上帝还让家庭"要生养众多，遍满地面，治理这地，……"，于是，社会就正式形成。婚姻是人类文明的独特标志，一男一女的结合更是独特，区别于所有的动物。上帝只造了一个女人夏娃作为亚当的配偶和助手，以及人类男女的自然出生比例总是大致相当，都说明了上帝设计的本意是一夫一妻的婚姻制度。因此，一夫一妻（一男一女）是婚姻家庭文明的最高形态，是人类通过向上帝负责的伦理道德而进行自我约束的成功表现。

因此，同性恋、堕胎、乱伦，属于反文明和反社会的一种方向，必然导致文明的堕落和人性的禽兽化。文明的堕落直接导致社会的腐败和缺乏创造力，罪性获得自由发作，个人和家庭的生活紊乱。

2、以色列人的《旧约》文明

《圣经·出埃及记》中的记载，说明了以色列作为一个民族，其文明进程是如何受到上帝的亲自教育和督促而形成的。通过**神性真理信仰为核心、人性责任伦理的律法、法治—宪政的管理制度**，犹太人的人性文明迅速提升，社会日益先进。

在《旧约》中可以清楚看到，每当人类在伦理道德上堕落，在人性上腐败，在神性上叛逆，文明就会降级或失落。最后，甚至导致上帝毁灭人类。例如，在挪亚时代上帝发大洪水毁灭人类之前，人们"终日所思的尽都是恶（创 6：5）"，"世界在上帝面前败坏，地上满了强暴（创 6：11）"，甚至，"耶和华就后悔造人在地上，心中忧伤（创 6：6）。"挪亚时代之后，上帝毁灭所多玛和蛾摩拉这两座城市，也是因为城里的人们在上帝面前"罪大恶极"。

以色列人在埃及沦为奴隶达 400 年之久，社会文明程度降到了最低点。然而，上帝带领他们出埃及并进入迦南之后，只经过两代人的时间，就将以色列教育培养成文明强国。这是非常珍贵的文明历史案例。上帝教育犹太人的方式，大致包括以下三个方面：

第一、建立神性的圣洁真理信仰：从亚伯拉罕开始，上帝就开始在犹太人祖先当中培养建立神性的信仰。到了摩西的时候，这种神性信仰的重申和强化，到达了历史性的新高度。上帝首先通过燃烧的荆棘向摩西显现，随后通过摩西行了许多伟大的神迹。这些神迹直接鼓励和巩固了以色列人的神性信仰——文明的源泉。

上帝行使了 12 个史无前例的神迹，惩罚埃及人，将以色列人从埃及政权的奴役下解放出来，赋予了他们人权、尊严和自由。同时，也让以色列人的神性信仰有历史事实根基，并产生敬畏之心。"敬畏耶和华是智慧的开端。"而智慧是文明的营养。当神迹出现在人类当中，人类出于人性的骄傲，容易忘记和不承认神迹的发生。

于是，上帝设立逾越节，让以色列人每年庆祝，纪念上帝行使了有目共睹的伟大神迹，将他们解放出来。同时，逾越节中还隐藏了一条数千年的预言，到了最后在耶稣的身上完全应验，从而交叉证明了逾越节的神性来源和意义。此外，出埃及之后，以色列人在旷野的 40 年飘荡中，无可否认的神迹，包括天降吗哪食品一直伴随着，继续巩固和深化了他们的神性信仰。

上帝以神迹的方式出现在人类当中，是为了促进神性信仰，提升人性的美好和社会的公义，从而促进人类的文明。人类的文明必须要有真理神性的源泉，否则就会被罪性污染腐败，甚至完全堕落，导致文明降级甚至丧失。上帝在旧约时代选择犹太人，因为他们是亚当-夏娃和亚伯拉罕-撒拉的直系后裔，代表着全人类，同时也是上帝持守对亚伯拉罕的应许和所立的旧约。

第二、律法赋予权利和责任：胜利离开埃及后，上帝就通过摩西颁布律法。这些律法也包括伦理道德的内容，从而有力保障了文明的健康成长。在犹太人体会到了从奴隶成为自由人的可贵之后，上帝通过摩西颁布了十诫命（出埃及记 20：1-17）和相对应的详细法规。

十诫命属于宪法性质，分为两部分：前四条是人应当怎样对待上帝——即神性信仰的责任，同时也是上帝在人类面前的**神权**；后六条是怎样对待别人——人性伦理的责任，同时也是基本的**人权**。以上帝真理为基础的神性信仰责任与人性伦理责任，同时也是神权和人权，两者之间的相互作用，直接缔造了犹太文明，同时也丰富了人类文明的内涵，提升了文明的层次。

颁布十诫命之后，上帝开始颁布详细的法律和法规。第一条就是怎样建造为上帝献祭的祭坛，即神性责任先行一步。然后，是关于怎样对待别人的典章，首先是怎样对待他们当中那些社会地位最为低下的奴仆。接着，上帝又颁布了大量细节性的法律条文，主要还是两个部分：对上帝的责任和对别人的责任。其中，《利未记》的条文主要是怎样具体履行人对上帝的信仰责任，旨在让人圣洁；然后，《申命记》主要是怎样具体履行对别人（包括邻舍）的权利责任，旨在让人行公义。当然，这两书在神性责任和人性责任的两个方面也有重叠交叉的部分。例如,《申命记》中也有强调神性责任的内容,还在 4:24 中特别提到"因为耶和华—你的上帝乃是烈火,是忌邪的上帝。"(同时参看《希伯来书》12:29)(节选自笔者的《神性与人性——燃烧的荆棘》)

在真理的神性信仰的基础上,责任和权利才能得到充分的促进,社会文明才因此提高。通过摩西传播上帝的话语,重申与亚伯拉罕的契约,颁布法律规定神性信仰和人性伦理的双重责任后,上帝将犹太人从奴隶的层次快速提升为文明的民族,并进一步繁荣强大,预备好进入迦南地区承受更伟大的赐福,建立国家,影响其它民族,荣耀上帝的圣名。

第三、法治与宪政确保社会公义:上帝颁布了法律,就开始严厉执行。上帝在执行法律的过程中,让以色列人明白,个人和社会团体是不可分割的,一个人违法,可能株连整个群体。同时,尽管是通过摩西颁布的律法,摩西和其它犹太人的最高领袖,不论是政治、宗教和军事领袖,都必须和人民一样遵守同样的律法。这就是为什么即使是摩西和大卫那样最有威望的政治领袖,在违背律法之后,也会受到惩罚,甚至摩西还失去了进入迦南的荣耀资格。同时,犹太人的政治领袖(国王)和宗教领袖(先知)的双重权威,形成了权力相互制衡的两权分立的政治管理模式。这就是宪政和法治文明的原始朴素模型,是上帝亲自传授给人类并进行实践指导的。

因为违背律法,出埃及的那一整代人也失去了进入迦南地区的资格,直到旷野流荡 40 年全部死去,新的一代人才进入了迦南,并且是在新的领袖的带领下。进入迦南后,上帝又实施了一系列严格的法律和伦理的强化教育方针,让以色列人从首领到平民,都因为大大敬畏而严格遵守律法伦理,严守上帝子民的身份并履行神性和人性的双重职责,导致整个民族在上帝面前视为圣洁,神权得到尊重,人权得到保障,公义在社会中彰显。因此,整体文明迅速提升,并蒙受上帝丰富的精神和物质的双重赐福。

有时候,这种雷电般严厉的律法执行不仅让犹太人感到恐惧,甚至也令他们感到气馁。例如,大卫王在运送上帝约柜的时候,忽略了只有利未人才是上帝膏立的祭司,才有资格接触圣洁的神性器具，于是就让一般的人运输。结果，悲剧发生了："到了拿艮的禾场，因为牛失前蹄，乌撒就伸手扶住上帝的约柜。上帝耶和华向乌撒发怒，因这错误击杀他，他就死在上帝的约柜旁。……那日，大卫惧怕耶和华，说：耶和华的约柜怎可运到我这里来？于是大卫不肯将耶和华的约柜运进大卫的城，却运到迦特人俄别以东的家中。（撒下6：6-7，9）"这种宪政制度和法治运行的初期，即使大卫王也不太适应，并且感到气馁。然而，他很快明白了问题所在，就严格按照上帝的律法规矩，让利未人运输约柜，并符合法规的要求，结果平安运到，还因此蒙受上帝的祝福（《历代志上》第15章）。上帝所拣选膏立的大卫王也必须臣服于上帝的律法，这就是宪政的原生精神所在。（节选自笔者的《神性与人性——燃烧的荆棘》）

正是这种宪政和法治的严厉性，导致了以色列人从奴隶层次的文化生态，迅速成为高度文明和强大繁荣的民族和国家。从约书亚带领以色列人开始征服迦南，经过了大约250年，到了所罗门王的时代，以色列就成为最为文明发达的国家，名声远扬，让外国使节和国王纷纷前来朝拜。根据《列王记上》10：23-25 的记载："所罗门王的财宝与智慧胜过天下的列王。普天下的王都求见所罗门，要听上帝赐给他智慧的话。他们各带贡物，就是金器、银器、衣服、军械、香料、骡马，每年有一定之例。"最令人惊奇的是，作为当时的文明古国埃及的法老，昔日犹太人的奴隶主，也将自己的女儿，嫁给了所罗门王（列王记上3：1）。所罗门执政期间，圣洁、公义、智慧、繁荣、富裕和军事强大，成为犹太文明的主要特征。耶和华的名大得荣耀。

以色列文明的败落：文明可以在一代人当中建立起来，也可以在一代人中失落。以色列文明发展的根基，是神性信仰。堕落也是从信仰开始。《列王记上》11：4，9-10记载了这一文明衰落的开始与原因："所罗门年老的时候，他的妃嫔诱惑他的心去随从别神，不效法他父亲大卫诚诚实实地顺服耶和华—他的上帝。……耶和华向所罗门发怒，因为他的心偏离向他两次显现的耶和华—以色列的上帝。耶和华曾吩咐他不可随从别神，他却没有遵守耶和华所吩咐的。"

信仰的背叛，人心的腐败，导致文明的衰落，帝国的崩溃始于内部。于是，以色列国的内部分裂，成为两个国家。之后，由于国力衰弱，外国敌人开始攻打，战乱不止。两国之后的历任国王中，再也没有出现大卫和所罗门那样的杰出人物，而上帝也不断通过先知反复警告那些悖逆的国王，内容主要涉及两点：**信仰的圣洁和社会的公义**。国王和先知的二权分立模式，仍然在维持着以色列的政治文明，尽管由于国王和人民对神性信仰的背叛和在人性伦理方面的堕落而导致大势已去。国王所代表的是人性文化，总是希望获得能够独立于神性信仰的自由和权力；而先知所代表的是神性信仰，意在让国王的权力和人民的自由都臣服在上帝的伦理框架下。

在大卫、所罗门等文明繁荣的时代，人性文化与神性信仰之间是彼此和谐运作，因此文明高度发达。但是，之后的时代，两者之间是彼此争斗制约的，从而导致文明的衰落。然而，那些国王中凡是重视神性信仰的，就获得上帝的赐福，文明就得到维护；反之，国家就遭殃。这样反反复复，但整体趋势是走向亡国，不可救药。除了谴责国王，上帝还派先知谴责民众的罪恶。不论是国王还是普通民众，在罪性上都是一样的（只是机会不同），都需要臣服于上帝的伦理约束。从这一点来看，如今西方政治自由主义者们所鼓吹的以"人民无误论"为假设前提的民主制度，是幼稚而可笑的，经不起实践和历史的检验。

根据《列王记下》22：1-2 的记载，所罗门王之后约 300 年，犹大的国王是约西亚，他是上帝所喜悦的，因为"约西亚行耶和华眼中看为正的事，行他祖大卫一切所行的，不偏左右。"这位约西亚王在位第 18 年的时候，下令修复圣殿，结果在圣殿发现了先祖留下的文明的秘诀——律法契约书。根据《列王记下》23：1-3 记载，于是，"王差遣人招聚犹大和耶路撒冷的众长老来。王和犹大众人与耶路撒冷的居民，并祭司、先知，和所有的百姓，无论大小，都一同上到耶和华的殿；王就把耶和华殿里所得的约书念给他们听。王站在柱旁，在耶和华面前立约，要尽心尽性地顺从耶和华，遵守他的诚命、法度、律例，成就这书上所记的约言。众民都服从这约。"
接着，约西亚王开始拆除偶像，废除异教，恢复真理的神性信仰，
圣洁又开始回到政治和文化中。

这是多么令人羡慕和肃然起敬的场景：国王和民众都与上帝立
约，复兴真理的圣洁神性信仰，遵守上帝的法律和伦理。这就是犹
太文明的秘诀，也是宪政和公民社会的基本思路。但令人遗憾的是，
好景不长，正如《列王记下》23：25记载说："在约西亚以前没有
王像他尽心、尽性、尽力地归向耶和华，遵行摩西的一切律法；在
他以后也没有兴起一个王像他。"因此，荒凉的结局已经定了。在
基督徒个人的生活中，我们也是常常如此，不知道错过了多少荣耀
上帝和获得赐福的机会。

小结

整本《圣经·旧约》也可以视为人类文明史的教科书。上帝在
人类文明史中扮演导师的角色。以犹太文明为例，上帝帮助以色列
人从建立个人和群体的圣洁神性信仰开始，然后颁布伦理法典，奠
定神权、人权、责任、自由的文化理念，接着通过二权分立，建立
法治和宪政的社会体制，最后强调社会的圣洁和公义。这是犹太文
明的发展过程和基本元素。

《旧约》记载的犹太文明主要包括神性信仰、伦理道德、法治
宪政。不可忽略的是，犹太文明也学习了当时埃及的一些先进文化，
包括科技、艺术，等方面的。摩西从小接受埃及的皇宫教育，成为
埃及文明中的精英，也就自然将埃及的一些社会文明带入犹太人当
中。同样，在《新约》时代，基督教文明的发展，不仅继承了犹太
文明，还吸取了希腊—罗马的逻辑思维哲学及其衍生的科学和政治
模式——属于纯粹的人性，从而将人类文明推向了新的顶峰。

法治的严厉让平民和国王都害怕，但这不是上帝的最终意图。
上帝希望人们能够自觉遵守法律，从内心自然乐意臣服于上帝的伦
理法典；这正是《旧约》时代上帝教育人类（犹太人为代表）所要
完成的意图。也可以说，人类的文明来自人类对罪性的自我约束，
而这种自我约束的最理想原则是上帝所赐给人类的伦理律法原则

——神权和人权，而最有效的约束是来自对上帝的神性信仰责任的忠实。这样的自我约束程度越高，文明的程度就越高。自我约束，落实到最深处，是对心理的自我约束。文明的大树，从心灵中发芽。（参看笔者的《中国基督徒的心理更新》）

二、西方欧美的基督教文明

基督耶稣来到这个世界，开创了《新约》时代。这一历史事件成为人类文明史的分水岭：上帝亲自来到这个世界，成为人的样式，并且有圣灵从此内住在基督徒里面，直接赋予神性和上帝儿女的身份，从而大大提升了人类文明。在《旧约》严格的伦理法治文明的基础上，《新约》要求人们的行为出自心灵的爱，而不是出于对律法和惩罚的畏惧。爱的动机和行为自然就成全了律法的宗旨，正如耶稣所说的："莫想我来要废掉律法和先知。我来不是要废掉，乃是要成全。"（太5：17）经过漫长的《旧约》时代的神性法治教育，人类文明终于上升到能够接受《新约》伦理教育的高度。

西方欧美的基督教文明，也可以称为人类的《新约》文明的代表，是人类历史中文明的最高峰，至今没有被超越。基督教文明的发展，与《旧约》犹太文明的发展模式，有相当的类似之处；此外，还结合了希腊-罗马的世俗文明。根据我的观察、体验和研究，西方现代文明的辉煌，是世俗罗马-雅典文明与犹太-基督教文明相结合而发展出来的伟大成果。然而，两者的结合并非通过自愿的合作，而是通过近2000年的竞争和斗争相互制约的结果，并主要是通过政教关系的竞技场和阵地。罗马-希腊文明的本质是以理性-法律为中心的世俗文化，犹太-基督教文明的本质是以律法-伦理为中心的信仰文化。伦理作为道德哲学体系，证明人类为什么需要和遵守道德，并为道德提供标准；而信仰意识形态为伦理提供标准。（笔者的《基督教与中国公民社会》）

1、柏拉图对摩西律法的借鉴

"亚历山大的革利免（Clement of Alexandria 公元 3 世纪）是一位哲学家，他认为柏拉图所代表的希腊政治观，特别是在立法方面，受到了摩西的影响。政治就是控制，是与人有关的，因此滋生国王的角色职责。国王通过法律管理，明白如何统治自愿的民众。柏拉图认为政治包括法律和政治正确；后者包括政治视野与政治和谐秩序。一方面，统治者需要调整自己适应被统治者；另一方面，被统治者要顺服统治者。这是摩西管理事务的方式所突出说明的。柏拉图还受到摩西教导的影响，认为法律是基于人的出生，而政治是基于结社和同意。"（参看笔者的《双重身份和双重使命》）

不仅是政治观点，对希腊政治彻底失望的柏拉图，在埃及等中东和西亚地区游学 10 年后回到雅典，他的哲学观点中突然出现了上帝的概念，并明显是出自《创世记》中上帝的形象——宇宙万物的创造者。这并非巧合与推测，因为当时的埃及和西亚地区的文化中，尤其是时逢犹太人回归故土且圣殿重建完毕，摩西五经（《圣经》的前五书）在这些地区传播甚广。《圣经·使徒行传》15：21也证明至少在犹太人居住的地区是这样的，"因为从古以来，摩西的书在各城有人传讲，每逢安息日，在会堂里诵读。"

柏拉图的学生亚里斯多德在此基础上，发展出《形而上学》，终于将门派林立的希腊哲学传统，归纳成一个整齐的在笼统神性框架中的人类理性思维体系。希腊哲学是人类自身探索真理的顶峰水平，除了犹太人的神性文明之外，超过世界上所有其它文明，但也只是属于一般性的人性真理，因为有关上帝的观念和知识，只有通过特殊启示真理，才能为人们所知。当柏拉图学习到了《摩西五经》中的上帝观、世界观和法治观，就将希腊哲学文明推向了新的高度。正如上古时期的神性文明对人类文明的提升："那时候有伟人在地上。后来上帝的儿子们和人的女子们交合生子；那就是上古英武有名的人。"（创世记6：4）

2、教会初期在罗马帝国的得胜——神性信仰的确立

正是在希腊哲学和罗马政治进入成熟时期、罗马帝国殖民以色列等民族并导致这些地区的希腊化的历史文明大环境中，耶稣基督降生在伯利恒，开创了伟大的《新约》时代，并注定要通过神性的教育，将人类的文明推向一个历史新高度。作为人类所创造的文明最高水平的代表者——希腊哲学和罗马政治，在借鉴了《摩西五经》从而得到了一点真理亮光的照射下，这个时候已经预备好了人的心灵和头脑接受耶稣基督的全备真理，尤其是通过《约翰福音》的诠释方式。

除了哲学政治文化的软件环境，罗马帝国前所未有的版图扩张、发达的交通、繁荣的贸易、强大的军事所保障的社会安定，也达到了人类历史中绝无仅有的辉煌，这无疑成为福音传播的最有利的硬件条件。在此基础上，根据《使徒行传》的记载，圣灵的大能工作，将福音从犹太人开始，迅速传播到其它民族和地区。安提阿教会，作为第一个非犹太人教会，差派了历史上的第一位宣教士——使徒保罗，通过三次宣教旅程，将福音甚至传到了罗马帝国的首都。尽管如此，基督教从一开始，就受到犹太宗教保守势力和罗马政治势力的联合绞杀。从耶稣被钉十字架开始，他的门徒们就不断遭受逼迫，并涌现了大批的男女殉道者，前仆后继。

在基督教获得罗马帝国政府许可的自由之前，即在公元 313 年颁布《米兰诏谕》的政令之前，尽管遭受残酷的逼迫，基督教对罗马文明还是产生了重要的影响。作为基督徒生活在罗马统治的境内，形成了许多执著的基督教伦理文化特征，与希腊罗马伦理文化形成了鲜明的对比。例如，罗马文化崇尚男性的健美和勇猛，因此，出生男婴如果看起来不健壮，就会遭到遗弃野外。但是，基督徒却拒绝遗弃自己的孩子（参看殉道者犹斯丁公元 2 世纪的著作《致丢格那妥的信》），无论是否健美。此外，尽管全世界当时都是一夫多妻制，基督徒却严格坚持一夫一妻制。基督徒对妇女和儿童权利的尊敬，远远超越已经领先于全世界的希腊罗马文明。这不是人类自身靠自觉所能达到的文明高度，而是神性信仰责任的启示性真理所带给基督徒的亮光和高层次的文明内涵，以及履行神性和人性的双重责任的强大心灵动力。

顺便提一下，即使在罗马帝国之外的古波斯（伊朗）甚至里海地区，接近中亚，基督教信仰在当地的文化中也如明灯照耀，远远超前于当地的依靠人类自身发展的文明程度。根据在罗马帝国和波斯帝国交界处的几度易帜的埃戴萨（Edessa）王国的基督徒巴代散（Bardaisan 154-222 后被定为异端）的《疆域之律法书》（Book of the Laws of the Lands）的记载，基督教当时向东传播之远，令人吃惊。他在书中记录了当地和东边地区的基督徒群体持守以信仰为基础、与当地文化格格不入的伦理风俗，说：

"我们在帕提亚（Parthia）的弟兄们，他们不娶两个妻子，犹太基督徒们也不行割礼。我们在吉兰（Gilan）和贵霜（Kushan）的姐妹们不与外邦人结婚，那些波斯的基督徒不和他们的女儿结婚。那些米甸（Media）的基督徒不抛弃死人，也不把他们喂狗，也不把快要死的人活埋。埃戴萨的基督徒不会杀死那些犯了奸淫的妻子和姐妹，哈特拉（Hatra）的基督徒拒绝用石头打死小偷。"（Our brothers from Parthia do not marry two wives; Jewish Christians are not circumcised, our sisters from *Gilan* and *Kushan* do not associate with foreigners; those from Persia do not marry their daughters; those from *Media* do not abandon their dead, nor do they give them to the dogs to eat, nor do they bury the dying while still alive, Christians from Edessa do not kill their wives or sisters who commit adultery, and those from *Hatra* do not stone thieves.）

基督教成为罗马国教之后，就给罗马希腊文化注入了真理的神性信仰元素。教会得到空前发展，教义和教会体制趋于成熟。公元476 年，罗马帝国包括首都在内的核心圈被北方的野蛮北欧民族所击败占领，西罗马消亡。在之后的 500 年里，由于教会对这些野蛮民族进行了成功教化，并结合东罗马-希腊文化在东欧的文明，才形成了以基督教信仰为核心的新西方文明的雏形，并最终通过西欧的由马丁·路德发动的基督教改革，将这种神性与人性有机结合的西方文明推向新高度。这个过程类似于《出埃及记》的模式——从文明形态最低级别的奴隶和野蛮人开始，通过接受神性信仰、伦理法典、国王和教皇的宪政二权分离，精神和物质文明程度就得到空前发展和提高。

那么，为什么基督教成为国教之后的一个世纪，巍然屹立 8 个世纪的罗马帝国却亡国了呢？这也是为什么当时许多人指责，是基督教导致了软弱的文化，因此罗马帝国衰落。伟大的神学家奥古斯丁目睹了西罗马的灭亡，出于为基督教辩护的动机，写下了历史巨著《上帝之城》，说明世界上的国度不是永恒的，衰败是不可避免的；而上帝之城跨越历史长河和国家民族的界限，永恒屹立。奥古斯丁的辩论是有力的。也就是说，基督教信仰和基督教文明并不是服务于国家，而是服务于人类，是以人为本、以耶稣基督为主的神性信仰文明，其宗旨是爱上帝与爱人。爱国主义是人性文明的产物，鼓吹国家是最高的负责对象，并因此有合法和"高尚"的理由践踏其它国家的人权与和平。

罗马帝国的衰败，并不是基督教所导致的问题。一方面，可以认为是拥有弓箭和快马优势的野蛮游牧民族对定居民族的武力战胜。在火器发明之前，是世界文明史中许多地区都存在的现象，并且在东方的中国也不例外。从另一方面，需要观察到的是，西罗马消亡了，对基督教有什么影响呢？"在西罗马灭亡和蛮族们铁蹄践踏的恶劣环境中，耶稣基督的教会却巍然屹立。修道院保存并抄写了大量的书籍和经典著作，使得西方文明的知识得以延续下去。并且，教会开始在战火的废墟上向这些野蛮的异教民族传福音。500年后，整个欧洲由野蛮入侵者建立的国家都皈依了基督教，被教会和福音真理所驯服，跨入文明社会的行列，并建立起新兴的国家，先后是法国（公元 496）、爱尔兰（561）、英国（697）、北欧和俄罗斯（公元 1000 年前后）等。"（参看笔者的《神性与人性——燃烧的荆棘》）

也就是说，上帝的智慧高于人类的见识。罗马帝国的西罗马的灭亡，导致野蛮民族有机会进入基督教文化环境，接受基督教信仰，并缔造出全新的西方文明。作为东罗马帝国，保留了希腊罗马文化，但是整体的基督教信仰和社会文明，却没有可观的发展；这是因为传统文化的局限性和束缚性。作为西罗马的地区，那些新兴的西方国家皈依基督教后，在经过神性的信仰之火锤炼后，由于没有文化传统的包袱，基督教迅猛发展。之后，西欧通过十字军东征才接触到并学习了东罗马的世俗人性文明（并导致文艺复兴运动），两者集合逐渐形成了理想的新文明模型，让西方文明在世界文明史中开始遥遥领先。

3、中世纪的文明——神性伦理对人性的驯化更新

"中世纪的黑暗"这种说法，是西方反基督教的人文主义阵营的批评。事实上，中世纪教会对社会的深刻控制和影响，是将野蛮的入侵游牧民族驯化成文明的欧洲人的重要原因。可以说，没有中世纪神性伦理烈火的炼净，就没有之后欧洲文明的辉煌。中世纪的基督教的错误，主要是神性伦理压制人性自由的神学错误和天主教会的错误机制。

从宏观的角度来看，一千年之久的中世纪（从公元476西罗马灭亡算起）的第一个500年，是驯化野蛮民族并建立基督教国家的过程，如同以色列人出埃及。中世纪的第二个500年里，由于政治与神性信仰的合一，在社会中严格执行基督教的伦理法典，是上帝提升人类文明的过程中的一个必经阶段，就如同出埃及之后在旷野40年的信仰和伦理的锤炼，主要也是通过政治与神性信仰合一且二权分离的模式。

中世纪的教会有许多腐败，亏缺了上帝的荣耀。这些罪行包括教皇职位可以买卖、设立宗教法庭残酷处死异端者、出售赎罪券，等等。正如奥古斯丁说明的，上帝之城是无形的，却永恒屹立，由圣灵所连接的众圣徒的心灵而组成的无形教会以及无形教会所组成的上帝国度，也是如此，圣洁而毫无瑕疵。有形教会的问题不断，主要是因为人的罪性，特别是教会领袖和神学家的错误。中世纪的教会和政府的关系，即国王和教皇的关系，属于《旧约》中的二权分立模式。国王和教皇之间的权力斗争导致相互的地位此伏彼起，是中世纪的主题之一。

然而，尽管有许多的错误，上帝仍然让他的教会不断成长和成熟，从而不断更新欧洲的文明程度。中世纪采用信仰和伦理的法律化，并通过严厉的惩罚迫使人们遵守。作为刚刚接受基督教的那些野蛮民族，正是通过这种包括国王在内的所有人都必须臣服在教会权柄之下的制度，没有躲避的空间，才被迫在生活中全方位地深刻实践基督教的神性信仰和人性伦理。这也是曾经为浪子的奥古斯丁的悔改生活历程模式。500 年的严格教育和实践，导致了人们的道德水平和个人灵性素质空前提高，悔改和敬虔成为社会文化公德，成为人们个人生活和生命的一部分，并结出圣洁的果实，从而形成了基督教文明的坚实社会基础和传统伦理文化环境，迎接中世纪后的第三个 500 年文明的全面升级。

在第二个 500 年里，从公元 1096-1291 年，西方欧洲国王们和教皇联合发动了七次十字军东征。在这个过程中，人性文明（文艺、建筑、科技等方面）十分落后的欧洲开始接触到东罗马的希腊传统文化，大开眼界，包括教皇在内的社会精英十分着迷。圣战结束后，从 14 世纪初期，旨在学习罗马传统文明的文艺复兴运动开始在欧洲兴起，一直持续到 16 世纪。"文艺复兴传到北欧，掀起了学术运动。因此使得一大批宗教领袖们成为学者，不仅研究古代神学文献，而且还积极思考研究当时教会的神学思想错误，从而大大促进了基督教神学理论的健康发展，为宗教改革的到来和成功打下了坚实的理论基础。"（参看笔者《神性与人性》）

这 200 年的文艺复兴运动，是在神性信仰的基础上发展人性文明的过程，正如以色列人从埃及等发达国家学习人性文明一样，上帝开始引导欧洲人进入成熟健康的文明形态。事实上，在十字军东征的后期，伟大的神学家阿奎那的托马斯，就将希腊哲学的精华——亚里斯多德的形而上学进行注释和发展，在思维模式方面和哲学相关的学术领域里促进了欧洲的文明。因此，文艺复兴运动不过是在此基础上的全面希腊-罗马化的过程。

这样看来，欧洲文明的发展模式与犹太文明发展的模式类似：将最初所处的社会文明模式推倒重建，首先确立严格的神性信仰（尊主为大），其次建立伦理法典更新个人和社会道德水平，并建立国王和教皇的二权分立模式，然后学习其它民族先进的人性文明，最后形成自身的独特而辉煌的高度文明。然而，两者共同的问题是——都是人的罪性所导致的，在获得高度文明之后，人们就开始骄傲自大，贪图享受，努力争取一种没有上帝及其伦理约束的罪性自由，最终导致神性信仰遭到遗弃。于是，文明就迅速堕落，荒凉的结局定了。

4、近现代的英美文明——西方文明的辉煌顶峰

基督教改革，让西方欧洲开始进入了迦南。社会文化的重点从单纯的神性敬虔转向"信徒皆祭司"和"职业皆呼召"的信仰在生活中的具体实践。神性与人性在个人生活和社会文化中都开始获得健康的平衡。文艺复兴已经导致了社会文化的丰富多样性，尤其是艺术类的成就，提升了整体文明层次。除了天主教团体之外，整个欧洲都沉浸在喜悦中。改革所带来的人性自由空气，不仅使普通信徒们从信仰的僵化形式中解放出来，也让国王贵族们长舒一口气，开始享受因天主教势力衰落而导致的政治自由和政权回到凯撒手中的快乐。

由于错误的神学、教义和教会体制得到纠正，不仅是教会，社会也发生了巨大的变化。基督教改革之后，始于 17 世纪的启蒙运动，让欧洲人的思想和创造力爆发出史无前例的生机，缔造了烟花般绚烂的新文明。在之后的二个多世纪里，欧洲的社会在神性与人性的平衡发展环境中，发挥出惊人的潜力，自然科学、艺术、经济、宪政模式、军事（火器的优势）等，全面高速发展，达到了人类文明史中自罗马帝国以来的最高点。其中，英国成为这些文明的代表性的中坚力量。尽管启蒙运动于 19 世纪初期通过学术界和政界转化成现代主义思想运动，在欧洲形成了公开挑战基督教信仰及其思想的势力，但其健康的发展还是一直持续了 400 多年，至第二次世界大战才放慢了脚步。

这 400 年的辉煌，是在神性信仰、基督教伦理主导的政权管理和社会文化的前提下，罗马-希腊传统的世俗人性文化，特别是科

技和文艺的发展，获得了足够自由的空间，综合作用而导致的。这是真理神性信仰文化和希腊式理性逻辑哲学的人性文化相结合的美好果实；同时，不可忽略宪政制度的重要作用。尽管当时的世俗文化是以反基督教的性质出现，但是以暗流的方式运作，并没有成为主导社会的势力，却正好弥补了当时欧洲人性文化的不足。这是一种注定的巧合。

此外，自 17 世纪中叶起，西方文明在欧洲文明之外，还发展出美国文明这一分支奇葩。美国文明的发展过程和模式，与犹太人在摩西的带领下的文明进程非常类似，因此其文明成果也是辉煌的，并在欧洲文明的基础上更上一层楼，达到人类历史中文明程度的新高峰。公元 1620 年，一批英国等地的清教徒，离开了逼迫他们的欧洲（埃及），乘五月之花号轮船，来到今天美国东北部的普利米斯登陆，正式进入这片迦南美地。

在登陆之前，船上的乘客集体同意制定签署了《五月之花号公约》——美国的第一份政治契约，内容如下：

"以上帝的名义，阿门。我们这些签约之人，是蒙上帝恩佑的大不列颠、法兰西及爱尔兰的威严的国王詹姆斯陛下的忠顺臣民，信仰之捍卫者，——为了上帝的荣耀、基督徒信仰的推广和我们的国王和国家的荣誉，我们航行渡海，为了在弗吉尼亚北部建立第一个殖民地，因此在上帝面前共同庄严签约，彼此自愿结为公民政治团体。为了使上述目的得以有序进行、维持和发展，亦为将来能随时制定、构建和规范最符合、最方便于本殖民地总体利益的一切公正和平等的法律、法规、政令法案、宪章与公职，我们全体承诺对此约完全的遵守与服从。据此，于主后 1620 年 11 月 11 日，我们的英格兰、法兰西、爱尔兰第十八世和苏格兰第五十四世的国王陛下在位之年，在鳕鱼角签署姓名如下，以此证明。"

在这份契约中，至少包含了理想文明生态的三大板块：1、"以上帝的名义"和"推广基督教信仰"，奠定了神性信仰基础。2、基督徒信仰同时也包括了基督徒伦理，还有"公正和平等的法律、法规、政令法案、宪章和公职"。3、然后"在上帝面前庄严签约，彼此自愿结为公民政治团体"，确定了宪政管理和公民权利。

《五月之花号公约》明确了理想文明的三大板块，并且共同签署，美国文明就是按照这个方向发展的。至于文明的第四因素——文艺发展，在前三大文明板块运作而提供的条件下，是顺理成章的。这个公约对于美国文明的形成，意义超过那份专注在政治和公民权利的《独立宣言》。《独立宣言》更多地是代表了罗马政治-希腊文化，而不是基督教神性信仰。因此，《五月之花号公约》和《独立宣言》构成了理想文明生态的两部分要素：**以基督教为基础的信仰神性文化和以理性逻辑哲学思维模式为基础的人性文化。**

在之后的 300 年里，美国文明迅速发展，在经历了独立战争和南北内战之后，文明走向成熟，并在 20 世纪初期一跃成为世界最发达的文明强国。美国文明在 20 世纪导致了全球化运动，因此对全世界产生了决定性的影响，涉及人类文明的各个方面：基督教信仰、科技、政治、经济、军事、教育、文艺、体育，等等。美国文明不仅是基督教文明史的最高峰，也是迄今人类文明的最高水平。

亚历西斯·德·托克维尔（Alexis de Tocqueville 1805-1859 法国政治思想家），在其名著《论美国的民主》的第十五章中，深刻阐明了基督教是美国公民社会—民主制度的不可分割的因素，并提倡政府应当遵守基督教的道德。对于基督教信仰在美国公民社会中的作用，他是这样阐明的：

"在美国，每星期的第七天，全国的工商业活动都好象完全停顿，所有的喧闹的声音也听不到了。人们迎来了安静的休息，或者勿宁说是一种庄严的凝思时刻。灵魂又恢复了自主的地位，并进行自我反省。

在这一天里，市场上不见人迹；每个公民都带领自己的子女到教堂去，在这里倾听他们似乎很少听到过的陌生的布道讲演。他们听到了高傲和贪婪所造成的不可胜数的害处。传教士向他们说：人必须抑制自己的欲望，只有美德才能使人得到高尚的享乐，人应当追求真正的幸福。

他们从教堂回到家里，并不去看他们的商业帐簿，而是要打开《圣经》，从中寻找关于造物主的伟大与善良，关于上帝的功业的无限壮丽，关于人的最后归宿、职责和追求永生权利的美好动人描写。

美国人就是这样挤出一点时间来净化自己，暂时放弃其生活上的小小欲望和转瞬即逝的利益，而立即进入伟大、纯洁和永恒的理想世界的。

我在本书的上一卷里考察过美国人的政治制度得以持久的原因，并认为宗教是主要原因之一。现在，我要研究的是宗教对个人的影响，并认为这种影响对每个公民的作用，并不亚于它对整个国家的作用。

美国人以他们的行动证明：他们认为必须依靠宗教，才能使民主制度具有德化的性质。美国人本身对于这个问题的看法，也是一切民主国家应当理解的真理。"

（该翻译版本来自 http://www.pacilution.com/ShowArticle.asp?ArticleID=4028）

令人遗憾的是，始于文艺复兴时期、在启蒙运动和现代主义运动中发展壮大并在二次世界大战后逐渐羽翼丰满的以抵挡基督教为主旋律的西方世俗自由主义意识形态，终于在进入后现代主义时期之后（1960-1970 年代）彻底控制了欧洲的社会文化，揭开了欧洲文明走向歧途并无法避免败落的序幕。同一种力量，来自欧洲但是步伐要慢大约 50 年，也在美国社会文化中逐渐渗透，同样是通过占领高等教育领域的方式，于 21 世纪初期取得了决定性的胜利，正高度自信地开始全面摧毁伟大的美国文明。

5、当代欧美文明的衰落——神性信仰及其伦理的失落

马丁·路德发动基督教改革之后，在神性信仰及其伦理和人性自由的健康社会文化环境中，欧洲文明在文艺复兴的基础上，迅速发展并通过启蒙运动而走向高潮。然而，正如主耶稣基督在《马太福音》13：24-26 所说的那样："天国好象人撒好种在田里，及至人睡觉的时候，有仇敌来，将稗子撒在麦子里就走了。到长苗吐穗的时候，稗子也显出来。" 在这种社会文化巨变的形势中，始于

17 世纪的启蒙运动，蕴藏了一股反基督教的世俗暗流，开始在欧洲慢慢集结并渐渐汹涌起来。这股力量代表了罗马世俗民主政治和希腊自然论（无神论或自然神论）的哲学，尤其是后者在被奥古斯丁的神学收编并沦为婢女长达 1000 年之后，终于利用基督教内部的分裂和国王政治势力的煽风点火以及民众长期遭受宗教律法压抑的不满情绪，抓住了历史机遇，开始号召人性解放并以此掩盖其反叛的计划，并最终于 19 世纪初期形成了现代主义思潮。

于是，这股暗流中的两大敌基督思潮，在现代主义的两大旌旗——达尔文的生物进化论和无神论的科学唯物主义——的号召鼓励下，终于登堂入室，成为社会文化潮流。前者是以科学的面孔出现，后者是以政治哲学的手段。20 世纪的两次世界大战标志着西方现代文明的分水岭，并于 1960 年代开始进入后现代时期，即当代时期。由此，西方文明从辉煌的顶峰开始走向衰落，是因为科学教育与政治哲学的阵地被反基督教的自由主义占领而导致的。如今在 21 世纪初期，西方文明的腐败性衰落开始浮出水面，如冰山一角。当然，西方文明的衰落，是相对于自己的辉煌顶峰而言的，相比于世界其它所有文明，西方文明至今仍然是遥遥领先的。

笔者在《神性与人性》中，对现代主义思潮的问题进行了如下分析：

现代主义思想运动的产生，主要是因为法国大革命和拿破仑的军事扩展，导致欧洲对启蒙运动思想文明的怀疑并试图寻找新的方案；同时，达尔文的进化论的出现，是现代主义思想运动形成的标志性大旗。现代主义思想运动主要包括两支：无神论的科学唯物主义和受其影响而产生的基督教自由主义思想。前者强调的是神性并不存在而"人定胜天"，后者强调的是人性不需要神性而自主。启蒙运动本质上促进了基督教人性文明的大跃进，并继续强调神性框架下的真理性和确定性，以及基督教伦理体系的不可缺少性，属于神性光照下的现实主义。而现代主义思想运动则是人性文明针对神性文明的大反叛，尽管仍然强调真理的概念，却抛弃基督教伦理，建立人性（和罪性）自由为原则的伦理体系。出于对人的高度自信，认为人能够不依靠神性成为美好的人，且没有神性的社会能够更加理想和文明，因此这是一种盲目幼稚的人性理想主义。马克思等人的共产主义理想，就是在这种思想的基础上进一步发展产生的。

现代主义思想的自信，主要是来自于现代科学的发展和世俗主义哲学，尤其是达尔文的生物进化论，有力挑战了基督教的创造论，并席卷学术界，成为一种新的信仰并衍生出新的思想意识形态体系。直到今天，科学已经发展到基因阶段，仍然有许多科学家相信进化论。最可笑的是，西方的学校从小学就开始教授进化论，与共产主义国家的洗脑式教育异曲同工。进化论为核心的无神论唯物主义思想在欧洲发展了还不到一个世纪，震惊全人类的两次世界大战爆发，人性自主和人定胜天的高度自信遭到完全摧毁。

第一次世界大战的爆发，只是给欧洲偏离神性轨道的骄傲且盲目的人性以警告。然而，欧洲社会却在错误的道路上越滑越远。第二次世界大战不可避免的爆发，其中德国、意大利和亚洲的日本扮演了罪恶的角色。日本是现代主义文明在欧洲之外的唯一门徒。现代主义浪潮对北美的影响比较肤浅和缓慢，因为清教徒建立并影响的美国文明高度重视神性，且十分坚固和强大。欧洲的现代-后现代主义文明发展比北美的总是快一步。

达尔文的生物进化论在欧洲摧毁了基督教的神性信仰文化，现代主义思潮摧毁了基督教的伦理法典权威，并因此奠定了欧洲文明走向衰落的文化土壤。二次世界大战之后，在种族问题上人们接受了教训，尽管不承认是由于生物进化论的影响，但是在实践上采取了政治自由主义政策（不是基督教的伦理，虽然表面相似，本质上是反真理的）。自由主义思想认为种族之间平等的观点，是基于世俗高尚主义的文明情感，认为人类本质是高尚的，因此能够解决自己的问题。基督教伦理是出于启示性真理，认为上帝创造的每个人都是平等的，但是强调每个人的罪性，以及人类无法自救。

需要高度重视的是，现代主义思潮中最有影响力的产物——达尔文的生物进化论和无神论的科学唯物主义的结晶——共产主义，是敌基督教势力和败坏欧洲文明的主要力量。马克思所称的这个"在欧洲上空徘徊的幽灵"，在上个世纪掀起了世界范围内的共产主义暴政运动，将大约三分之一的人类奴役在暴力和贫穷为主旋律的枷锁下，践踏了人类的基本尊严。冷战后，人们欢呼共产主义政权的连锁垮台，但是由于对共产主义本质的忽略，导致共产主义幽灵在欧洲再次趁机复苏反扑，这次是以政治自由主义的面孔，通过以和平演变的方式，正在大获全胜。

共产主义的本质，并不是独裁和计划经济——这些只是共产主义政权建立之后的执政方式。共产主义的本质在于其政治社会哲学理念：资本家追求商业利润造成社会分配不公平；穷人的问题总是富人和精英造成的；普通民众是历史的创造者，而不是社会精英；需要暴力手段进行社会资源平均分配。

二十世纪的共产主义运动，就是基于这样的假大空理念，特别是仇富心理，成功煽动了民众的物质欲和权力欲的罪性，导致革命运动的成功，消灭了社会精英阶层，开始了共产主义政权时代。共产主义在灵界背景中，是人类罪性通过高尚的借口而自由发挥的伪善道德和邪恶政治，因此其罪恶之任意妄为的惨重代价是必然的。于是，民众很快发现，共产主义革命的口号完全落空了，因为人民更加贫穷，社会更加不公正，政治更加腐败。由于精英阶层被系统性的消灭，整体社会生产能力和运作效率大大降低。而且，新的精英群体从人民中脱颖而出，尽管能力远远不如他们之前所消灭的贵族精英，但是对于权力和财富的渴望与贪婪，却有过之而不及；他们对人民专制的凶狠，达到历史的新高度。因此，通过暴力革命而产生的共产主义暴政，很快由于自身的运转失灵以及遭到人民的反对而垮台，或苟延残喘。

令人惊奇的是，共产主义运动并没有因此消亡，而是在欧洲和美国继续通过和平演变的方式进行。自从 1960 年代后，由于政治自由主义和反基督教世俗力量的联合运作，通过教育系统和大众媒体，对人民逐渐实施系统性的洗脑式教育，让民众不知不觉地接受了共产主义的本质理念。其中，因为暴力革命的方式已经遭到普世谴责，共产主义理念的鼓吹者就号召通过民主制度的投票进行颠覆，然后制定新法律，通过法律暴力推行社会资源的平均分配，践踏了多劳多得的自由经济的公平原则，同时鼓励了不劳而获的偷盗和寄生文化。这正是如今欧洲和美国正在进行的共产主义和平演变，全方位毁坏着西方基督教伦理中"敬虔、公平与爱"为基础的文明生态。

笔者在《基督教与中国公民社会》中，通过政治与宗教之间关系的角度，阐述了西方文明遭到敌基督教思想潮流的腐蚀并产生恶果的原理：

包括《独立宣言》在内的美国的立国政治哲学和宪政体系，几乎借鉴了英国伟大的基督徒学者约翰·洛克的基于基督教伦理的全套理论体系，涉及宪政制度、政府教会分离、公民权利，以及宗教容忍，都是从"上帝创造人人平等"这一基督教的神学命题出发。作为《独立宣言》的主要起草人——自然神论者、罗马文明的杰出代表者杰弗逊（美国第三任总统），裁减了洛克的原装体系，忽视了经济财产方面的理论，并用"上帝"和"不言而喻"这样的语言，"忽悠"了善良的清教徒们，导致美国政教分离的程度，从开始就一直是模糊不清的。根据杰弗逊的《圣经》观和自然神论信仰，他所说的上帝，其实就是亚里斯多德的形而上哲学意义的上帝。这是非常巧妙的概念偷换。当时似乎只有后来成为杰弗逊的政敌的约翰·亚当斯——基督教文明的代表者，看出了其中的"猫腻"。这位美国的第一任副总统和第二任总统，他的观点很清楚："我们的宪法是为持守道德的宗教人士所设立的，而对于不是这样的人民所组成的政府而言，是完全不济于事的。"[30]（Our constitution was made only for a moral and a religious people. It is wholly inadequate to the government of any other.）这里的"宗教人士"，在当时指的是基督徒。美国的政教关系模式，是西方和世界文明史中最先进的制度，但仍然有发展的空间。

此外，西方的宪政思路在最初形成的时候，其方向主要是限制国王和政府滥用权利，怎样保护公民权利。然而，基督教的神学认为国王和草民同样是罪人，都需要制约；面对上帝人人平等；受害方并不一定是正义的。如今西方文明经过 300 多年的努力终于限制了君王和政府的权利，却吃惊地发现人民的权利也需要限制，尤其是在面对国家（或民族）之间利益冲突的情况下。那些民主万能论者的假设是，人民和多数人总是正确的。但事实并非如此，民众可能通过暴力革命和民主制度而滥用参政权利，并集结成"可拉一党"，满足自己的权利欲和罪性（《圣经·民数记》第16章）。例如，以爱国和追求自由平等为口号的法国大革命、二战时期崇尚种族爱国主义的德国和日本法西斯、共产主义暴政的苏联-东欧-中国-朝鲜、当今中东茉莉花革命后一些国家的民主暴政，以及非洲一些国家的宪政公民—民主政府的集体腐败。因此，二战后联合国的建立和国际法-公约的制定发展，都是旨在保护超越国家公民权利概念的人权（这也是一个非常基督教的概念）。然而，事实上国际法是难以实现的，因为在将神权和王权去除之后，国家就被爱国主义神化，公民就被民主制度神化，成为最高的权威。这又是一个怪圈。

西方延续始于19世纪的现代主义思想运动的反基督教的世俗无神论的信仰意识形态，借着怀疑主义和世俗存在主义的哲学（标志性口号：上帝死了），在整个20世纪横行霸道，并在1960-1970年代的西方达到高潮进入后现代主义-相对主义（postmodernism-relativism）时期，如今已经在欧洲大获全胜，且正在美国挺进。这个时代的特点是，人们不再相信有绝对的真理，甚至不相信有真理，因为一切都是相对的；大声宣告美与丑、善与恶之间的对立消失，甚至不相信邪恶的存在；心理学、精神病学和大脑科学解释并定论所有人类的行为现象，精英和民众都盲目崇尚多元主义。这种可怕愚昧的哲学思潮席卷学术界、政界和社会其它公共领域，形成不可挑战的政治正确的偶像。然而，2011年挪威于特岛和2012年美国纽敦镇的邪恶而恐怖的枪声，标志着后现代主义在西方已经破产。

当欧洲人抛弃了基督教的信仰及其伦理文化，在政府与教会分离的基础上，进一步实现了政教（政治与基督教）的彻底分离、教育世俗化，就将人民和祖国神化，或将欧洲共同体神化。反基督教的世俗和自由主义势力，还在1960年代后的欧洲通过在社会政治文化中提倡和实践信仰文化的多元主义，大量移入非基督教文化的外国群体，并在公共教育中灌输这一信仰意识形态。然而，这是一项失败的实验。短短的几十年，伊斯兰教社会力量就在英法等国崛起，导致欧洲传统文明一元主导的格局被打破。尤其是穆斯林社区对伊斯兰教伦理和教法的强硬推广，以及穆斯林人口比例的迅速增加，就对欧洲世俗自由主义信仰意识形态中的"普世价值观"（例如，一夫一妻制、男女平等）产生了强有力的挑战。尽管不愿意承认，欧洲的精英们和民众应当开始意识到，即使是西方反基督教的世俗价值观，也有基督教文化洗礼的印记，因此并不是其它非基督教文化和信仰意识形态都会承认的"普世价值"。这样看来，美国的 911 悲剧和英法德等穆斯林社区对欧洲文明的挑战，标准着多元主义在西方已经破产。

可见，世俗后现代主义-相对主义和以不同信仰为基础的多元文明主义，在西方通过人口比例的变化和民主制度，悄悄成为推翻既定一元主导文化而建立新一元主导文化的平台，因此是一个无法静止和平衡的过程。信仰多元主义秩序的理想只能在世界范围内，由不同国家之间的和平共处来实现，但超越国家界限的信仰文明的扩张和国家利益至上所导致的冲突，让这样的局面难以在长时间范围内和（或）大面积地实现。

如今，在西方社会中的基督教社区严重缩小和后现代主义-多元信仰文化崛起的情况下，反基督教的世俗和自由主义通过民主的方式占据上峰，并逐渐通过新法律的制定，演化成为公开反对和压制基督教信仰文化对社会的合法影响。这种现实还导致民主制度会成为微弱多数的一半公民统治另一半公民甚至强加于令微弱少数群体良心不安的信仰意识形态，而且是通过社会文化中的政治正确和国家法治的冠冕堂皇，从而将宪政掳到罗马，将民主劫持到雅典。

令人鼓舞的是，一些寻求真理的学者已经开始抛弃后现代主义，并反思信仰多元文化（多元文明）的困境和基于这种文化环境的民主制度的失灵和尴尬。

小结

西方文明的衰落，如果不悬崖勒马，就会成为定局。欧洲将沦为伊斯兰教的天下，伊斯兰教通过和平演变的策略，终于即将实现了自公元 8 世纪伊斯兰教的阿拉伯人经过血腥刀剑之争企图占领欧洲却无法成功的梦想。在不久的将来，欧洲就可能重蹈今天的南非和津巴布韦的社会变革模式及其覆辙。而美国，随着来自落后国家移民数量的激增和政府继续增加福利投资，将可能沦为**亚**共产主义的国度，从而将陷入如今拉丁美洲的政治、社会、经济模式。

西方文明的衰落和所表现的伦理道德的耻辱，根本原因并不在于敌基督教的势力强大，而是在于文明中的一系列根本因素的多米诺骨牌式的腐败效应：首先是神性信仰的衰落——这是因为教会和神学的衰落——因为精英教会的衰落——因为精英基督徒数量的减少——因为神学家和教会领袖的错误。神性信仰的衰落，导致伦理道德的堕落，然后是法律和法制出现问题，最后宪政制度成为微弱多数的一半人口的变相独裁、实施合法暴力的工具。此外，今天的欧洲和美国，在文艺领域中一直没有历史性突破，尽管科技在日新月异，不断划时代。

精英教会是西方近现代历史中的最为重要的社会积极力量和创造文明的基督徒团体。从英国的宪政推行者们到美国独立战争——美国内战的领导者们，都是精英基督徒和精英教会起到了决定性的带领角色作用。然而，如今的教会也普遍接受了共产主义的理念，忽视甚至排斥精英基督徒的重要作用，竭力让五千两银子才干的基督徒和一千两银子才干的基督徒，做同样的工作，扮演同样的角色。问题是，五千两银子的基督徒们，将来当如何在主的面前交账呢？

三、教会和基督徒在中国创造新文明

中国人至今对文明的理解仍然异常困难，因此很难证明这个高智商的民族是否有足够的思想、智慧和伦理道德来成功管理社会。中国的传统文明，是属于低级、愚昧、儒释道等邪灵文化的大杂烩。食与色，仍然是中国人文明的核心，属于**类人**文明，或高级动物特征。再加上中国人至今还有吃胎盘的习惯，所以中国文明还未脱离野蛮习俗。令人遗憾的是，正如许多文明层次低的民族那样，中国人也缺乏清楚的自我意识，不知道与高端文明之间的光年差距，自我感觉良好。

许多中国人认为文明发达的因素是：经济富裕、公平的社会体制、高等教育、普及科学知识、勤奋劳动、高的智商。然而，在过去的 30 年里，中国人一直在这些领域中积极努力，在某些方面取得了一些成就，但整体社会文明程度反而倒退了。于是，人们将所有的问题都归咎于中国不公平的社会体制和政府的腐败。这些当然是重要的因素，但仍然不是决定性的。

高度文明有一个明显的标志是，重视自我批评，听取别人批评。低级文明正好相反，不允许任何人批评，认为自己的问题全是别人造成的。高度文明偏重于提倡爱人，特别是爱自己国家的公民，低级文明偏重于提倡爱国，却残酷对待自己国家的公民。造假（包括有毒的婴儿奶粉）、盗版——其最高形态是山寨文化，还有蓬勃的色情行业，等等，这些都是文明的疾病，是动物般贪婪导致走捷径的直接后果。

文明是什么？打一个比方：人们造出一辆汽车，这是模仿性创造。当美丽的车模以主人的角色站在车旁的时候，这就是文明了；当车模站在那里充当车的配角的时候，文明又失去了。再一个比方，鲜花与假花之间的区别，就在于是否有生命，而这种生命就代表了文明。

没有圣洁的神性信仰及其伦理，人类依靠人性、良知和头脑所能达到的文明高度，顶多就是奥古斯丁所说的那样，会因为共同分享美好而感到高兴。然而，在个人与个人、群体和群体、国家与国家之间的利益冲突的情况下，才能显示出文明的质量和层次。理想的高级文明形态可以称为"橄榄文明"，而低级的文明是"荆棘文明"。（参看笔者的《基督教与中国公民社会》）

中国基督徒要利用自身优势，从现在开始，有意识地参与促进新文明在家庭和社会中的诞生。基督教文明在中国发展的要素包括：**个人建立基督教神性信仰，在社会中推广基督教伦理文化，在家庭和社会中促进人性自由，更新心理与思维模式，建立宪政法治保障公民权利，基督徒持守双重身份并忠心履行双重使命。**

1、在个人生活中建立基督教神性信仰

要想提高整体的个人、家庭和社会文明，中国人需要在个人生活中建立以《圣经》为根基的基督教神性信仰。这种信仰的建立和成熟并不是孤立的，而是与教会生活联合在一起的。教会是在中国缔造新文明的平台，基督徒是在这个平台上的工人，通过**伦理的桥梁**参与社会，履行着推进上帝国度和社会文明的双重责任。

一旦超过30%的中国人成为基督徒，社会新文明的成长就具备了良好的土壤。这些数量的基督徒的出现，必然伴随着教会的复兴，而教会的复兴是上帝国度在这个世界得胜扩大的标志。教会的复兴在灵界中起到一种洁净更新社会、积累正能量的作用，并进一步支撑和推进个人的信仰质量。

在这个过程中，要重视建立精英基督徒群体和精英教会。首先，建立精英团契。这种团契可以是松散型的、以社会背景和个人关系为纽带的基督徒朋友圈子，也可以是在教会中的正规团契。其次，当精英基督徒群体的人数足够的时候，就当建立专门的精英教会。在北京、上海等大城市，精英教会已经开始崛起，这是教会和个人信仰走向成熟的一个重要标志。

精英基督徒群体本身就代表着社会中的最高文明形态，能够充当合格的带领和规划的角色，因此缔造社会新文明是他们的优势。今天的中国人，由于共产主义思想中对精英憎恨意识的灌输洗脑，甚至精英自己也认为普通民众是历史的创造者。正确的解读应当是，中国的民众只有顺服基督徒精英的领导，才能够改变和创造历史，从而享受文明的美好成果。没有基督徒精英的领导，民众是盲目的，即使基督徒民众也不例外。同时，没有民众的支持、配合和服从，精英也无计可施。注意，那些非基督徒的精英们，他们常常是利用、勒索和欺骗民众，因此只是头脑的精英，而不是文明的精英。

个人信仰的建立和成熟，与教会和团契的生活密不可分。同时，要重视个人信仰在家庭中的实践。家庭是社会的单元，美好的基督教文明可以在家庭中首先实现，而不必等到整个社会实现之后。精英基督徒家庭要首先实现基督教文明，否则，就无法证明精英基督

徒的身份。精英基督徒还要积极在社会精英当中传播福音，将人心夺回，归于基督，影响教会也影响社会。

精英是相对而言的一个社会群体。在不同的阶层、文化和民族群体中，都有自己的精英团体。因此，精英是广泛分布在社会中的，并非高高在上的唯一小团体。精英意识是文明的重要动力，崇尚精英的社会文化是符合《圣经》教导的。上帝在《旧约》中，重视选择精英来完成伟大的历史使命。在《新约》中，上帝既拣选草根也拣选精英，因为基督教所面对的不只是以色列人，而是全人类各民族不同的社会阶层。于是，上帝安排精英履行精英的使命，普通人履行普通人的使命，如同身体的不同部分联合运作，荣耀耶稣基督的圣名。作为当时精英基督徒的代表保罗，他所完成的使命是最伟大的，包括书写《新约》的三分之一和开创对非犹太人的宣教事业。同样，上帝也使用彼得、约翰那些没有学问的小民。

正如《哥林多前书》第 12 章的教导，身体的每个部分都有同样的价值，都有各自独特的职责，尽管有体面和不体面之分，俊美不俊美之分，但都有同样的价值和尊贵。眼睛要做眼睛的工作，手脚要做手脚的工作。因此，在教会中和社会中，基督徒们的职责有的体面一些，例如，精英的工作；而有的则不太体面，例如，社会基层人士的工作。但是，在基督里他们都是一样重要的价值和角色。精英和草民都要谦卑下来，不要互相指责和鄙视。然而，需要注意的是，精英们不要扮演非精英的角色，非精英人士也不要做精英的工作，否则就会导致"身体"的功能紊乱。这就是共产主义意识形态和西方自由主义的问题所在。

中国基督徒应当奋起，争做主耶稣基督的**精兵**，在这场宏大的历史性的属灵争战中，打那美好的胜仗。正如已经强调过的，一千两银子恩赐的人，不要企图扮演五千两银子才能的角色；同样，五千两银子才干的人，也不要只从事一千两银子才干的职责。根据主耶稣基督的呼召和恩赐，履行自己的职责，这才是个人信仰实现最大效率发光的方式。基督教的发展，主要是普通基督徒民众的责任；基督教对社会文明的更新，主要是精英基督徒的责任。中国教会的巨大发展，是草根民众基督徒信仰运动的伟大成果。因此，缔造基督教文明的教会平台已经搭好了，却迟迟不见精英基督徒们的身影。

2、在社会中推广基督教伦理文化

基督教伦理对于个人来说，是知罪悔改导致生命被圣灵洁净更新的理性原则；对于社会来说，是清除文化中的罪性而洁净社会文明的公德标准。一位来自中国家庭教会的年轻牧者在给我的电子邮件中，对于罪与文明的问题，是这样深刻分析评论的：

"我突然感到清除罪恶是一个极为复杂和需要极大代价的事。我现在重新看待中国教会中对于'圣俗分开'的喜爱，是盼望一步到位的拜偶像心态。信徒们很喜欢接受我是'新造的'，却没有热情'不断改造'。罪性在人生命中是交织的，也必然交织在文化中，稗子无法拔除，会伤及麦子。对世俗文化中罪性的改造，如同基督徒生命中对罪性的根除。如此看来，文明的进程应该就是一个螺旋上升的过程。这样，上帝的救赎在个人和人类文明的整体上达成一致。"

一个社会中不可能所有的人都接受基督教信仰，但是，一个社会必须要有统一的伦理体系，否则，社会就会混乱。在过去 2 千年的人类文明史中，已经证明了基督教伦理是最理想的个人、家庭和社会伦理。基督教文明的建立，并非一定要在全民归主的基础上。当一个社会中的大部分人（70%）成为基督徒后，基督教伦理就可以深入推广并植根在社会中。也就是说，一个人可以不接受基督教信仰，但是应当接受基督教伦理。这种推广是不需要强迫的，因为基督教伦理通过基督徒的美好作为，以及如今普世价值（世俗版的基督教伦理）的推广，是容易被人们接受的，除此也没有更高明的伦理与之相比。例如，没有人可以否认爱人如己的基督教伦理——耶稣的教导："你们愿意人怎样待你们，你们也要怎样待人。"基督教的伦理优势，也是如今的中国民众普遍赞赏基督教的一个重要原因。

　　基督教伦理包括尊重神权和保护人权。其中，在人权方面，在个人的道德规范和社会公德中，弘扬公义和爱人如已，是总的原则。基督教还强调勤奋劳动的美德，说明作工的当得工价（罗 4：4）、不作工就不可以吃饭的原则（帖后 3：10）。有趣的现象是，并不是每一种社会文化和文明都在同样程度上强调勤奋劳动的美德和付诸实践。任何一种文明，最终都要落实到人的具体工作中。因此，依靠勤奋劳动而致富的原则，也是约翰·卫斯理在美国早期移民中所大力提倡的信仰实践方式，极大促进了美国早期物质文明的发展。约翰·卫斯理的影响美国早期基督教社会文化的口号是：竭尽所能地挣钱、竭尽所能地存钱、竭尽所能地捐钱。

　　基督徒的工作伦理是荣耀主名，并承担供养家庭的责任，帮助有经济缺乏的人。物质文明是社会文明不可缺少的基础，因此，工作和纳税是每个公民的责任。文明程度越高的群体，人们就越崇尚勤奋劳动，并且视依靠接受社会福利和政府援助而生活为耻。由这样的群体而组成的社会，在法治的原则下，就一定会成为物质发达的社会。根据保罗的教导，个人的重担要个人承担，在此基础上，还要分担彼此的重担。这是非常合理的原则。

　　伦理文化既可以成为文明的资本，也可以化为文明的成本，正如政治制度一样。中国人勤奋劳动，但是伦理文化和政治制度成本太高，因此物质文明仍然在世界最差的行列中，而精神文明也是如此。推广基督教伦理，能够改良文化环境，并最终改变不合理的社会制度。除了公义和爱的总原则之外，勤奋劳动也是重要的美德。

　　此外，家庭和婚姻的伦理也是极其重要的。一夫一妻制是基督教的伦理，并且如今被广泛接受，提升了人类的整体文明。然而，一夫一妻制是基督教文明的产物；如果文明层次达不到，人们就会排斥一夫一妻制。就中国如今的社会来看，一夫一妻制已经通过法律实行了 60 多年了，但是，上至国家领导人，下到平民百姓，只要有机会和条件，都会在实质上实践"一夫多妻"的传统婚姻文化。文明好比是戴在美女脖子上的珍贵项链，如果戴在猪脖子上，文明就消失了。因此，文明是一种艺术。

基督教信仰及其伦理和希腊罗马式的理性思维模式，是西方文明的联合载体。敬畏神权才能保护人权，理性思维才有创造性。许多人误以为，作为工具性的民主制度、宪政法治、公民社会、科技，才是西方文明的载体，并导致了对人权的尊重保护和社会的发达安定繁荣。然而，在非洲的殖民地国家纷纷独立、政权从欧洲殖民者移交到本地人之后，尽管继承了民主体制和宪政法治，社会文明程度却大幅度降低，法治紊乱，经济一落千丈，这又如何解释呢？津巴布韦和南非，是两个最典型的例子。中东尽管有源源不断的石油出卖而获得巨额财富，但文明程度还停留在一夫多妻制的程度，科技和教育也极其落后。然而，基督徒比例很高的许多拉丁美洲国家的文明程度，也远远低于美国和加拿大，尽管自然资源和社会制度没有什么区别；这主要是因为缺乏理性思维模式和及其实践应用，因此导致管理模式和效率低下；解决方案应该是在民众中普及罗马-希腊理性文明影响下的当代高等教育。在中国，虽然高等教育、科学技术和经济有了较大的发展，理性思维模式也逐渐普及，但是人们的生活质量仍然非常低劣，并且伦理道德的严重缺失导致社会中的罪恶严重泛滥。即使是亚洲最发达的日本、台湾、新加坡和香港，采用全套的西方民主、宪政、经济和教育制度，其文明程度与西方仍相差甚远。韩国是一个有趣的例子，其传统的孔孟文化束缚了基督教伦理的发挥，其传统的佛教思维方式牵制了理性逻辑思维模式，从而导致了基督教文明被传统文化荆棘所挤压。

因此，高层文明不只是简单的体制和可以模仿的技术，其核心是基督教的信仰伦理和希腊罗马式的理性逻辑思维模式。两者缺一不可。注意，在基督教文明的成长中，戴着基督教面具的异端邪教是相当危险可恶的属灵病毒和心理顽疾，需要坚决抵制和清除。

基督徒在中国社会中，主要是通过个人的社会圈子、教会圈子和私人圈子，以身作则，推广基督徒的伦理文化。此外，教会和基督徒还要通过所居住的社区、无形化的团契社区，建立起基督徒的文化社区，将基督教伦理植入社区，形成新的社区文化。

3、在家庭和社会中促进人性自由

中世纪的欧洲尽管是全民归信基督教，但是文明程度却没有突破。在文艺复兴运动开始后，尤其是马丁路德的基督教改革之后，在天主教和基督教之间相争导致的教会势力的狭小真空中，人们找到了人性自由的乐园。然而，罪性也乘机发展，最终走向抵制神性的极端。

在悔改归主之后实践信仰的过程中，神性和人性的平衡，是基督教文明中的关键。笔者在《神性与人性》中，分析说明了神性前提和人性自由健康发展的重要性、神性与人性平衡的原理。

人类文明的发展是人性文明不断被《圣经》及其信仰的神性文明更新提高的过程。人类历史是上帝不断教育人类和升级人类文明的过程。通过神性的启蒙、滋养、塑造和丰富人性，让人类文明以个人、家庭、社会和族群的形式不断提高，发挥出上帝创造的人性潜力，成为光和盐，驱散罪恶的黑暗势力，荣耀上帝的圣名。

神性是烈火，或者是阳光，适当的距离能够给人性以温暖的美好支持供应，但是距离过近就会令人性干渴，甚至被烤干。神学和教义以及信仰实践，要给人性留下足够的空间让神性的阳光照射进来，才能促进人性的果实生长并荣耀神性。

基督徒需要意识到，是美好的人性献在祭坛上，成为馨香蒙上帝悦纳的祭。为什么上帝说，他喜爱怜恤，不喜爱祭物。耶稣说献祭之前，要首先谋求与弟兄的和睦。上帝是多么重视人性，但太多的人只注重追求神性，并因此忽视甚至压制了人性。另外一个极端则是，基督徒受到世俗文化的影响，对自己拥有的神性不自信，从而冷落甚至抛弃神性，导致人性的枯竭，令上帝失望和谴责。

在中国的家庭中，由于儒教和佛教的影响，家庭文化普遍压抑人性，严肃过度，活泼不足，尤其是对孩子的教育和管理。由于以升学为硬指标，中国父母对孩子的培养主要是追求高分数和高智商，从而扼杀了重要的心灵活力和头脑创造力。文明是人类心灵的美好和头脑创造力的结晶，而不是简单的知识学习和高智商累积的成果。

创造和提升文明的重要因素，除了真理神性信仰和伦理之外，是人的智慧，这是与智商几乎没有关系的概念。

文明的程度受到两个因素的影响：圣洁的真理神性信仰和理性逻辑辩证思维文化；具体来讲，就是基督教信仰和希腊罗马文化。文明-文化也有优劣之分，有发展中的文明-文化和发达文明-文化，正如国家一样。人类文明在西方欧美文明的基础上，还会有很大的发展空间。

智慧的缺乏，在基督教信仰和伦理确立后，是可以弥补的。《圣经·箴言》9:10 教导说："敬畏耶和华是智慧的开端；认识至圣者便是聪明。"这是非常重要的开端，之后就要重视人性的自由。人性的自由主要表现在心理的自由和思维模式的自由。基督徒只有在家庭中首先实践人性的自由并获得成功，才能在社会中推广。一些加尔文主义者认为，整个社会都应该被基督教信仰所占领，这其实是错误的神学观点。社会中必须要有世俗文化的空间，以保持社会的人性自由，否则，就会回到中世纪的社会模式。然而，世俗文化的空间必须要臣服在基督教伦理的框架下，不可喧宾夺主。否则，人的罪性就会借自由之名发作而反叛，突破上帝的命令去偷吃禁果，从而导致上帝的惩罚和人类文明堕落的苦果。

4、更新心理与思维模式

笔者在《中国基督徒的心理更新》中，详细阐明了更新的原理和方法。更新心理能够从根部铲除和压制一个人的罪性。中国人的心理人格的主要问题是**胆怯**与**虚谎**，只有用基督徒的**信实**与**爱**才能克服。中国人的心理行为的两大问题是**情绪控制头脑**和**心理寄生**，可以通过心理顺服理性头脑的模式，并在上帝的真理和圣灵动力的帮助下，实现克服和更新。

下面是《中国基督徒的心理更新》中的开头与结尾的部分内容节选：

参考心理学的知识，可以将心理模型简单分为两个组成部分：**心理人格**和**心理行为**。下面就从这两个方面，来反省中国文化中传统的心理模型，并提倡通过基督教真理、伦理和圣灵的工作，来建立与基督徒生命配套的心理模型。

我个人成为基督徒后，靠着主耶稣基督的恩典，花了许多年才意识到自己的错误心理模式，然后就开始致力于改变和更新心理，过程缓慢而漫长，但总是不断受益良多。我还明白了一个重要的道理：**真正的我，其实就是我的心理。**

……

圣灵和真理使我们得自由，属于生命得自由，主要表现在心理获得并感受到健美的自由。换而言之，心理的自由与健美，是一个生命是否得自由的标准。在真理的基础上，公义和爱是基督徒心理模式的核心。爱和公义，既是心理内涵，也是心理行为。圣灵赋予我们永恒的爱和生命，如甘泉滋养我们的心理内涵。我们的心理有多么宽广，头脑和生活就会同样宽广。

对于基督徒来说，信仰是在心理、灵魂和头脑中同时运行的综合性活动。信仰也可以被视为是始于灵魂的、对心理模式和思维模式进行系统性更新建设的过程。对于基督徒来说，信仰是在耶稣基督及其真理中的生命成长的过程。《哥林多后书》4：7 说："我们有这宝贝放在瓦器里，要显明这莫大的能力是出于上帝，不是出于我们。"圣灵就是瓦器（基督徒）里的宝贝，教会是耶稣基督的身体。也就是说，我们的心理有强大的圣灵做支撑，在基督里的信心是我们的心理支点，而教会是我们的心理后盾。圣灵和教会，通过我们的信仰，帮助我们完成心理的更新重建。

基督徒要有意识地反省和打破自己的固有心理模式（习惯），接受圣灵和真理的更新，提升心理境界，以便让新酒装在新皮囊里。基督徒们常说的"老我"，可以理解为是旧的心理模式，是罪恶势力在生命中最后的堡垒。因此，必须要下决心将自己的旧心理模式，钉死在十字架上，然后在耶稣基督的真理和圣灵中复活，成为一个彻底新造的人。正如《加拉太书》2：20 所说明的："我已经与基督同钉十字架，现在活着的不再是我，乃是基督在我里面活着；……"

据说，在英国伦敦的威斯敏斯特教堂的墓地中，有一个墓碑上刻着这样一段墓志铭：

"当我年轻的时候，我梦想改变这个世界。当我成熟以后，我发现我不能够改变这个世界，我将目光缩短了些，决定只改变我的国家。当我进入暮年以后，我发现我不能够改变我们的国家，我的最后愿望仅仅是改变一下我的家庭，但是，这也不可能。当我现在躺在床上，行将就木时，我突然意识到：如果一开始我仅仅去改变我自己，然后，我可能改变我的家庭；在家人的帮助和鼓励下，我可能为国家做一些事情；然后，谁知道呢?我甚至可能改变这个世界。"

我想说明的是，改变自己的心理模式，就能真正地改变自己，更新自己。积极拓展自己的心理模式，人生才会相应地发展。基督教信仰是对心理模式进行良性改变的最佳方式。在此基础上，随着基督徒人数的增多，逐渐形成健康的教会社区心理模式，并影响社会文化心理模式得到改变和更新，最后逐渐形成健康卫生的社会心理，从而提高了社会文明。人类文明的大树，是从人心中开始发芽。

最重要的是，我们并非盲目和情绪化，而是有理性兼灵性的信心根据，因为《约翰一书》4：4 教导我们说："小子们哪，你们是属上帝的，并且胜了他们；因为那在你们里面的，比那在世界上的更大。"

理性思维模式容易在科学的体系中发挥，因为在既定的理性思维体系中进行微观的逻辑推理，仍然属于模仿性的思维。但是，在非理性的心理模式，理性思维模式却难以发挥出来，这正是许多中国知识分子的思维创造性匮乏的原因所在。也就是说，理性思维模式需要有配套的心理模式，才能够充分发挥。通过有意识地更新心理模式，就能够降低生活和工作中的心理模式成本，以及所导致的思维模式成本，并逐渐获得清洁正直自由的心理模式和富有创造力的思维模式。

5、建立宪政法治保障公民权利

正如前述，《圣经·旧约》提供了原始朴素的**国王与先知**的二权分立的宪政模式，并且是在对上帝的神性信仰和遵守伦理律法的基础上运作的。上帝通过摩西颁布的伦理法典，主要分为两部分——**神权和人权**。法制和法治，是连接神权与人权的桥梁。

人们只有首先保障神权，才会有尊敬人权的意识与动力。基督教文明的社会也是如此，必须要同时尊敬神权和保护人权，并通过法治来确保基督教伦理的主导性，才能实现社会最高效率的良性运作。笔者在《基督教与中国公民社会》中，论证了公民社会和宪政法制起源于基督教的神性文化，是基督教伦理的产物和基督徒精英政治的作品。如今，中国教会和基督徒已经促进了中国宪政和公民社会的发展，尽管总体上来讲还是无意识的行为。下面是部分节选内容：

基督教对当前中国公民身份-权利的促进，主要是基于无形化的教会社区，通过以"公义和爱为核心的基督教伦理"为基础的教区文化，教会和基督徒坚守信仰意识形态及其实践原则，不停止聚会，推广法律维权模式，影响教会与社会。这种模式推动了公民社会在中国的发展，并催生了新型的政教关系。总之，作为从西方借贷来的制度文化资本——宪政公民社会和政教关系模型，正在中国通过基督教新文化运动而良性本地化，并将避免当代西方公民社会模型中伦理体系的缺失。

......

欧洲现代公民身份-权利（citizenship rights）的形成发展，得益于在 17-18 世纪英国社会的资本主义进程中，产业工人们争取权利的运动，并主要是通过基督教的教区（pastoral regions），并且是在"法律、社区和政治文化"（law, communities and political culture）这三大因素之间的机制性关系模式的结果；因此，公民身份是一个不断发展的机制化过程，并非静止的定义（玛格丽特·索默斯 Margaret Somers ,1993）。

现代公民身份拥有三大权利（T. H. Marshall 马歇尔，1964）：民生权利（civil rights 工作权、法律权，等）、政治权利（political rights 选举和被选举权利，等）和社会权利（social rights 社会福利权、受教育权，等）。中国公民正在争取的有五大权利，还包括生育权利和宗教权利（birth rights and religious rights）。

基督教在中国的发展，尤其是"无形化教会社区"（invisible and unstructured church communities）的不断壮大成熟，通过基于基督教伦理的教区文化（Christian ethical culture of the communities），与现行的"伪宪政法制"（pseudo-constitutional law infrastructure），共同构成了塑造和推动中国公民身份-权利和宪政公民社会（constitutional citizenship society）发展的三大要素板块，并主要是通过坚持聚会和法律维权这两种手段，来实践争取宗教权利（信仰意识形态权利）。

……

如今，中国基督教无形化社区的快速发展和壮大，已经提供了推动公民社会发展的基督教伦理板块。所以，以争取公民宗教信仰权利为出发点的教会法律维权运动，通过无形化教区，与"伪宪政法制"和"基督教伦理为核心的教区文化"一起，推动了中国公民社会的实质性发展。在这个过程中，基督教伦理赋予中国基督教精英团体崭新的视角，来理解并实践公民权利，并因此能够站在足够的高度，对国家侵犯公民的权利进行批评，从而形成朴素的教区政治文化。但是，这又触及到另外一个必须解决的神学和政治哲学问题：基督教在中国的发展，需要怎样的政教关系——即政治和宗教的关系（包括政府和教会的关系）。

需要注意的，本文探讨的是中国的实际情况所导致的公民社会发展方式，不同文化背景的国家都有可能在自己的信仰意识形态体系中发展出公民社会，尽管运行效果会参差不齐，甚至面目全非。但是，基于现代公民社会是从西方的基督教文化环境中形成的原理，这种借鉴的社会制度模型，将在中国通过基督教的新文化社区实现理想效果的本地化。这种公民社会制度文化资本的输入和良性本地化，还可能在未来中国带来意外的红利：形成以基督教伦理（保守的《圣经》伦理）为纽带的政教联合关系，并用宪法的形式固定下来。

这种政教关系模型，将会修正当代西方式宪政公民—民主社会制度的弱点——伦理缺失导致的一系列困境，因为基督教的伦理向我们解释说，"因为全律法都包在'爱人如已'这一句话之内了。"（《圣经·加拉太书》5：14）甚至，耶稣还教导说："只是我告诉你们，要爱你们的仇敌，为那逼迫你们的祷告。"（《圣经·马太福音5：44》）这种不以国家、民族、公民身份为最高负责对象，而是面对上帝和人（邻舍）负责的"世界公民伦理"体系，能够更好地解决正义论、道德论、公民身份-权利论、民主论、多元信仰文明论、国家主义、种族主义、民族主义、国际和平论、生态公义论的等等困境，提供美好的出路。同时，在这个体系内部，仍然会出现左右两翼，即相对保守和相对自由的两种竞争制约势力。

由于政权和信仰意识形态的不可分割性，中国精英和民众在未来有权做出选择，采用所认为正确的信仰意识形态体系作为立国思想之本。基督教对中国公民社会的影响和最终得胜，将可能导致未来中国社会采用以保守基督教伦理（《圣经》伦理）为基础的洛克契约主义和美国清教徒主义的宪政模式，实现公民社会模型的理想本地化，并合成衍生新型的政教关系模式。这将是一种避免当前崇尚无主导信仰秩序的多元主义的西方宪政民主制度的缺陷、基于基督教伦理的一元秩序为主导标准的、崇尚现代科学的理性文明、重视西方式（雅典式）的高等教育模式、鼓励世俗文化、容忍其它宗教的有限多元社会结构。这种以基督教伦理为基础的社会结构，为个人的生活提供神圣的保护伞，并将所组成的社会运行在神圣的上层建筑穹顶下（Peter Berger, 1967）。这相当于在传统的美国宪政文明的历史基础上，又迈进了一步——政府与教会仍然保持分离，但政治哲学与基督教伦理融合，形成基督教信仰意识形态所支撑的政权。这种宪政文明的特点是，宪法中具有清楚的、决定性的神性位置（美国的《独立宣言》中只有模糊的神性）和以此为基础的丰富人性。（《圣经·旧约》中"十诫命的宪法结构"具有启发意义：参看笔者的《人性与神性》）

......

总之，这种对英美的基督教信仰及其伦理影响下的宪政公民制度文化资本的借贷，在基督教本土化并迅猛发展的有力平台上，不仅从思想和实践方面解决了不断受到限制—逼迫的教会和基督徒精英们的困境，促进了中国公民身份-权利和公民社会的本地化发展，还进一步开始产生政教关系的红利——政府与教会分离，政治与基督教通过伦理联合。这个原则还可以从现在就指导中国的教会和基督徒，在与政治的接触中，要从基督教伦理的角度来决定应该做什么，不应该做什么，而不是按照"是否参与政治"这样的误导性思路。

6、基督徒忠心履行双重使命

教会和社会文明的发展，都无法离开基督徒们的忠心和对使命的勤奋履行。中国境内的基督徒们，需要有意识地承担起双重使命——影响教会和影响社会，因为这是基督徒的双重身份——天国的公民和社会的公民——所决定的。其中，影响教会的职责包括：传福音，门徒培训，建立教会，发展神学，执行大使命，建立基督徒团体机制模式，等方式。影响社会的职责包括在政治、商业、社会文化、学术教育，等方面。

基督徒要做忠心的仆人。下面是笔者在《基督徒的双重身份和双重使命》中的部分节选内容：

《圣经》中所教导说明的信仰责任和伦理责任，确定了基督徒的教会身份（基督徒身份）和社会身份（公民身份）。由于责任决定身份的《新约》原理特点，基督徒需要忠实地履行双重责任，并且，通过履行信仰责任影响更新教会，履行伦理责任影响更新社会。履行责任的途径有两种：个人的方式和团体的方式。

基督徒在中国要做上帝忠心的仆人，还要将上帝赐给我们的才干发挥出来，忠心于自己的双重身份——地上国度的公民和天国的公民，履行上帝交托我们的双重职责——信与爱（爱上帝和爱人）。通过信仰和美好的作为，将责任在履行过程中升华，成为信仰使命

（教会使命）和伦理使命（社会使命）。这是中国基督徒需要肩负的双重使命，并当竭尽全力，以此荣耀上帝的圣名。

在教会历史中，教会领袖和基督徒曾经犯过严重的错误。例如，中世纪基督教对人性的压抑、17-19 世纪美国和英国的奴隶制得到许多教会领袖和基督徒的认可、二战时期德国纳粹对犹太人的屠杀也得到许多教会和基督徒的认可、二战之后东欧共产主义国家的东正教和中国三自基督教体系对敌基督的共产主义政治的信仰妥协，等等（参看《警惕中国教会里的爱国主义异端》）。然而，在这些历史错误中，总有一些教会领袖和基督徒站起来反对，没有盲从，他们的秘诀是——在社会中坚持"爱邻舍如己"的伦理责任原则。

总结可知，造成教会在上述历史错误中蒙羞的主要原因和方式有两种：1、政府和教会关系的认识错误，导致要么教会绑架政府，要么教会被政府绑架。2、神性信仰与人性文化的界限混淆，导致要么信仰压制文化，要么文化异化信仰。通过本文的探讨可以明白，教会领袖和基督徒如果以忠实履行信仰责任和伦理责任的角度为原则，不仅能够让上帝儿女的教会身份和社会公民的身份实现有机和谐，还能最大程度地避免上述两种错误，从而在各种政治、社会和文化的潮流中保持头脑清晰，不致迷失，站立得稳，荣耀主耶稣基督的圣名。

通过在耶稣基督里的信仰，靠着圣灵的大能更新工作，不仅能够给个人的生命和生活带来革命性的变化，作为教会和基督徒群体，也会给社会带来生命性的影响和更新。这种影响和更新的结果是，在中国缔造出全新的社会文明。基督徒认真实践双重身份和双重使命，会直接导致对教会和社会的深刻影响，从而在教会中结出美好的属灵果实，在社会中结出美好的文化果实。毫无疑问，基督教正在并将继续成为塑造中国新文明的主要力量。

也就是说，基督徒通过履行双重使命来实践自己的双重身份，荣耀主的名，就会缔造出新的社会文明。不仅如此，基督徒在中国还要有意识地积极参与对社会文明的更新，释放上帝通过神性信仰和伦理而带给人类的全面祝福。当中国境内的教会和基督徒缔造了全新的美好文明和辉煌的社会成就，并让世界有目共睹，那么，中国教会全面对外宣教的时代就到来了。

在中国社会里缔造基督教新文明，基督徒个人的努力无法脱离教会、团契、基督徒社区等单元的平台，个人和团体应当共同努力。基督徒个人文明的提升，到了一定程度就难以长进，这是因为文明的群体社会属性，因此需要依靠基督徒团体，个人文明才能够进一步提升。群体性的观点、意见和标准，能够赋予个人积极保持与团体相配的身份的心理动力；换而言之，由于这种身份导致对群体负责的心理，以及通过学习和彼此督促而受到鼓励，个人的自我约束和追求生命更新的动力就大大提升。当一个群体的文明到达一定程度，也会难以突破。这时候，作为这个群体的一些代表性的个人，需要进入更高文明层次的教会和社会群体（例如，来到美国），通过学习和接受熏陶，就能够将先进的文明内涵标准和模式作为文化资本，带回原属的文明群体，并转化成该群体文明的新标准和方向。

结束语：文明的属灵意义

基督教在中国需要缔造新的文明，实现从信仰到创造的跨越。在此基础上，要进一步积极影响世界文明的进程，正如历史中所有的基督教文明，荣耀主耶稣基督的圣名。

基督教信仰，或者说，基于整本《圣经》的信仰，本身就是一整套提升人类文明的最高真理：以福音为核心，涉及个人的生命包括灵魂、心理和头脑的悔改更新，还有婚姻、家庭、团契、教会、社会等文明机制，以及基督徒的教会和社会的双重身份、做光做盐，对教会和社会的影响更新，等等范畴。上帝通过启示性真理教育人类，使人类不断创立更高层次的文明；人类文明的进程是螺旋式上升发展的，正如基督徒个人生命的成长过程。

注意，只有基于《圣经》的真理神性信仰，才能最大程度地促进文明，并不是所有的真理都能促进文明，也不是所有的信仰都对文明有正面作用。正如《大秦景教流行中国碑颂》所指出的，"惟道非圣不弘，圣非道不大；道圣符契，天下文明。"意思是，真理没有神性就影响有限，神性缺乏真理也非伟大，两者相符和谐，才会天下文明。这是相当深刻的有关信仰、神性、真理与文明相互作用关系的原理。

基督教信仰在个人、家庭、教会和社会中，必然会产生美好的效果。这不是一种机械式的效应，而是如同溪边树上结出的甜果实。这样的果效在个人生活中，表现为新造的丰盛生命；在家庭中，有圣洁的浪漫婚姻；在教会中，形成火焰般的神性文化；在社会中，产生清泉似的人性文明。基督教影响社会文明的关键是神性与人性的平衡。基督徒在中国要实践信仰真理，更新心理与思维模式，严格自我约束，遵守《圣经》伦理，从而改变传统和现行文化的基因。我们要在个人、家庭和教会平台的基础上，有意识地更新社会，承担起在中国的环境里缔造基督教文明的使命。基督徒要履行更新教会和更新社会的双重使命，这是神圣的呼召。

此外，上帝还在历史中不断通过神迹奇事来启蒙和教化人类。然而，基督教社会的文明程度越高，上帝用超自然方式的直接介入和接触就越少。因为，基督教带动人类文明程度的不断提高，是人类通过信仰上帝及其真理而向罪恶斗争并胜过魔鬼撒旦诱惑和破坏的有力证明，是上帝所期盼和喜悦的。那么，所有来自上帝的神迹奇事，最终都可以视为是旨在提高人性文明。从这一点来看，千禧年作为人类文明自伊甸园里堕落之后、经过接受漫长的神性教育和人性发展而到达顶峰之后的历史结束点，是合理的，可称颂的。

2013 年 06 月 21 日星期五 （夏至）初稿

2013 年 09 月 11 日星期三终稿

《中国法律与宗教观察》内含中国颁布、发行的涉及法律、政治、政府的政策文件、学术作品及其完整的英文译本。

欢迎访问对华援助协会中文网站：http://www.ChinaAid.net

中国观察网：http://www.MonitorChina.org

——完——

Chinese Law & Religion Monitor

July – December 2013

Vol. 9, No. 2

Table of Contents

July-December 2013 Vol. 9, No. 2

Chinese Law & Religion Monitor

ISBN-13: 978-1493512294 ISBN-10: 1493512293

Address: 1300 Pennsylvanian Ave. NW, Suite 700, Washington, DC 20004

Telephone: 1-888-889-7757

The *Chinese Law & Religion Monitor* is a biannual publication containing policy documents and academic works involving law, religion, and politics in China, with English translation.

Editor's Note

By "Bob" Xiqiu Fu

This is the last issue of China Aid Association's *Chinese Law and Religion Monitor*. Initially a quarterly, it later became a semi-annual publication. A total of twelve issues have been published, all devoted to innovations in theories on religion and the law as well as testing these theories by putting them into actual practice through ChinaAid's causes and activities. The integration of the empirical methodology of science and the Christian ethics upheld by ChinaAid has markedly promoted freedom of religion, the rule of law, and civil society in China, whether in ideological concepts or actual practice.

The four papers in this Fall-Winter 2013 issue of the *Chinese Law and Religion Monitor* explore the relationship between religious freedom and the law, as well as the socio-cultural effects of their interaction. The topics include key academic research points from the sociological perspective, the influence of Christian faith and ethics on the Western judicial system and the free market, the Christian theological view of "man's evil nature" as the original rationale for constitutional government, and Christian faith and ethics as the foundation of constitutional government and the resulting elevation of human freedom and social civilization.

1. In "A Research Agenda for Religious Freedom in China," prominent Chinese-American sociologist Yang Fenggang points out that research on religious freedom in China has great potential, but it needs to be centered around three key points: conception, regulations and civil society. In China, [because] atheism is the basis for the concept of religious freedom, it has not kept up with the laws and regulations on religion and Communist Party policies, all of which greatly interferes with the implementation of laws and regulations on religion and results in [China] falling short of international standards. As for the third

point, a grave shortage exists of research studies on religious groups and civil society organizations defending religious freedom.

2. In "A Response to the Dual Challenge of the Free Market and Social Justice: Christian faith and the Western legal tradition in the context of globalization," well-known Chinese scholar of constitutional philosophy. Yang Shen argues and shows that various social ideologies and movements criticizing the free market and constitutional democracy arose in Europe and the United States during the Enlightenment. On one side were Nazism and the Stalinist model, which rose up and were defeated, while on the other side, the social welfare ideology emerged in Europe and the United States. In the tide of globalization, Asian countries as a whole have unique characteristics when compared with constitutional governments that originated in Britain and the United States. Are Christianity and the Christian church outdated? Is Christian justice monism still applicable? This paper points out that Christian ethics and public engagement, along with systematic and multi-layered judicial justice, regulate the "game" between capital and labor by way of interactions among multiple communities, better achieving balance and control of the free market and social justice.

3. In "Christian Constitutional Government and Theories of Human Nature," well-known Chinese house church pastor Man De (pen name of Baosheng Guo), who lives in the United States and pastors a Chinese church there, points out the close relationship that exists between the theory of human nature, i.e. the determination of man's moral nature and rational capacity, and the theories and practices of constitutionalism. Man is completely morally depraved, is powerless to attain salvation and perfection through his own efforts, and has limited reason and knowledge. In short, by expounding on that, the Christian theory of human nature surpasses that of other religions, naturally becoming the foundation for building the theory of constitutionalism. From the three perspectives of Biblical text, Christian doctrine and theology, and the history of theological thought, this paper explores the influence of the Christian view of human nature on the concept of constitutionalism. In Christian doctrine and theology,

4

the total depravity of human nature after the Fall and the view of "salvation by God's grace alone" emphasize man's evil nature. As far as the history of Christian theological thought is concerned, whether it was the Apostle Paul, Augustine, Aquinas, Martin Luther or John Calvin, they all expounded brilliantly on the evil of human nature and the checks and balances upon it, profoundly influencing Western ethics and the history of Western political thought.

4. In "The Advance of Civilization: the deepening growth of Christianity in China," well-known Chinese house church scholar Mark Chuanhang Shan, currently living in the United States, expounds on the four components that make up the ecosystem for an ideal social civilization: divine faith, a code of ethics, constitutional government, and human freedom. This model of Christian civilization shows that constitutionalism is not "water without a source" but rather that it can function normally only upon a foundation of faith and the ethics of that faith, thereby safeguarding citizens' rights and human freedom. From this, we can also see that Christian civilization is the native environment for constitutionalism and human rights.

To sum up, the central topic of the four papers is religion, in particular Christianity, and the significance of religious freedom for constitutionalism and social civilization. It is inevitable that the development of Christianity in China, including government-sanctioned churches but in particular the increasingly mature house churches, will exert a broad influence on people's awareness of faith, produce socially progressive ideologies, and as a result, advance China's political ecosystem, civil society, and the rule of law, and promote China's overall social civilization.

As some scholars have pointed out, the corruption of human society and the decline of powerful nations, if not caused by interference from outside forces, always begins with ethical and moral corruption within a society. Christianity created a glorious civilization in the West, but today, the Christian-influenced ethical system is facing unprecedented challenges from political pride and democratic bias and is rapidly declining in Europe and the United States. "Desolations have been decreed."

On the other hand, Chinese society is at the point of going through a [process of] fission and re-composition of its civilization; Christianity is sprouting like buds in the spring and roaring like the surging tides. Who can stop such a robust advance of civilization? Not only that, to our great amazement, the ethics of the Orthodox Church is already being resurrected in Russian society on the platform of the church, and this once-glorious civilization is on the verge of shining again. Thus is the curtain slowly rising to reveal a new era in the history of human civilization.

Editor-in-Chief:

Rev. Bob Fu, PhD, founder and president, China Aid Association

December 31, 2013 Midland, Texas, USA

A Research Agenda for Religious Freedom in China

Fenggang Yang

Religious freedom in China, a subject that has appeared frequently in international news, governmental documents, and the reports of nongovernmental organizations (NGO), has been understudied by academic scholars both inside and outside China. [1] Inside China, and to some extent outside China as well, many scholars seem to fear that the Chinese Communist authorities regard religious freedom as a politically oversensitive topic that is too risky to discuss in print. While scholars in China commonly fear political censure and consequences for writing about religious affairs, scholars outside China are sometimes concerned about losing access to China if they openly comment on the impalpable situation of religious freedom. I believe that religious freedom in China can be a topic with good potential for fruitful studies if scholars are equipped with suitable theoretical and methodological tools. To move the field forward, some thought liberation is in order.

---

[1] I would like to acknowledge the assistance of Jiayin Hu, Min Gao, Zhe Liu, Ying Hei, Chao Wang, Hongping Nie in collecting relevant literature. The paper benefited from suggestions by Jiexia Zhai Autry, Stephen Bailey, Dennis Hoover, and Zai Liang.

First of all, to follow the principle of *shi shi qiu shi* 实事求是, to seek truth in facts, as promoted by Deng Xiaoping since the late 1970s as a new Chinese Communist policy principle, scholarly research ought to find facts and develop theoretical explanations of the facts. Fact finding and explaining does not have to become "political" in the narrow sense of antagonism or holding an ideological position. Rather it would be political in the best and broadest sense of politics, which is of, relating to, or concerned with the public interest. Indeed, properly understood, the subject of religious freedom is unavoidable for conscientious citizens in the world today.

Moreover, religious freedom is arguably the first freedom in a constitutional democracy, that is, it comes first before the other freedoms and may serve as the basis or wellspring for other freedoms (see, e.g., Balmer, Grogerg and Mabry 2012). I have come to believe that until the Chinese elites gain a better understanding of and appreciation for religious freedom, further democratization in China will be difficult, if possible at all. The deficiency of religious freedom undermines economic development and social order. On the other hand, if religious freedom advances before the other freedoms, such as freedom of the press and freedom to organize political parties, it may significantly contribute to a smoother, or less volatile, transition toward democracy.

Three Aspects of Religious Freedom: Conception, Regulation, and Civil Society

Some sociologists have attempted to develop theories of religious freedom and examine it cross-nationally (Barker 2003; Richardson 2006; Grim and Finke 2011). In reviewing the situation in China and some other countries, I think issues pertinent to religious freedom may be distinguished into three major aspects on the social level: conception, regulation, and civil society. To attain and retain this freedom in a society, these three aspects have to be synchronized, which, in reality, is difficult to achieve and maintain in any society.

In the West, it is common that the idea of religious freedom may come first before it becomes law that is enforced by the state and defended by civic organizations and individual citizens in civil society. The idea has to be accepted by the citizens, especially by the cultural and political elites, before the law can be put in place and implemented in practice.

In societies where the modernization process was triggered by external forces and challenges, the law in writing might be adopted from or imposed by the external or international bodies before the idea is accepted by the citizens. This is the case in China. Although "freedom of religious belief" has been included in the Constitution since the establishment of the People's Republic of China (PRC), this constitutional right has not been fully realized in practice. This is primarily due, I propose, to the lack of some common understanding of religious freedom, especially among political and cultural elites, and the underdevelopment of a civil society that consciously defends religious freedom.

This paper suggests that each of these three broad areas needs more empirical research and theoretical reflection: the changing religious regulations, the common understanding of religious freedom among Chinese elites and ordinary citizens, and the rising civil society that contributes to greater freedoms. In the existing literature, there have been a significant number of legal or policy analyses, perhaps because the written regulations are tangible for analysis. However, few studies have examined the conception of religious freedom among the people, or the civil society pertaining to religious freedom.

Conflicting Conceptions of Religious Freedom and Atheisms

In China today, it is not that the political and cultural elites all fail to understand the meaning of religious freedom. In fact, some of the public statements in Chinese Communist Party's-state documents are beautifully phrased. For example, in the 1982 Document Number 19 of the Chinese Communist Party (CCP), entitled "The Basic Viewpoint and Policy on the Religious Question during Our Country's Socialist

Period," which sets the foundation for the religious policy since then, it includes this paragraph:

> What do we mean by freedom of religious belief? We mean that every citizen has the freedom to believe in religion and also the freedom not to believe in religion. S/he has also the freedom to believe in this religion or that religion. Within a particular religion, s/he has the freedom to believe in this sect or that sect. A person who was previously a nonbeliever has the freedom to become a religious believer, and one who has been a religious believer has the freedom to become a nonbeliever.

This is a set of enlightened statements about the freedom of religious belief, including the freedom of conversion to or from a religion or a sect of a religion. This is very much in line with the common understanding in modern societies and with the international norms as reflected in the United Nations treaties, even though it lacks clarity about religious practice and organization (Evans 2002).

However, immediately following this enlightened paragraph, this CCP edict insists that the Chinese Communist Party members must be atheists and unremittingly propagate atheism. In other words, CCP members are excluded from holding this constitutional right of PRC citizens and must be committed to atheism. This in itself is not necessarily a problem if the CCP were one of the political parties that one could voluntarily join, because citizens may or may not have to join this party. In reality, however, the CCP holds exclusive political power and joining the Party is most often the prerequisite for public service positions and leadership opportunities in almost all social institutions and organizations throughout China. Anyone with an aspiration for public service or a leadership position almost has no choice but to try to join the CCP, and therefore has to denounce religion and declare oneself to be an atheist.

In reality, this requirement for CCP members to uphold atheism is impossible to enforce. According to our analysis of the Chinese Spiritual Life Survey in 2007, it shows that about 84 percent of CCP members and 85 percent of the general public admitted holding some religious beliefs and/or participating in some religious practices (Yang 2010), which surprised Chinese scholars and the media.[2]

Despite the impossibility of enforcing atheism among the CCP's own members, this atheist ideology is mandated by the CCP to serve as the foundation of the Party-state's religious policy for *all* Chinese citizens. No matter how the authorities may justify it, such a foundation is bound to undermine the above quoted paragraph of enlightened statements of religious freedom. The contradiction between the "freedom of religious belief" in CCP policy (and the Constitution) and its atheist ideology is a perpetual problem, confusing not only to ordinary citizens and CCP members, but also to Party-state officials in charge of managing religious affairs, who are often ambivalent, torn and waver between the contradictory principles.

Adding to the confusion is that there have been different versions of atheism: which have been referred to as militant atheism, enlightenment atheism, and mild atheism (Yang 2011a). The Chinese Marxist official ideology of atheism holds that the essence of religion is that it is the spiritual opium of the people and that its destiny is to wither away. Using the same set of vocabulary, however, different versions of atheism are distinguishable and have different policy implications.

> Enlightenment atheism regards religion as an illusory or false consciousness, being both non-scientific and backward; thus, atheist propaganda is necessary to expunge the misleading religious ideas. In comparison, militant atheism treats religion as the dangerous opium and narcotic of the people, a wrong political ideology serving the interests of the exploiting classes and the anti-revolutionary elements; thus,

---

[2] Many scholars at the conference in Beijing where we presented the findings expressed surprise and it took some courage for Chinese journalists to report it in a newspaper and a newsmagazine in China (Ning 2010; Zhou 2010). On the other hand, a scholar of religious studies commented that even the remaining 15 or 16 percent might not be genuinely atheist.

the political forces are necessary to control and eliminate religion. (Yang 2011a: 46)

The different versions of atheism are important to religious freedom in China. Although enlightenment atheism is embodied in the 1982 Document Number 19, militant atheism, which was once dominant during the Cultural Revolution (1966-1976), has perpetuated through the CCP organizational machine, especially the CCP schools that provide periodic training to CCP members for promotion to leadership positions. More important, it seems that a large proportion of the party-state officials in charge of religious affairs are retired military officers and their perception of religion is often crude and hostile. Given how widespread militant atheism is among these officials in the middle and lower ranks, it is not surprising to learn of cases of local officials suppressing religion and yet to also hear party-state officials at the center nonetheless claiming that those [actions] are not endorsed but in violation of the set policy. Both are simultaneously true, as both enlightenment atheism and militant atheism coexist among the policy makers and administrators.

In other words, even though the CCP Center's Document Number 19 granted significant freedom of religion based on the enlightenment version atheism, such limited freedom has not been fully implemented in practice in part because rank-and-file cadres in charge of religious affairs tend to hold the militant version of atheism. How widespread are the militant and enlightenment views of atheism among officials in charge of religious affairs? In what ways does it matter to policy implementation? These questions can only be answered with empirical studies such as surveys, interviews, observations, and case studies with officials.

In 2000, CCP General Secretary Jiang Zemin made a speech to the cadres of the CCP United Front Work Department, expressing a bold new conception of religion. While insisting on the atheistic rhetoric, he suggested that the demise of religion might not happen until after the presumed disappearance of social classes and the state in the far future. Based on this view, atheistic propaganda and anti-religion campaigns would not be necessary at present. This is an interesting conception.

However, most of the CCP theoreticians appear to have chosen to ignore it, except for Pan Yue, who published an essay in line with Jiang's speech called "Marxist View of Religion Must Advance with the Times" (2001). Marxist theoreticians quickly rose to criticize Pan and successfully muffled his view. Not until 2007 did a scholar of religious studies at the Central Nationalities University, Mou Zhongjian, publish an essay called "The Chinese Socialists Ought to be Mild Atheists." Mou advocates mild atheists (*wenhe de wushenlunzhe* 温和的无神论者) not believing in religion but holding a rational attitude toward religion. Instead of attacking religion directly, they should strive to eliminate the alienating natural and social forces that lead people to religion. Instead of engaging in anti-religious campaigns, they ought to respect religious faith, hold notions of cultural pluralism in modern society, and protect human rights. Mou asserts that this should be the orthodox understanding of Marxism on religion. Unfortunately, Mou's idea of mild atheism has been frozen by the CCP propaganda system. Upon my probing with the editors of the newspaper and some scholars, I learned that no further public discussion about this concept was allowed.

Before the end of Jiang Zemin's term in 2002, some people had hoped for some breakthroughs for greater religious freedom, such as allowing CCP members to be religious believers, just like the breakthrough of allowing business owners or capitalists to join the CCP. The latter was formalized by the CCP Sixteenth Congress in late 2002, but the former has never happened. Given the dominance of militant atheism and enlightenment atheism among CCP theoreticians and officials, the failure of [achieving] a breakthrough in religious policy was probably inevitable.

Since 1999, along with waves of crackdowns on "evil cults," there have been atheism propaganda campaigns through schools, the Communist Youth League, the Young Pioneers for school students, and the mass media. As part of the anti-cult efforts, a new magazine, *Science and Atheism* (*kexue yu wushenlun* 科学与无神论) was launched in 2000, which has become the mouthpiece and bridgehead of militant atheists. They have also established a new division in the Academy of Marxism as part of the Chinese Academy of Social Sciences. Such campaigns may be effective to a significant extent.

My personal interactions and observations in various parts of China indicate that enlightenment atheism seems widespread among college students, graduates and faculty, and militant atheism seems widespread among government officials. Systematic studies are needed to verify this tentative assessment. I believe the prevalence of militant atheism among rank-and-file cadres of religious affairs has especially limited the implementation of the religious policy inscribed in the CCP's 1982 Document Number 19. Merely changing the formal regulation may not be enough for real change. It also requires changing the minds of the agents in the control apparatus.

Differentiation of Religion, Superstition and Evil Cults

Even though "freedom of religious belief" is inscribed in the Constitution and CCP documents, Chinese authorities have granted legal status to only five religions: Buddhism, Daoism, Islam, Catholicism, and Christianity (Protestantism). This limitation is legitimized by the conception of religion in a very narrow sense, in which they insist on categorical differences between religion and superstition (*mi xin* 迷信), and between religion and the "evil cult" (*xie jiao* 邪教). By stating that superstition and "evil cults" are not religious, they thus assert that freedom of religious belief does not apply to superstitious or cultic beliefs and practices.

The differentiation between religion and superstition may be traced back to the turn of the twentieth century when Chinese elites began to strive to modernize China under the military pressures of Western and Japanese powers (Nedostup 2010; Goossaert and Palmer 2010). Carrying on this modernist legacy but aggravated by the atheist ideology, the CCP has launched waves of political campaigns to eliminate superstitions. In the 1950s, all traditional folk religious groups that could not be classified as Buddhism or Daoism were banned as "reactionary sects and cults" (*fandong hui dao men* 反动会

14

道门), traditional folk religious beliefs and practices that were diffused in daily life were regarded as "feudalistic superstitions" (*feng jian mi xin* 封建迷信) and people holding such beliefs and practices were subject to public admonishment. Even the five religions have to undergo cleansing of "feudalistic superstitions" and "antirevolutionary forces" from within.[3]

In 1966, the so-called Cultural Revolution began with the campaign to destroy and sweep away the "Four Olds" – Old Customs, Old Culture, Old Habits, and Old Ideas, which expanded to include all religions. Following Mao's call, Red Guards ransacked traditional architectures, burnt scriptures and classical books, and shattered various antiquities. All religious buildings were torn down or closed down. For 13 years between 1966 and 1979, there was no legally allowed religious gatherings for Chinese residents.

The ban against all religions was lifted in 1979 when the CCP under Deng Xiaoping began to focus on economic reforms. Some venues of the five religions were allowed to reopen for religious services. However, the differentiation between religion and superstition was restated through official Party-state documents or statements (*Renmin Ribao* 1979; Ya 1981).[4] In the 1990s, another label was adopted in the official Party-state discourse -- "evil cult" (*xie jiao* 邪教). This label has been applied to traditional folk religious sects and cults, new religious movements imported from other countries, and Christianity-inspired indigenous sects emerged in China. In 1999, Falun Gong was designated an "evil cult" and it has remained the main target of anti-cult campaigns. Since then, other major *qigong* groups have fallen into this category as well (see Yang 2011a: 114-118). The imported new religious movements include the Unification Church, Children of God (The Family), the True Buddha Sect, etc. Some new religions, such as

---

[3] Cleansing "superstitions" in government sanctioned religions has continued even to today (Blanchard 2013).

[4] Nevertheless, nowadays so-called "superstitious" beliefs and practices are widespread throughout China. It has been reported that even more than half of the middle-and-above ranked officials would admit having participated in some form of "superstition." (*Kexue Shibao* 2007).

Mormonism and Baha'i may not be officially designated as "evil cults," but nonetheless are banned. Christianity-inspired indigenous sects are a mixed bag that includes both Christian heresies such as the "Established King," "Three-Grades of Servants" and "Almighty God," as well as sectarian groups that many overseas Christians would regard as orthodox although somewhat extreme in certain teachings and practices, such as "All Scope Church" and "South China Church." The current list of officially banned Christianity-inspired "evil cults" includes at least 16 groups (see Yang 2011a: 103-105).

It seems that most people in China today, including both the elites and ordinary citizens, accept the two differentiations and find little problem in government crackdowns on "evil cults" or "superstitions." This is not merely acquiescing to authoritarian rule but an internalization of the conception and discourse of the Party-state. Such an unquestioned conception contributes to maintaining the status quo of limited freedom of religion.

In China today, most people seem content that only five of all the religions in the world are legally allowed and that restrictions are stricter on certain religions than on others. Even among those people who express discontentment with the existing religious policy and who call for some modification, such as legally allowing this or that particular religion, most nonetheless think that some restrictions are necessary and that the restrictions need not be applied equally to all religions. Once again, minor adjustment of the formal regulation may not be enough for real change. It also requires changing the minds of the religious players in the overall religious scene in China.

Religious Regulation: The Constitution and Administrative Ordinances

Formal regulations of religion have been analyzed extensively by China watchers in the West and some scholars of the law in China. However, few studies of the regulation have clearly articulated the mechanisms and relative weight of the three major forms of formal regulation in the PRC: party policies inscribed in the CCP documents or circulars, state laws passed by the National People's Congress, and administrative ordinances enacted by central, provincial or local governments or governmental agencies. The policy, the law and the ordinance should be examined carefully because their statuses are very different from those in democratic societies. The law is commonly regarded as the most important regulation in a democratic society under the rule of law. In the PRC, however, CCP policies are above, underwrite and override the law. "The Constitution of the PRC represents a formal articulation of Party policy" (Potter 2003: 324). While modification of formally passed laws are slow [due to] the complexity of the [legislative] process of the National People's Congress, party policies may be adjusted quickly by a stroke of the [pen by the] CCP. The administrative ordinance is supposed to implement the law. In reality it has replaced the law and carries out CCP policy.

Many analyses of the regulations have pointed out the limits of religious freedom in the 1982Constitution. Article 36 states:

> Citizens of the People's Republic of China enjoy freedom of religious belief. No state organ, public organization, or individual may compel citizens to believe in, or not to believe in, any religion; nor may they discriminate against citizens who believe in, or do not believe in, any religion.

> The state protects normal religious activities. No one may make use of religion to engage in activities that disrupt public order, impair state. Religious bodies and religious affairs are not subject to any foreign domination.

It is important to note that Article 36 is about "freedom of religious belief" rather than "religious freedom." Some Chinese political and cultural elites articulate that citizens may be free to believe in their heads whatever they want to believe, but practice and organization must be restricted for the purpose of maintaining social harmony (see Ye 1998:2-3). In principle, putting certain restrictions on religious practice and organization is in itself not necessarily a violation of international norms, as there is no responsible government in the modern world that has not put in place some kind of regulation of religion (Beaman 2003; Beyer 2003; Gill 2003). The problem lies in what is considered to be "normal religious activities," which the Constitution does not define but leaves to the cadres of religious affairs to decide. While variations in interpretation exist in different localities, this is often used by rank-and-file cadres who tend to hold militant atheism to impose strict restrictions on religious activities.

Another problem with the constitutional article is that "the courts cannot rely on or refer to provisions of the Constitution in their adjudicative work" (O'Brien 2010: 376; see also Kellogg 2009). Because the Constitution cannot be used in court cases, violation of the constitutional right may not be litigated in court. Consequently, disputes involving religious freedom have to be resolved by the party-state administrative authorities, which further compromises the constitutional protection of freedom of religious belief.

Since the 1980s, as some top CCP leaders have advocated gradually increasing the rule of law instead of the rule by the personal will of the leaders, there have been voices from administrators and religious leaders calling for establishing a law of religious affairs (Ying 2006; Yang 2006; Liu 2008). However, the attempts have produced no results because of a failure to reach agreement on some basic principles and concepts, including the definition of religion (which religions ought to be legalized), normal religious activities (which ones ought to be allowed), the role of the Constitution versus CCP policies, the role of the National People's Congress versus CCP organizations, the supervision of the administration, the government sponsored mass organizations, and the cyclical administration (O'Brien 2010). Instead of a formal law, the authorities have resorted to administrative ordinances. After many years of experimenting with "temporary ordinances" by provincial governments, the State Council decreed a comprehensive "Regulations of Religious Affairs" that took effect in 2005.

Immediately following the enactment of the "Regulations of Religious Affairs" in 2005, Eric R. Carlson (2005) published an analysis along with the full English translation in appendix. Carlson offers a balanced analysis, pointing out that "the regulations are an improvement by providing more predictability and clarification as to how religious groups and the government interact through the application and approval processes" (758). On the other hand, he also points out, there are significant shortcomings in the new regulations: continuing strong state control over religion through registration requirements for religious bodies and sites, supervision of religious personnel, doctrine and practice, and continued discrimination against certain religious groups, and harsh and arbitrary penalties.

By comparison, James W. Tong (2010) begins by acknowledging serious problems in China's religious policy, but then argues that the 2005 regulations represent significant progress in a number of aspects, such as no requirement that religious organizations support socialism and the leadership of the CCP, Christians no longer prohibited from worshipping at home, property rights of religious communities affirmed, increased institutional autonomy given to religious communities and the power of the state to intervene in religious affairs circumscribed. He argues that the progress has been possible because of the demise of orthodox Communist ideology and the systemic political and social reforms launched by the party-state that are aimed at separating state from society, to protect human and civil rights, and to govern by law. This is a relatively optimistic assessment for structural progress toward greater religious freedom.

Examining the actual practices since 2005, however, Lauren B. Homer (2010) sees nothing more than empty promises in the 2005 Regulations. "Unregistered congregations and their leaders continue to face beatings, jail, fines, destruction of property, and other often horrific abuses. Those who have been brave enough to venture into a government office to try to register their congregations have been rebuffed, and some have even been arrested for prior unregistered activities. Indeed, many lawyers representing house churches have themselves been jailed or disbarred for 'anti-state activities'" (2010:55). That is, even though the 2005 regulations include some promising potential, they have not been put into practice. Again, I would attribute this failure of implementation in part to the conception problems discussed above.

Religious Regulation: Measuring up against international standards

In the regulation studies, one question is: has there been progress in Chinese religious regulation? Progress is evident if the current policy is compared with that during the Cultural Revolution (1966-1976) when religion was eradicated from the whole of society (Tong 2010), or the restrictions are somewhat understandable if compared with that during the imperial times of traditional China (Qu 2011). However, when measured against international laws and norms, to which the PRC has expressly committed, the existing regulations clearly fall short.

In an article published in 1994, Eric Kolodner reviews the international human rights system regarding religious freedom, examines various provincial ordinances, and explains in some detail how the Chinese authorities restricts "activities of religious adherents, places of worship, the construction of new religious sites, contacts with foreign organizations, religious training for students, and the distribution of religious literature. It also limits the number of religious leaders, prohibits 'superstitious activities,' imposes penalties on violators, and creates government departments to administer religion laws" (Holodner 1994:490).

In a similar study but using updated regulations, Carolyn Evans (2002) provides a detailed analysis of Chinese and international formal laws regarding religious freedom. It carefully and thoroughly measures the specifics in the Chinese Constitution and other formal laws against United Nation's treaties, including nuanced discussions of the negotiation processes and disagreements over the Charter of the United Nations, the Universal Declaration of Human Rights, the International Covenant on Civil and Political Rights. The author argues that even though the Chinese government's restrictive actions against self-harm of cultic believers or mixing of ethnic politics with religion may not be totally unjustified, the measures against such acts are doubtlessly excessive. The paper concludes (773-774),

> While all four of China's communist era constitutions have included protections for freedom of religion and belief, the

reality is that religious freedom has not been respected either by past Chinese governments or by the one presently in power in Beijing...in the area of state control of religion, it is clearly that China is in breach of the international standards that protect religious freedom. China has claimed that it recognizes the value of religious freedom and that it adheres to its international obligations to treat all people equally regardless of religion or belief. Its own record, however, shows that the Chinese government still has a long way to go before its rhetoric matches the reality.

Pitman B. Potter's 2003article provides a comprehensive analysis of regulations in various forms: the CCP policy statements, the Constitution and relevant laws, ordinances imposed by governmental agencies, and varied treatments of different religions (also see Cheng 2003). Potter argues that the deliberate distinction between religious belief and religious practice actually poses challenges for the regime's efforts to maintain political control while preserving an image of tolerance aimed at building legitimacy. He concludes, "Regulation of religion reflects Party policies granting limited autonomy for accepted practices while attempting to repress activities that challenge political orthodoxy" (Potter 2003: 337).

Recently, some Chinese legal scholars have joined the effort to analyze formal regulations of religion. An excellent example is the article "Religious Freedom and Its Legal Restrictions in China" by Qianfan Zhang and Yingping Zhu (2011), professors of law at Peking University and East China University of Political Science and Law, respectively. Published in an English academic journal, the authors offer detailed criticism of the 2005 "Regulation of Religious Affairs" and conclude (795),

> Overall, the Regulation authorizes many restrictions on—and in some cases, even deprivations of—the freedom of religious belief and practice protected by Article 36 of the Constitution without providing for sufficient remedies to check against potential abuse of power" by the administrators of religious affairs.

The article comprehensively analyzes problems of religion-related provisions in the Military Service Law, the Criminal Law regarding "evil cults," the Law of Ethnic Autonomous Regions, the Law of the Protection of Consumer's Rights, and the Prison Law. In addition, the authors examine a number of cases in which the Chinese government violated the [principle of] separation of church and state, including governmental interference in the construction of religious buildings, religious seminaries or academies, appointment of religious personnel, and religious associations. The review and analysis are very much like a systematic indictment of the Chinese Party-state for its violation of religious freedom.

In a focused analysis of the laws concerning "evil cults," Guobin Zhu, who received his higher education in China, Hong Kong and France and is a faculty member at the City University of Hong Kong, concludes that there are serious problems in the current formal law (2010: 500).

> First of all, the system of law currently in place intends to regulate, manage, and control religious beliefs and activities. Second, legal rules and measures dealing with irregular or unlawful activities are harsh and sometimes arbitrary. While the executive branch is granted discretionary power, there is no check on the exercise of this power, and no judicial control over administrative action. Third, the measures taken by the government have often been excessive and disproportionate. Most importantly, the actions taken against borderline cases or "unlawful" activities are generally very harsh, with no mercy or no sense of tolerance, to an extent that at the end, they violate the right to belief, as well as the rights of the person.

Two points are worth noting with regard to the last two articles by Chinese authors: First, under the current strict press censorship, it would be impossible to publish these critical analysis papers in China. Second, such papers have been published in scholarly journals outside China and, as far as I know, the authors have not been penalized by the Chinese authorities or been denied access to China for research trips.

This indicates that, in the globalization era, there is a significant level of freedom of scholarship and it has become possible for scholars inside and outside China to do serious research on religious freedom and publish articles outside China.

Civil Society and Religious Freedom

The relationship between civil society and religious freedom in China is complex, and it varies considerably by region and ethnicity. On the one hand, "There is no doubt that today in China two important ethnic minorities, the Tibetans and the Uygurs, experience severe limitations when they want to practice their traditional religion.... The intense fear of the Chinese Communist Party (CCP) of a possible link between religion and ethnic separatism has put many restraints on the constitutional guarantees of the right to freedom of religious belief" in Tibet and Xinjiang Autonomous Regions" (Wellens 2009, 434). On the other hand, for ethnic minorities in Yunnan Province, "the picture of religious freedom for minority nationalities becomes markedly more nuanced. It might be argued that in several instances minority nationalities have greater freedom in practicing religion than their Han Chinese neighbours" (435). Some ethnic religions, such as the Dongba among Naxi people, have been encouraged and supported by the local government for the purposes of tourism and economic development. Indeed, even "Buddhism and Islam have been able to ride the wave of government support of ethnic tourism" and the local government has sponsored the rebuilding of major monasteries and mosques (451). More important, the revival of ethnic religions has strengthened their social cohesion and ethnic pride, thus protecting these ethnic groups from Christian evangelism. "An unconditional liberalisation in this respect would certainly disadvantage indigenous religions when they have to compete in a globalized 'marketplace of ideas'" (453). Wellens raises an important question about religious freedom. If preserving ethnic distinctiveness is valuable, or more valuable than individual freedom of religious choice, the government restriction of Christian and Islamic proselytizing would be justifiable in China and other countries. This question needs careful examination and serious debate.

With regard to religion among the majority Han people, there have been many studies of various religions and religious life in various parts of China, some of which have touched upon issues of religious freedom. For example, under the current religious regulation, how is it possible for a Catholic church in a Hakka village in Guangdong province to endure social and political hardships (Lozada 2002), for a Christian church to survive and revive in a remote village in Gansu province (Huang and Yang 2005), for a Buddhist temple in Hebei province to establish on the ruins of an ancient Buddhist site that had been abandoned for decades and thrive to become a nationally and internationally influential center (Yang and Wei 2005), for a folk religious temple in northern Shaanxi province to expand to become a multi-functional social center (Chau 2006), and for Christian entrepreneurs in the coastal city of Wenzhou to negotiate with the authorities and enlarge their social space for practicing religion (Cao 2011)? Even though these studies do not focus on religious freedom *per se*, they offer rich descriptions of and insightful analyses on the level of religious freedom practiced in the current social and political contexts.

The research on religion and civil society is directly relevant to issues of religious freedom because, conceptually, religious freedom is an integral part of a civil society. Richard Madsen (1998) pioneered this research in his examination of China's Catholics in the emerging civil society. Some recent studies show that there is evident change among house churches, from avoiding discussing political issues to actively defending constitutional rights for Christians and others (Hong 2012).

Through analyzing the contents of an online publication, *Aiyan* 爱筵, Gerda Wielander (2009) shows that some house churches have engaged resistant politics by raising rights awareness and engaging in efforts toward a liberal democracy. Many authors in *Aiyan* have argued that "freedom of religious belief is considered a God-given right which is guaranteed in the Chinese Constitution and which no lower administrative body has the right to limit" (175). Some "Christian lawyers" have taken on cases of Christians whose religious freedom rights have been violated. The Association of Human Rights Attorneys of Chinese Christians has been formed and the names and contact numbers of its members were published in *Aiyan*. They are all leading scholars in the field of constitutional law with the country's foremost research tanks or universities. Inboden and Inboden (2009) also report in the *Far Eastern Economic Review* on the rise of Christian lawyers and their striving for the rights of religious freedom.

Indeed, in the first decade of the twenty-first century, some new developments in religion have made civil society in China lively. For example, there has been a rapid increase of large house-church congregations in urban areas and they have become public (Yang 2011b). Meanwhile, the numbers of Christian entrepreneurs, professors, lawyers, journalists, writers and artists have grown, and they have formed fellowship groups or associations and spoken up in the public square on social and political issues. Many Christian books have been published (Kennedy 2012), as have many Christian magazines and journals online or in printed form. Many materials and data have become available for more empirical studies examining religious freedom and civil society developments.

Conclusion

I have proposed that three areas are especially important for the scholarly study of religious freedom in a society: conception, regulation, and civil society. So far most of the scholarly attention to religious freedom in China has been on formal regulations and CCP policies. The conception of religious freedom is another area that has been developed recently, which may be germane for further empirical studies through surveys, interviews, and content analysis. The least studied area is the actual practice and defense of religious freedom by religious communities and civic organizations in civil society, even though many empirical studies of religious communities have touched upon issues relevant to religious freedom.

Many topics are waiting to be studied. For example, the conceptions of religion and religious freedom among various categories of people, especially cultural and political elites, may be studied through surveys, interviews, and content analysis of speeches and publications. It should be interesting to examine religious freedom notions and practices by the officially sanctioned religious communities, Protestant house churches and underground Catholic churches, Tibetan Buddhists and Muslim ethnic minorities, and what has been called "evil cults" by the Chinese authorities. It would also be interesting to study the impact on religious freedom in China of expatriate religious communities, international NGOs and charity organizations, the dialogues with or sanctions by foreign governments and international bodies, etc.

In summary, if scholars are seeking truth in facts analyzed with social scientific theories and methods, religious freedom in China can be a topic with great potential for fruitful research.

References

Balmer, Randall, Lee Grogerg, and Mark Mabry. 2012. *First Freedom: The fight for Religious Freedom*. American Fork, UT: Covenant Communications.

Barker, Eileen. 2003. "And the Wisdom to Know the Difference? Freedom, Control and the Sociology of Religion." *Sociology of Religion* 64 (3): 285–307.

Beaman, Lori G. 2003. "The Myth of Pluralism, Diversity and Vigor: The Constitutional Privilege of Protestantism in the United States and Canada." *Journal for the Scientific Study of Religion* 42 (3): 311–325.

Beyer, Peter. 2003. "Constitutional Privilege and Constituting Pluralism: Religious Freedom in National, Global, and Legal Context." *Journal for the Scientific Study of Religion* 42 (3): 333–340.

Blanchard, Ben. 2013. "China's 100 Million Religious Believers Must Banish Their 'Superstitions', says official." *The Independent*, April 21.

Cao, Nanlai. 2011. *Constructing China's Jerusalem: Christians, Power, and Place in Contemporary Wenzhou*. Stanford, CA: Stanford University Press.

Carlson, Eric R. 2005. "China's New Regulations on Religion: A Small Step, Not a Great Leap, Forward." *Brigham Young University Law Review* 2005 (3):747–797.

Chau, Adam Yuet. 2006. *Miraculous Response: Doing Popular Religion in Contemporary China.* Stanford, CA: Stanford University Press.

Cheng, May M. C. 2003. "House Church Movements and Religious Freedom in China." *China: An International Journal* 1 (1): 16–45.

Evans, Carolyn M. 2002. "Chinese Law and the International Protection of Religious Freedom." *Journal of Church and State* 44 (4): 749–774.

Gill, Anthony J. 2003. "Lost in the Supermarket: Comments on Beaman, Religious Pluralism, and What It Means to Be Free." *Journal for the Scientific Study of Religion* 42 (3): 327–332.

Goossaert, Vincent, and David A. Palmer. 2012. *The Religious Question in Modern China.* Chicago, IL: University of Chicago Press.

Grim, Brian J., and Roger Finke. 2011. *The Price of Freedom Denied: Religious Persecution and Conflict in the Twenty-First Century.* New York: Cambridge University Press.

Homer, Lauren B. 2010. "Registration of Chinese Protestant House Churches Under China's 2005 Regulation on Religious Affairs: Resolving the Implementation Impasse." *Journal of Church and State* 52 (1): 50–73.

Hong, Zhaohui. 2012. "Protecting and Striving for the Rights to Religious Freedom: Case Studies on the Protestant House Churches in China." *Journal of Third World Studies* 29 (1): 249–261.

Huang, Jianbo, and Fenggang Yang. 2005. "The Cross Faces the Loudspeakers: A Village Church Perseveres Under State Power." In *State, Market, and Religions in Chinese Societies*, edited by Fenggang Yang and Josphe Tamney, 41–62. Leiden: Brill Academic.

Inboden, Rana Siu, and William Inboden. 2009. "Faith and Law in China." *Far Eastern Economic Review*, September 4.

Kellogg, Thomas. 2009. "The Death of Constitutional Litigation in China?" *China Brief* 9 (7): 4–6.

Kennedy, John W. 2012. "Discipling the Dragon: Christian Publishing Finds Success in China." *Christianity Today*, January 20.

Kexue Shibao (Science Times). 2007. *"yiban yishang xianchuji gongwuyuan nan ju 'mixin'"* ["More than Half of Public Service Officials at the County or Above Levels Have Difficulties to Resist 'Superstitions'"]. Accessed May 11, 2007. http://www.sciencetimes.com.cn/htmlnews/2007511193241656179151.html

Kolodner, Eric. 1994. "Religious Rights in China: A Comparison of International Human Rights Law and Chinese Domestic Legislation." *Human Rights Quarterly* 16 (3): 455–490.

Liu, Peng. 2008. "Zhongguo zongjiao fazhihuade lichen" ["The Course of Legalisation of China's Religions"]. In *Blue Book on China's Religions 2008*: 261-277, edited AQ7 by Jin Ze. Beijing: Social Science Documents Publishing House,

Lozada, Eriberto, Jr. 2002. *God Aboveground: Catholic Church, Postsocialist State, and Transnational Processes in a Chinese Village.* Stanford, CA: Stanford University Press.

Madsen, Richard. 1998. *China's Catholics: Tragedy and Hope in an Emerging Civil Society.* Berkeley, CA: University of California Press.

Nedostup, Rebecca. 2010. *Superstitious Regimes: Religion and the Politics of Chinese Modernity.* Cambridge, MA: Harvard University Asia Center.

Ning, Er. 2010. "Magic Thrives when Religion is depreciated: Chinese Beliefs and the Reconstruction of Ethics and Morality." *Nanfang Metropolis News* (Guangzhou), August 8.

O'Brien, Roderick. 2010. "Two Chinese Commentators on the Slow Progress towards a Law on Religions." *China: An International Journal* 8 (2): 374–385.

Potter, Pitman B. 2003. "Belief in Control: Regulation of Religion in China." *The China Quarterly* 174(2): 317–37.

Qu, Hong. 2011. "Religious Policy in the People's Republic of China: An Alternative Perspective." *Journal of Contemporary China* 20 (70): 433–448.

Renmin ribao (People's Daily). 1979. "Zongjiao he fengjian mixin" ["Religion and Feudal Superstition"], March 15.

Richardson, James T. 2006. "The Sociology of Religious Freedom: A Structural and Socio-Legal Analysis." *Sociology of Religion* 67 (3): 271–294.

Tong, James W. 2010. "The New Religious Policy in China: Catching up with Systemic Reforms." *Asian Survey* 50 (5): 859–887.

Wellens, Koen. 2009. "Negotiable Rights? China's Ethnic Minorities and the Right to Freedom of Religion." *International Journal on Minority and Group Rights* 16: 433–454.

Wielander, Gerda. 2009. "Protestant and Online: The Case of Aiyan." *The China Quarterly* 197 (1): 165–182.

Ya, Hanzhang. 1981. "Carry Out the Policy of Freedom of Religious Belief and Oppose Feudal Superstitious Activities." *Guangming ribao* (Guangming Daily),April 20.

Yang, Fenggang. 2010. "Quantifying Religions in China." Paper presented at the seventh annual conference for the social scientific study of religion in China, Beijing, July 26–27.

Yang, Fenggang. 2011a. *Religion in China: Survival and Revival under Communist Rule*. New York: Oxford University Press.

Yang, Fenggang. 2011b. "Chinese House Church Goes to Public." Sightings, an online magazine published by Marty Martin Center for Advance Study of Religion at University of Chicago, May 12.

Yang, Fenggang, and Dedong Wei. 2005. "The Bailin Buddhist Temple: Thriving Under Communism." In *State, Market, and Religions in Chinese Societies*, edited by Fenggang Yang and Joseph Tamney, 63–87. Leiden: Brill Academic.

Yang, Junfeng. 2006. "Guowuyuan 'zongjiaoshi tiaoli' shuping [An Evaluation of the State Council 'Religious Affairs Regulations']." In

Blue Book on China's Legal System 2005, edited by Li Lin et al. Beijing: Social Science Documents Publishing House.

Ye, Xiaowen. 1998. "Zongjiao yu pufa – Zongjiao gongzuo pufa duben xu" ["Religion and the Propagation of Legal Knowledge"] (Preface). In *Zongjiao gongzuo pufa duben* [A Reader in the Promotion of Legal Knowledge in Religious Affairs Work]:1-15, edited by Policy and Regulation Department of the State Council Religious Affairs Bureau. Beijing: Religious Culture Press.

Ying, Fuk-Tsang. 2006. "New Wine in Old Wineskins: An Appraisal of Religious Legislation in China and the Regulations on Religious Affairs of 2005."*Religion, State & Society* 34 (4): 347–373.

Yue, Pan. 2001. "Marxist View of Religion Must Advance with the Times." *Newspaper of Shenzhen Special Zone*, December 16.

Zhang, Qianfan and Yingping Zhu. 2011. "Religious Freedom and Its Legal Restrictions in China." *Brigham Young University Law Review* 2011 (3):783–818.

Zhongjian, Mou. 2007. "The Chinese Socialists Ought to be Mild Atheists." *China Ethnic News*, January 16, p. 6.

Zhou, Hualei. 2010. "Chinese Believing Gods." *China News Weekly* (Beijing), August 30.

Zhu, Guobin. 2010. "Prosecuting 'Evil Cults:' A Critical Examination of Law Regarding Freedom of Religious Belief in Mainland China." *Human Rights Quarterly* 32 (3): 471–501.

A Response to the Dual Challenge of the Free Market and Social Justice: Christian faith and the Western legal tradition in the context of globalization

By Yang Shen

(from *Justice Monism: from the condition of the people to law and government*, Wuhan University Press, 2012, pp. 193-235)

Modern society has witnessed the emergence of various social reforms and revolutionary movements critical of the liberal market economy and the constitutional democratic system. Almost all thinkers participated in a grand, century-long discussion and debate around this topic, touching upon the advantages and disadvantages of the liberal market theory, the possibility of social justice, the philosophical relationship between freedom and justice, and whether and how mankind's various existing systems can, to a limited degree, prevent already existing phenomena. Various social theories were formulated, including liberalism, socialism and conservatism. As for economic systems, there were the planned and market economies, with market economy further sub-divided into the Keynesian, Chicago and Austrian schools, as well as supply-side economics and monetarism, etc.

Multi-structured analytical paradigms, such as "'an open society' with the church" and "a social structure of Christianity and law-based politics," attempted to use the example of political development in the

Anglo-American constitutional era to reveal the operational logic behind the transformation into political states of "open society" from small communities that value the individual. Is this explanatory paradigm still applicable to the economic life of these nations? If so, how do social entities interact with one another and how is today's market civilization established by their interactions? In response to these questions, this paper attempts to point out that, through the interaction of market communities and other communities, the public spirit of an "open society," Christianity's market ethics, and common law-centered judicial justice regulate the "game" between capital and labor in a multi-dimensional way that reflects justice monism, which is relatively better at striking a balance between the market economy and social justice.

I. Small Community System and the Development of Capitalism: the academic criticism of sociologists by legal scholars

If Marx is said to have devoted himself to criticizing the Western tradition and development of modernity, then [sociologist Max] Weber in another sense diligently defended the Western tradition. Although Weber in his academic studies rarely criticized Marxism directly, it is actually easy to discover Marxism being targeted in Weber's thoughts. Weber's most renowned contributions were in the academic fields of religious sociology and political sociology. Contrary to the assertion that "religion is the opiate of the people,"[1] Weber pointed out in *The Protestant Ethic and the Spirit of Capitalism* that in certain ascetic Protestant denominations, especially Calvinism, Christian doctrine had gradually evolved and began to view the rational pursuit of economic gain as a manifestation of being blessed by Jesus Christ. Weber also argued that capitalism based on and aided by this rational doctrine would grow ever more colossally, quickly coming into conflict with the original [form of the] religion, and religion would ultimately and

---

[1] Karl Marx (Germany): *Introduction to a Critique of Hegel's Philosophy of Right*, 1843-1844. *Marx and Engels: Selected Works, Volume One*. People's Publishing House, 1995, p. 2.

inevitably be abandoned. Therefore, rather than the mature spirit of capitalism, Weber was actually concerned with the spirit of capitalism in transition times, i.e. contemporary times. To thoroughly elaborate on his views, in addition to *The Protestant Ethic and the Spirit of Capitalism*, Weber also wrote *The Religion of China: Confucianism and Taoism*, *The Religion of India: The Sociology of Hinduism and Buddhism*, and *Ancient Judaism*.

Such views are also reflected in Weber's research in political sociology. In his lecture "Politics As a Vocation," Weber defined the state as an entity that "lays claim to the monopoly of legitimate physical violence".[2] He also believed that a politician cannot be regarded as a [so-called] truly moral Christian and cannot be as noble and selfless as described in the Sermon on the Mount. Such saint-like politicians do not exist in real politics; neither can such politicians be given room to act. A politician must adopt ethics that balance morals and political goals ("a sense of proportion"), adopt the ethics of responsibility ("a feeling of responsibility"), and have strong passion for his vocation, all the while learning to maintain a distance between personal feelings and preferences and realistic goals. On this basis, Weber proposed three forms of formal political domination and authority: charismatic domination (family and religion), traditional authority (sovereign, patriarch, and the feudal system), and bureaucratic domination (modern law and state, bureaucrats).[3] By dividing the validity of authority into three categories, Weber purged sacredness from politics and demonstrated the Christian spirit of the secularization of politics.

Weber defended Protestant Christianity on this basis, asserting, "In my opinion, the view of historical materialism, frequently espoused, that the economic is in some sense the ultimate point in the chain of causes is completely finished as a scientific proposition."[4] [Harold J.] Berman,

---

[2] Max Weber, *On Law in Economy and Society.* Translated by Zhang Naigen. The Encyclopedia of China Publishing House, 1998. p. 43

[3] This is a summary of *On Law in Economy and Society* by Max Weber (Germany).

[4] Proceedings of the First Conference of German Sociologists,1910, quoted in Max Weber, *Economy and Society*, ed. Guenther Roth and Claus Wittich (New

an expert in Western legal history, commented thusly of Weber, "Although he subsequently achieved fame as a sociologist, and especially as a sociologist of politics and religion, his sociological theories always drew heavily on legal history, and among his most important works was a book on the sociology of law. Karl Marx, by contrast, although he too (sixty years before Weber) had taken his first degree in law, studying in Berlin under Germany's greatest jurist, Carl Friedrich von Savigny, rebelled not only against Savigny's approach to law but also against legal history and jurisprudence altogether."[5] If we acknowledge Berman's criticism of Marx as factual and recognize the obvious fact that Marx's core concern was not judicial justice but something else, we will have no difficulty understanding why Marx as a cross-disciplinary encyclopedic thinker demonstrated such striking limitations, and we will be able to understand that the set of explicit morals and moral aspirations of pursuing the freedom and liberation of mankind were so slow and had such trouble developing into implicit morals and moral obligations, from whence the justice monism system that reflects institutional-procedural justice developed. Comparatively speaking, Weber was obviously far superior [than Marx]: in Weber's thoughts and research, law and justice were always indispensable elements of human civilization and they had to be transformed into institutional civilization.

Nevertheless, because Weber failed to explicitly point out in his thought system whether the fruit of the secularization of Protestant ethics deeply influenced by Calvinism and its core values was a pluralistic view of justice or two different manifestations of Christian justice monism in different spatial and temporal orders, Weber and

---

York,1968), I, lxiv. Quoted from *Law and Revolution: The Formation of the Western Legal Tradition* by Harold J. Berman (U.S.A.), p. 535. Translated by He Weifang, Gao Hongjun, Zhang Zhiming and Xia Yong. Law Press China, 2008.

5 Harold J. Berman (U.S.A.), *Law and Revolution: The Formation of the Western Legal Tradition*. Translated by He Weifang, Gao Hongjun, Zhang Zhiming and Xia Yong. Law Press China, 2008, p. 538. Regarding the part on Marx, see "The Metaphysics of Law: An Essay on the Very Young Marx" by Donald R. Kelley, *American Historical Review*, 83(April 1978), pp. 350-367.

Marx arrived at the same point by different paths. "For Weber, as for Marx, Western law is bourgeois law, capitalist law, or in Weber's peculiar terminology, bureaucratic law, formally rational law "[6] So, "...ultimately Weber traced both ideas and law to politics, and politics itself to domination and coercion. Charisma, tradition, and rationality were, for Weber, primarily sources of legitimation of political authority, whereby coercion could be more effectively exerted."[7] To some extent, such an understanding is colored by German Lutheranism. In this way, Weber took a great leap, from being an affirmer and admirer of the Protestant spirit to being an advocate of political order in a nation-state, starting on the journey in his political thought of gradually moving toward pluralism. The "leviathan" that Hobbes spoke of was an armed guard protecting human rights, within which exists the absolute dilemma between freedom and coercion; only justice carried out by the law can join the two. Considered the "father of the Weimer Constitution," Weber was very clear about this. Prior to the end of World War I, he conducted in-depth studies of parliament.

Weber thought that German society lacked "organized democracy" or "representative democracy" but had a rich tradition of non-democratic agitators and mob rioting. He further pointed out that there is bound to be conflict between a head of state elected by the people and a parliament elected by the people, i.e. the incompatibility of "popular democracy" and "representative democracy." However, a parliament can at least stabilize power relationships, bring controllability to the president's position of power, retain the legal means of government-by-the-people to resist the president and provide orderly ways of improving bureaucratic systems, and when the president loses the trust of the populace, Caesarian dictators can be eliminated through peaceful means.[8] Nevertheless, with Weber's support, Article 48 of the Constitution granted the president the power to "take the necessary measures" when "public safety and order [are] seriously disturbed or threatened." Article 48 was an emergency act, but prior to 1933, it was often used to pass legislation without the consent of parliament, thereby

---

[6] *Law and Revolution*, p. 539.
[7] *Law and Revolution*, p. 540
[8]Max Weber, Parlament und Regierung im neugeordneten Deutschland, in Max Weber Gesamtausgabe, Band 15, Hrsg.von Horst Baier..., 1984 J.C.B. Mohr (Paul Siebeck) Tübingen, S. 538ff

making it easy for the Nazis to unify the nation. For instance, Article 48 was invoked to pass the Reichstag Fire Decree.

The situation would have been relatively safe if no expectations had been placed on academia or ideology to simply bring about a political transition to freedom and democracy. This would involve issues evaluating the Enlightenment and its moral decisiveness. Compared with various unenlightened conditions, the progressive significance of the Enlightenment goes without saying. Kant, [writing] before Weber['s time], defined enlightenment this way, "Enlightenment is man's emergence from his self-imposed nonage. Nonage is the inability to use one's own understanding without another's guidance. This nonage is self-imposed if its cause lies not in lack of understanding but in indecision and lack of courage to use one's own mind without another's guidance." "Freedom" is "the freedom to make public use of one's reason in all matters." "By 'public use of one's reason' I mean that use which a man, as scholar, makes of it before the reading public." "Such a contract, concluded to keep all further enlightenment from humanity, is simply null and void even if it should be confirmed by the sovereign power, by parliaments, and the most solemn treaties." "And to give up enlightenment altogether, either for oneself or one's descendants, is to violate and to trample upon the sacred rights of man." "I have emphasized the main point of the enlightenment—man's emergence from his self-imposed nonage— primarily in religious matters... Above all, nonage in religion is not only the most harmful but the most dishonorable."[9]

However, the paradox in such statements might also have been overlooked. In other words, enlightenment may be able to act on social reality and change social structure, but is this kind of change actually the result of this moral decisiveness of enlightenment or is it due to some other factors? People cannot do a quantitative analysis of this, that is, an accurate explanation using precise statistical methods in the natural science sense would be difficult. "The Lord does not look at

---

[9] Kant(Germany), "Answering the Question: What is Enlightenment?" From *What is Enlightenment? Eighteenth-Century Answers and Twentieth-Century Questions* by James Schmidt (U.S.A.), translated by Xu Xiangdong and Lu Huaping. Shanghai People's Publishing House, 2005.

the things people look at. People look at the outward appearance, but the Lord looks at the heart." (1 Samuel 16:7) Because a lack of clear standards results in uncertainty in understanding, this kind of judgment of a person's level of "maturity" and "rationality" has almost become the basic way of understanding human civilization. When people make constitutionalism an "idol" to be worshipped, believing that enlightenment holds supreme status in the process of realizing constitutionalism, that's when the serious problem of enlightenment becomes clear and obvious. As a religious sociologist, Weber made the same mistake when he held higher expectations for [the ability of] this kind of secularized and rationalized flavor of Christianity (which is hardly the Noahic Covenant's promise of divine providence that "all things work together") to improve Germany, because in the end [his expectations were] placed on moral decisiveness (almost entirely out of wishful thinking, which is both the hero-dominant historical view and the opportunistic historical view, similar to the Chinese people saying that "the saintly king creates history" and "the mandate of heaven is constantly changing.")

This relates to the basics of game theory. These are the basic presuppositions: the absolute scarcity of resources, the absolute limitedness of human reason, the absolute limitlessness of desire (only limited when self-examination and self-restraint are exercised), and the absolute imbalance of information. As a result, "Catch-22 dilemmas" beyond our imagination exist everywhere in human society. The elevation of mankind's morality and intellect by "enlightenment" or religion, as a way to expand understanding and to cultivate the ability to acquire knowledge, certainly can reduce the non-rational elements of these "Catch-22 dilemmas" and help people create and maintain the rational situations of the "Nash equilibrium" and of "cooperative games." This, however, is nothing more than a possibility. Moreover, in times of transformation and while transitioning from an old regime to a new one, mankind—due to its own absolute limitedness—often gets caught up in a certain kind of jungle warfare. The "Catch-22 dilemma" of such circumstances is not just the game between prisoner A and prisoner B; in actuality, the more the participants, the more extensive the game. For example, Germany after World War I experienced domestic religious and ethnic conflicts, conflicts among different political forces, and conflicts between Germany and other countries, in addition to facing a nationwide economic crisis (which involves conflicts between man and nature). For an individual in society, there were also conflicts between him and those around him, and conflicts within his small community itself. One could say that nearly all of the successful transformations so far have been similar to this kind of "collaborative solution" in which multiple games are intertwined.

In other words, Weber committed the classic [mistake] of overlooking the positive correlation inherent in moral decisiveness and political transformation, an oversight that [was typical] of the liberal enlightenment camp ever since the anti-Christian Enlightenment Movement came into being. In essence, it is human heroism. It was under the guidance of the kind of spirit of moral decisiveness presented in "The Vocation and Mission of Politicians" and *Politics as a Vocation* that Weber's views on World War I and the expansion of the German empire changed as the war situation steadily deteriorated. In 1918, Weber became a member of the German Armistice Committee, and in 1919, he travelled to Versailles where he represented Germany at the Paris Peace Accords negotiations. Later he joined the drafting committee of the Weimer Constitution. The Weimer Republic operated as a parliamentary democracy. [Its] parliament was filled with great numbers of small parties, each with a certain [number of] seats. Due to the ever-changing external environment (such as the poor economic situation, severe border crisis, frequent revolutionary workers movements [breaking out] domestically, and diplomatic crises [experienced by] the vanquished nations), it was almost impossible for these small political parties with differing political views to reach effective consensus, which made the formation of a stable and strong government in Germany difficult. For example, at the end of March 1930, the last majority government formed under the leadership of Hermann Müller of the Social Democratic Party fell apart simply because of a debate over how to fund unemployment insurance. It was out of fear of war-induced chaos that Weber supported adding to the Weimar Constitution the "Article 48" provisions for emergency presidential powers.

Let's set aside for the moment the various discussions with regard to specific problems in Weber's theory and the Weimer constitutional government, and let's do an analysis by comparing England and the United States at the time they were setting up their constitutional governments, [looking at] the public sentiment about and the institutional reasons [for constitutionalism]. In addressing Weber's ailment, Berman pointed out, "To the question whether law is to be viewed as part of the material base or as part of the ideological superstructure, the answer is once again that in the West law is both— which is to say that Western law shows that the dichotomy itself is wrong... . The fact that law, in its very nature, is both material and ideological is connected with the fact that law both grows upward out of the structures and customs of the whole society and moves downwards from the policies and values of the rulers of the society. Law helps to integrate the two. Thus theoretically at least, a conflict between social-economic conditions and political-moral ideology, which Marx saw as the primary cause of revolution, may be resolved by law."[10] Nonetheless, at what level does a nation's political culture, philosophy and faith interact with one another? This is an important topic in comparative political studies and comparative legal studies. Therefore, we must look at the Anglo-American [experience] and [the experience in] continental Europe as represented by Germany and France to uncover the differences in social structure and folk customs and public sentiment.

It was on the foundation of the rich public sentiment of Protestantism and of small communities, and under a broad and deep consensus on justice monism—in other words, on the dual foundation of the social structure of small communities and the conceptual structure of justice monism—that countries such as England and the United States went through smooth transformations rather than experiencing prolonged upheavals. It was not that moral decisiveness was missing in these countries. In English history, Cromwell's Puritan Revolution and the target of its fight had tried all along to be morally decisive. In American history, [Thomas] Paine and [Thomas] Jefferson can also certainly be [regarded] as representatives of moral decisiveness.

---

[10] *Law and Revolution*, pp. 545-546

Jefferson, who drafted "The Virginia Act for Establishing Religious Freedom" and The Declaration of Independence, repeatedly made the point that "From time to time the tree of liberty must be watered with the blood of patriots and tyrants," and "God forbid we should ever be twenty years without such a rebellion." [11] Paine made similar statements after the publication of *Common Sense*. The Chinese people certainly are very familiar with such statements. Mao Zedong once said that a "Cultural Revolution" should occur every seven to eight years in order to prevent bureaucratic authoritarianism. As objectionable as bureaucratic authoritarianism is, should the grassroots be mobilized to directly assist in a revolutionary war so as to advance human dignity? According to Jefferson's logic, if not for the presence of the transcendent, would the United States not have fallen into cyclical jungle warfare, alternating between revolution and "stability maintenance," ultimately becoming a Western version of "the principle of blood payment," which was discovered by the Chinese historian Wu Si?

II. The Struggle of the Working Class and the Civilization of Capital: a fair evaluation of various socialist ideologies and movements

In moving from theory to protest, and from protests to organizational systems, socialism changed the course of human development. Repudiating Marxist theories became a particularly important mission of Western political philosophy in the 20th century. In the preface to his 1963 *Karl Marx*, [Isaiah] Berlin spoke highly of [Karl] Popper's *The Open Society and Its Enemies*. In Popper's view, history has already proven false many of Marx's important prophecies. As a form of historical determinism, Marxism is bound to result in an arrangement of comprehensive and long-term plans for social practices. The most systematic and influential criticism of socialism was undoubtedly that of [Friedrich] Hayek. Hayek's ideas

---

[11] Merrill D. Peterson (U.S.A.), *Thomas Jefferson: Writings*. Translated by Liu Zuochang and Liu Hongfeng. Beijing Joint Publishing Company, 1993, p. 1021

can be summarized from the titles of his books, i.e. the "fatal conceit" of socialism in epistemology violates "the constitution of liberty" and damages "individualism and economic order," and as a result, it produces totalitarianism and leads to "the road to serfdom."

Nevertheless, the former Soviet Union, Eastern Europe and some Asian countries certainly are not the only Stalinist models in this world. And certain ideologies and ideals with social justice aims (various socialist ideologies, such as democratic socialism and social democratic ideologies, and not [John] Rawls' equality- and justice-oriented liberal ideology) and the socialist movements that grew out of them under the leadership of socialist political parties do not necessarily lead to totalitarian regimes. Take Norway in northern Europe as an example. On the eve of World War I, democratic socialism emerged from among the supporters of Marxism. Social democrats and democratic socialists shared the same political organization: the Socialist International. After the Russian Revolution, "social democracy" became the specialized term referring to non-revolutionary socialists. Modern democratic socialism emphasizes using the legislative process to reform the capitalist system and making it more fair and humane.

The Socialist International was an organization shared by social democracy and democratic socialism. The Socialist International viewed democratic socialism as a form of parliamentary democracy, able to resolve the problems emerging from an ordinary liberal democracy. The Socialist International stresses the following: "democracy" is not just individual freedom, it also includes freedom from discrimination and from abuse of political rights by the capitalists who control the tools of production; "equality and social justice" is not just equality before the law, it also includes economic and cultural equality, and the provision of equal opportunities to the physically and mentally disabled as well as other underprivileged people in society; finally, uniting in sympathy with those who have been unjustly or unfairly treated. Sweden is a model of a country that has put democratic socialism into practice. With a high tax rate, Sweden's economy is still vibrant compared with some other countries; its economic structure is quite robust, [having everything] from sole proprietorships to transnational corporations; and it boasts the world's longest average life span, low unemployment and low inflation, low national debt, low infant mortality, low cost of living, and relatively fast economic growth. In fact, the governments of the British Labor Party, the Australian Labor Party, the Socialist Party of France, the Social Democratic Party of Austria, the Socialist Party of Belgium, the Social Democratic Party of Germany, the Labor Party of Holland, and the Labor Party of Norway have not in one single case changed the constitutional systems of these long-time market-economy nations, nor led them—as described in Hayek's his social-economic theory—onto to the road to serfdom.

A theory of constitutional government that is conceptually consistent internally should not, in this ideological system, attach to "justice" other core values, such as equality, democracy, freedom, rights, and ethnic and community interests, other than "justice" itself. If these values are regarded as the criteria for justice, then the diversification of justice will be hard to avoid. The central issue is, if justice and the way to achieve justice become diversified, in a competitive "law of the jungle" society, the weak will be forced into a system that is the most unjust to them. This kind of secular "justice" is not relative justice but relative injustice.

Citizens have the right to freedom from want; capital liberalization and the free market cannot manufacture a [false] panic of this kind and use it to fulfill the purpose of capital. Those who participate in capital and the market are not the source of legitimacy. Both capital and the market take part in specific divisions of labor in society based on the specific demands of the individual, and both follow the logic of survival of the fittest and the law of the jungle. Of course, this is not to say that this logic is definitely unjust. Rather, the logic of the market must be confined to certain domains; once it goes beyond these domains, it likely will undertake functions that it is unable to perform. The inherent limitedness of resources and the limited nature of knowledge and reason that Hayek emphasizes mean that no matter how sufficient the market competition environment is, sufficient market competition in a liberal market free of government restrictions and with capital's logic carefully safeguarded by the law [still] is not able to meet the many needs of mankind. Oftentimes, economic freedom is not able to meet even its own objectives. This is called "the dysfunction of market." Certainly, "government dysfunction" can be used to argue for the acceptability of "the dysfunction of market." But this kind of acceptability must be carefully discussed in an open system which has more interested parties than just the government, the market and the entrepreneurs, and the working class.

Especially in the various labor-intensive enterprises where manpower is simply viewed as a labor resource, the comprehensive and all-pervasive enslavement of people by industrial capital is all the more likely to result in alienation of the people. Industrial capital allows for even less contact between skilled workers and capitalists, and for even less social and public interaction on the part of workers. "When a workman is unceasingly and exclusively engaged in the fabrication of one thing, he ultimately does his work with singular dexterity; but at the same time, he loses the general faculty of applying his mind to the direction of the work. He every day becomes more adroit and less industrious; so that it may be said of him that in proportion as the workman improves, the man is degraded... . The territorial aristocracy of former ages was either bound by law, or thought itself as bound by usage, to come to the relief of its serving-men and to relieve their distresses. But the manufacturing aristocracy of our age first impoverishes and debases the men who serve it and then abandons them to be supported by the charity of the public."[12] Concretely speaking, without a weekend to rest, workers are deprived of the right to go to church and worship, and in this way industrial capital becomes a threat to religious small communities. As workers' social lives shrink, other social problems arise, such as compromised ability to engage in various forms of public expression, including defending one's rights.

---

[12] Tocqueville (France), *On Democracy in America*. Translated by Dong Guoliang. Commercial Press, 1988, pp. 687-794 (quote in English taken from *Democracy in America, Vol. II*, New York: D. Appleton and Company, 1904, pp. 645, 648, accessed at
http://books.google.com/books?id=KO8tAAAAIAAJ&dq=editions%3AuhiaS MxLNn4C&pg=PR1#v=onepage&q&f=false April 27, 2014)

In consideration of various factors and propelled by the orderliness inherent to a multi-dimensional social structure, mature "open societies" impose serious and comprehensive limitations on industrial capital. This is the "monopoly" that socialism has long criticized. Even in the United States, a country that puts more emphasis on "small government" and the "night watchman state" than does Britain, as early as in 1890, when Lenin was asserting that monopoly had become characteristic of capitalism (that is, imperialism), the U.S. Congress passed the first act authorizing the federal government to control and intervene in the economy, i.e. "Sherman Antitrust Act", (its full name is "An Act to Protect Trade and Commerce against Unlawful Restraints and Monopolies"), which is still in force in today in this nation with a common law system. According to this Act, any contract entered into in the form of a trust and the implementation of a merger or conspiracy in restraint of trade are illegal; any person or organization that violates this law is subject to civil or criminal punishment. Since the 20th century, various forms of market interventions have proliferated, and Western society has not headed down the path to tyranny. By leaning moderately to [the side of] labor rights in the area of social welfare, a significant fact about human society resulted: following the end of World War II, the Western world has not experienced another large-scale violent revolutionary movement. Compared with the Stalinist model that is daily being bankrupted, the constitutional and democratic political system exhibits strong vitality.

Still, it is precisely within this modern system of ethnic groups becoming states, and in those societies governed by the rule of law and having distinctive Christian characteristics that inevitable changes occur in the situation of industrial capital and worker alienation when the bourgeoisie and the capitalists realize that they cannot do whatever they want in their own countries. Specifically, they begin to move to "colonial and semi-colonial" countries. Just taking the second half of the 20th century as an example, there was a shift to "the Third World." This became what Zygmunt Bauman called the "absentee landlordship" of the "global elites." Through this pattern, the capitalist class shakes off the workers around them, such as in Detroit, and via multinational companies and the make-to-order production method, they use the absentee landlord model—becoming a fluid, nimble, and easily disposable modernity.

Proponents of Hayek-ism seem able to refute from the philosophers' perspective the various theories of social criticism that are often labeled "postmodern"; Heyek's awareness problem lies in his concern that, in a society in which value propositions similar to democratic socialism are the value standards accepted by all in society and that all must accept, [these values] rise and become the nation's political views, the spirit of its governmental system, and the legal system. Of course, the risk might be real, but it is just a "possibility, not a "certainty." For a political view to become a totalitarian state system takes very complex social conditions, which must be revealed by what David Easton calls a "systematic analysis of political life." Take, for example, the socialist party movements previously mentioned that have socialist values as their objectives. Because the constitutional democratic political system with judicial justice at its core was established long ago, the governments formed by various labor parties and socialist parties did not in reality cause these countries to abandon the institutional arrangements of constitutional democracy; these working class parties that believed in Marxism were prodded by the long-standing existence of justice monism and its resulting civic education functions toward eventually abandoning the use of violent revolution to seize political power and the political ideal of scientific socialism. This reality in itself amply demonstrates that Marxism and democratic socialism also are important players in the human civilization of constitutional government.

The Socialist International, made up of social democratic parties (social-democratic political parties, labor parties and democratic socialist parties) had a profound impact on the development of human history. Members of socialist parties led the following social movements of major impact: in 1889, the Second International, founded in 1889, declared May 1 International Labor Day; in 1910, it declared March 8th International Women's Day. After the Second International fell apart, its members continued working under the name International Socialist Commission. In 1923, the Labor and Socialist International was founded. After World War II, the social democratic parties and democratic socialist parties in Europe that were oppressed by the Nazi regime founded the Socialist International. When Portugal and Spain went from being dictatorships to democracies in 1974 and 1975, respectively, the Socialist International earnestly supported the organizational restructuring of the social democratic parties in these two countries. In June 2007, the Socialist International's diverse member parties and organizations numbered 161, making it the largest international political organization in the world. The European Socialist Party, which operates in the European Parliament, is an ally of the Socialist International. Parties that are members of the Socialist International have governed at least the following Western developed countries: Australia, Austria, Belgium, Germany, Italy, Holland, Portugal, Spain, Switzerland, Britain, France, Sweden, Israel, Greece, Denmark, Canada and Norway. In contrast with those that have held the reins of power, there is also a long list of countries in which members of Socialists International are non-governing parties, advisory parties or parties with observer status. After the fall of communism in the former Soviet Union and Eastern Europe, members of Socialists International formed governments in at least these countries that had previously been ruled by communist parties: Bulgaria, Montenegro, Estonia, Hungary, Lithuania, Mongolia, Slovakia, the Ukraine and the Czech Republic.

We can go back to the criticism of Weber by legal historian and writer Berman to understand the limitations of economic liberalism which discredits the struggles of workers. Economic liberalism views a free market and capital liberalization as natural yardsticks of human justice, which is in fact making capital and market—which according to Christianity are carriers of mankind's "sinful" nature—the source of the community's legitimacy. In the view of the Christian justice-monism system, economic liberalism is the attempt by social theory and values to build a liberal Utopia in the human world. If Christ is regarded as the source of human justice and Christianity as the standard for faith, then economic liberalism is obviously heresy. The core doctrine of this "heresy" is that it entrusts the mission of realizing human justice to the market and capital, which are far from able to take up this mission and which are guided by the pursuit of profit and human inequality.

Liberalism, including economic liberalism, political liberalism, cultural liberalism and other forms of liberalism, shaped the ideological imagination: the ruling party of a country with a constitutional government must be a certain form of democratic party, liberal party, liberal democratic party or constitutional democratic party; and a party of this kind must put "freedom and democracy," written in capital letters, in its name and charter. If we acknowledge as scientific truths the political theories for which Britain's Berlin and Popper, China's Hu Shi and other "sound individualists" agitated, then we will never be able to understand how the Federal Republic of Germany after World War II was able to establish a constitutional-democratic order which had a relatively solid foundation and was highly approved of by the general public. [The ruling party] was not a liberal party nor a democratic party in the classic sense, but rather, it was a democratic socialist party and a Christian democratic party taking turns holding power—specifically, the Social Democratic Party of Germany (SPD) and the Christian Democratic Union (CDU)/Christian Social Union (CSU) holding power. The circumstances of the populace was a deciding factor in the formation of this kind of party politics structure. Protestants and Catholics each number 26 million (Protestants are concentrated in the north and east, with the majority belonging to the Lutheran denomination, i.e. the Protestant Evangelical Church in Germany; Catholics are concentrated in the south and west). There are also 900,000 Orthodox Christians (mostly Serbs and Greeks), 3.3 million Muslims (mainly Turks and Kurds from Turkey), 230,000 Buddhists and 90,000 Hindus (mainly Chinese, Indians and people from other Asian countries), and 120,000 Jews, almost all of whom believe in Judaism.

The following examples will help us understand the constitutional politics of the northern European countries. When Norway's constitution was adopted in 1814, it was considered the most democratic constitution at the time. It had a series of provisions, including ones about religion and politics. Article 1 says, "The Kingdom of Norway is a free, independent, indivisible and inalienable Realm. Its form of government is a limited and hereditary monarchy." Article 2 says, "All inhabitants of the Kingdom shall have the right to free exercise of their religion. The Evangelical-Lutheran religion shall

47

remain the official religion of the State. The inhabitants professing it shall be bound to bring up their children in the same." Article 3 and Article 4 declare that "The Executive Power is vested in the King" and "The King shall at all times profess the Evangelical-Lutheran religion." Article 9 says, "As soon as the King, being of age, accedes to the Government, he shall take the following oath before the Storting: 'I promise and swear that I will govern the Kingdom of Norway in accordance with its Constitution and Laws; so help me God, the Almighty and Omniscient.' If the Storting is not in session at the time, the oath shall be made in writing in the Council of State and be repeated solemnly by the King at the first subsequent Storting." Article 12 says, "More than half the number of Members of the Council of State shall profess the official religion of the State." Sweden, another northern European country, has five constitutional documents: the 1809 Instrument of Government, the 1810 Act of Succession, the 1949 Freedom of the Press Act (originated in 1766, adopted in 1810, and modified significantly in 1949), the 1809 Riksdag Act, and the 1991 Fundamental Law on Freedom of Expression. Article 4 of the 1810 Act of Succession says, "In accordance with the express provision of Article 2 of the Instrument of Government of 1809 that The King shall always profess the pure evangelical faith, as adopted and explained in the unaltered Confession of Augsburg and in the Resolution of the Uppsala Meeting of the year 1593, princes and princesses of the Royal House shall be brought up in that same faith and within the Realm. Any member of the Royal Family not professing this faith shall be excluded from all rights of succession."

The Catholic Church, having learned lessons from the Nazis' rise to power and having more widely accepted freedom and democracy as values, launched a historically unprecedented religious reformation under the pope's leadership, and Christian democracy emerged. Later, political parties endorsing the position of Christian democracy formed an international organization of political parties, i.e. Christian Democrat and People's Parties International, which is second only to the Socialist International as the world's largest international political party organization. Europe's Christian democratic parties and the regional European People's Party have formed the largest political party organization in the European Parliament. The French

Democratic Alliance joined the European Democratic Party, embracing a more pro-European Union stance. Christian democratic parties in Latin America are more inclined to leftist values compared with their counterparts in Europe. Like the Socialist International, Christian democracy is also a mix of diverse ideologies, and is therefore able to combine various characteristics of liberalism, conservatism and socialism, while emphasizing transcendent morality and Christian doctrine as its broad framework.

It is due to these factors that the God-man relationship, God's sovereignty, man's sinful nature and "separation of church and state" (goodness and justice), which are emphasized by Christian justice monism, are overlooked. The theory of "a social structure of Christianity and law-based politics" confers legality and legitimacy to the struggles of the working class and to the various small communities (such as workers protest groups, the legal community, the academic community, traditional religious communities, and regional government systems) that take part in and promote the realization of the secular justice of a rule-of-law civilization; in this way, the spirit of the legal experts reaffirms the rights of the citizens. Economic liberalism, however, uses the free market and capital liberalization as moral principles to reject the morality and rights of traditional small communities and the collective struggle of the working class. Because of that, economic liberalism manifested in justice monism is indebted to Christianity in the Western world and to the Christian tradition of law and politics; it was this tradition that redeemed the liberal reputation of economic liberalism—specifically, it was not the simple democracy of capitalism nor the democracy of other ideologies, but the democracy of a constitutional government. In developing countries that have yet to establish a constitutional government system, adherents of Hayek-ism who do not demand judicial justice in the general sense are actually the *de facto* creators of social injustice. The more strongly economists of this kind object to "populism," the more they show their dictatorial colors.

III. Justice in Autonomous, Intersecting Small Communities Can Be Realized: interaction between market communities and other communities

Using descriptive illustrations is a way to more clearly define the multiple operational states of a constitutional democracy. By looking at a few majorly significant transformational events in human history and at their written records, we can open up a fairly detailed case study to illustrate and prove the point. After Mary I, Queen of England, ascended to the throne in 1553, she earned the nickname "bloody Mary" for ruthlessly persecuting religious Reformers and having up to 300 Protestants burned on the stake. In 1603, James I started another round of persecution of Puritans. As a result, in September 1620, 100 Puritans who had boarded the *Mayflower* to sail to the new continent of North America signed the Mayflower Compact during the voyage. The compact detailed their willingness to build a community in the New World and to obey its laws.

One-hundred-and-two passengers were on board when the Compact was signed, 35 of whom were of the [English] Separatist church; the rest were craftsmen, fishermen, poor peasants and 14 bond servants. Pastor Brewster was their leader. These people could hardly be called outstanding economists, entrepreneurs, or reformers, or widely published critics of "populism" who were researchers and professors in national institutes. "There are different kinds of gifts, but the same Spirit distributes them. There are different kinds of service, but the same Lord. There are different kinds of working, but in all of them and in everyone it is the same God at work." (1 Corinthians 12:4-6) This small community was composed of members from various small communities, such as the factory, farm, and church. The core entity of this community was the church; each of the various small communities participated in unique ways and had a specific identity in the core entity. These interactively participatory citizens signed a new political contract to defend personal liberty and to place restrictions on their future community.

While the Mayflower Compact was signed mainly by English dissidents in exile overseas, several hundred years earlier in England, in the struggle [that resulted in] Magna Carta, the participants were leaders and representatives of various small communities [who brought] an institutional element to the struggle. The primary reason for Magna Carta was that England's King John and feudal barons from all over the country disagreed on the rights of the monarch. On June 10, 1215, the English feudal barons gathered in London and took King John by force. John was forced to agree to the Articles of the Barons proposed by the barons. On June 15, John placed the royal Great Seal on The Articles at Runnymede and four days later the barons renewed their oaths of fealty to John. Scribes of the royal court formally recorded the agreement between King John and the barons, which became the original manuscript of Magna Carta, duplicates of which were sent to the rest of the country and were kept by designated royal family members and bishops. The most important article of Magna Carta is Clause 61, known as the "security clause." Clause 61 established a committee of 25 barons who could at any time meet and overrule the king's dictates, through force by seizing his castles and possessions if necessary. This was based on a medieval legal practice, but applying it to a monarch was historically unprecedented.

This then raises a question: if the king was evil and trust no longer existed between the two sides, why would one side choose to compromise rather than "wipe out" the side that was evil? The answer to this question, in light of the limited history of mankind, had to be a mechanism that transcended the two parties in conflict, that reaffirmed the rights of the monarch's subjects in a systematic and orderly way, and that would restrain the rebellious impulses of the subjects after reaffirming their rights. Some moralists today would immediately think of strengthening citizens' moral character and moral cultivation, but this approach is too far-fetched. The fact is, in this country that highly esteems tradition, traditional ethics, especially the Christian faith, played a foundational role. Magna Carta consists of a preamble and 63 clauses, and the preamble has a [distinctly] religious flavor:

> John, by the grace of God, king of England, lord of Ireland, duke of Normandy and Aquitaine, and count of Anjou, to the archbishops, bishops, abbots, earls, barons, justiciaries, foresters, sheriffs, stewards, servants, and to all his bailiffs and liege subjects, greetings. Know that we, having regard

to God and for the salvation of our soul, and those of all our ancestors and heirs, and unto the honor of God and the advancement of his holy Church and for the rectifying of our realm, we have granted as underwritten by advice of our venerable fathers, Stephen, archbishop of Canterbury, primate of all England and cardinal of the holy Roman Church, Henry, archbishop of Dublin…and of the illustrious men William Marshal, earl of Pembroke, William, earl of Salisbury, ... and others.

Magna Carta then quickly enters into legislation that can be judicialized, the main points of which were: "in perpetuity... the English Church shall be free, and shall have its rights undiminished, and its liberties unimpaired," such as "freedom of the Church's elections"; "The guardian of the land of an heir who is under age shall take from it only reasonable revenues, customary dues, and feudal services. He shall do this without destruction or damage to men or property"; "No 'scutage' or 'aid' may be levied in our kingdom without its general consent, unless it is for the ransom of our person, to make our eldest son a knight, and (once) to marry our eldest daughter"; "The city of London shall enjoy all its ancient liberties and free customs, both by land and by water. We also will and grant that all other cities, boroughs, towns, and ports shall enjoy all their liberties and free customs"; "Ordinary lawsuits shall not follow the royal court around, but shall be held in a fixed place," with judicial authority independent of the Crown; "The writ called *precipe* shall not in future be issued to anyone in respect of any holding of land, if a free man could thereby be deprived of the right of trial in his own lord's court"; "No free man shall be seized or imprisoned, or stripped of his rights or possessions, or outlawed or exiled, or deprived of his standing in any other way, nor will we proceed with force against him, or send others to do so, except by the lawful judgement of his equals or by the law of the land." Finally, Clause 63 stipulates: "It is accordingly our wish and command that the English Church shall be free, and that men in our kingdom shall have and keep all these liberties, rights, and concessions, well and peaceably in their fulness and entirety for them and their heirs, of us and our heirs, in all things and all places for ever, " namely that, when necessary, force would be used to compel everyone in the land to respect the freedom of all, both king and subjects.

Modern-day pluralists may find the punitive clauses regarding the king's violations of Magna Carta very offensive. But the principle that is utterly chaotic in some political philosophies and is endlessly debated over in some ideological trends is actually basic common sense in jurisprudence: and that is that any contract or any law or constitution that serves as a social contract must be accompanied by guarantees of a compulsory nature. In other words, the consistency of the logic in the text of a contract and the compulsory nature of the implementation of the contract reflect justice monism. How Magna Carta transitioned in a clear and logical way from its opening religious proclamations to clauses of a legislative nature that can be judicialized is an important topic in constitutional law. A successful exploration of this topic would offer great insights to our discussions about how some ideologically oriented traditional countries have transitioned to judicially neutral and procedurally just constitutional politics.

Empirical experience has shown that, in order to restrain two parties that share a balance of power but are in political conflict and to compel them to quickly and logically respect the status quo, the two parties in conflict must be made to become sensible people. This means that both parties in the conflict are made aware that they are limited in their actions and also morally limited, and that they do not necessarily have any special right or ability to "enforce justice on behalf of Heaven," and then, full of the love of that comes from Jesus Christ on the cross, they forgive those brothers and sisters who had once persecuted them. Therewith, the two parties that share a balance of power will quickly enter into a contract that provides mutual protection through mutual restraint: clauses of a compulsory nature are what we call obligations; clauses of a protective nature are what we call rights; what connects the two is justice that comes from God, which must be put into effect on earth in the form of written laws and developed into documents of a constitutional nature. To reform the "blood lust" of politicized fighting, Clause 62 of Magna Carta rationally interprets the Christian spirit of forgiveness:

We have remitted and pardoned fully to all men any ill-will, hurt, or grudges that have arisen between us and our subjects, whether clergy or laymen, since the beginning of the dispute. We have in addition remitted fully, and for our own part have also pardoned, to all clergy and laymen any offences committed as a result of the said dispute between Easter in the sixteenth year of our reign (i.e. 1215) and the restoration of peace.

However, a single small community alone is insufficient to substantively defend the perpetual interests of the small community, especially that of letting citizens try to vote with their feet, using freedom of movement to extricate themselves from certain small communities that oppress personal freedoms. Due to the loss of an inherent spirit of justice and the tendency toward hierarchy in structure, it is hard for small communities to avoid becoming corrupted and turning into a platform for oppressing individuals. Worshiping a single small community is tantamount to worshipping the iron law of oligarchy. A social system that is civilized must reject any form of the cult of personality, cult of the group and cult of the small community. If an individual wants to give full consideration to the values and specific demands of the various interest groups in society in a more detailed and comprehensive manner, he must be relatively familiar with the values and specific demands of other small communities and have some knowledge of other people's mode of thinking and lifestyle. What this actually means is, a small community that is capable of being the foundation of a constitutional democratic system must be composed of members from various other small communities; the more diverse their backgrounds, occupations and geographic locales, the better. This is how it was with the signers of the Mayflower Compact and Magna Carta. In this paper, the state of interactive participation of Jesus Christ's visible churches is called "autonomous intersecting small communities."

It was upon this foundation that the United States was able to build a social welfare system that can co-exist with the nation's emphasis on freedom and small government and not cause the United States to go down the road to totalitarianism. A relative lack of knowledge of the sociology of religion created a huge blind spot in the thinking of the economist Hayek. Take for example the vividly Christian Republican Party in the obviously Protestant-leaning United States. This party highly values a *laissez faire* approach to the economy, but is an advocate of cultural conservatism. This odd arrangement of values actually advocates the Christian church and community rather than the government assuming most of the social welfare and community charity functions. In this way, government remains a small government while society does not lack for love and charity. The public's welfare and Christian tradition are inextricably linked. In the Christian world, wealth is privately held in the legal sense, but at the spiritual level, wealth beyond what is needed for basic life is society's. Charity is a tradition of Christianity and the Christian church. Nearly all the major welfare states of the world are Christian countries. Mother Teresa devoted her entire life to serving the poor and was awarded the Nobel Peace Prize in 1979. Although secular businesses are driven by profit, companies and society can still have a heart for charity. Charity and public welfare are values shared by the world's major religions; it is just that Christianity integrates charity and the rule of law somewhat better. The United States already has a rather sophisticated estate tax system and a rather sophisticated management system for charitable funds. For one thing, the United States uses a high progressive tax rate for estate and gift taxes, with up to 55% levied on an inheritance of more than $3 million, which the beneficiary must pay before receiving the inheritance. The law also gives tax deductions to people who donate to charities, including tax write-offs, income tax exemptions and tax cuts on the donations—[all] to encourage people to donate [to charities]. At the beginning of the 21st century, the U.S. tax rate was gradually reduced but charitable donations has continued to rise. This is why the United States, which has a fairly large income gap, has had few outbreaks of large-scale class conflicts. This situation allows the U.S. government to not have to assume too much of the burden that governments of the European welfare states do, enabling it to undertake the responsibility of preserving world peace, including the arduous mission of leading the world in the fight against fascism. Just imagine, if a constitutionalist United States had only economic liberalism without the wealth-sharing spirit born of the Christian faith and without the common law tradition, struggles between labor and capital would quickly break out and be hard to contain.

What needs to be emphasized is that, from the point of view of the Christian faith, any "expenditure" in any sense of the word that a person makes in this life does not necessarily give him any moral advantage over other people. Charity is regarded as a kind of faith-based social responsibility and does not in any sense give credence to the argument that it validates the moral superiority of philanthropists (or entrepreneurs) over other people (especially those of a much lower economic status: the working class and the middle class). The logic behind this is very simple: the size of the "expenditure" often is related only to the share of the social resources that a social group possesses. Furthermore, regardless of whether an entrepreneur's operational mechanism is legal or reasonable, or even entirely [in line with the Confucian exhortation to] acquire [wealth] in the proper way, he still is not entitled to a "justification by philanthropy" kind of right. Based on our understanding of human competition today, it's not hard to see that the practice of "justification by philanthropy" inevitably leads to the natural tendency to argue in favor of the affluent social class in capital-labor struggles, which causes more social inequality and creates the "Matthew effect" in social competition. With this kind of logic, any "philanthropy" that looks like "love" can ultimately be manipulated into a social mechanism to control and oppress. Conversely, the charity mechanism of "justification by faith" and its various secularized concepts of philanthropy and related mechanisms have effectively alleviated the contradiction between labor and capital in the West's employment system.

Northern European nations have still been able to establish and maintain constitutional democracies. When Lutheranism was made the state religion, the spread of Christianity in Northern Europe took on different characteristics from that in the United States. Lutheranism is conducive to the development of the democratic socialist movement. In terms of values, it has blood ties to socialism; the medium is the state religion of Lutheranism. What determined the Lutheran view of church-state relations was the theological understanding of Lutheranism as a Protestant denomination. Although Christian democracy and democratic socialism are isomorphic, if it can be said that Christian democracy has any shortcomings, it is that it entrusts the state (government) with the responsibility of aiding people at the bottom of society. This kind of democratic value system (which is actually a variant of nationalism's system of values) naïvely believes that a government orientated towards democracy and welfare and the participation in government of particular morally aware groups make it possible for the government to take on greater responsibilities, thus systematically rejecting "small government" and "night watchman government" models of governance. Christian democracy and democratic socialism can be said to be the West's version of [the concept of] "government by good men" [put forward by the philosopher and scholar Hu Shi and other political reformers in a 1923 manifesto].

Originally, the church—moved by the Holy Spirit, obeying the Bible and for the sake of the Gospel—took up the charitable work in society. For the church, charity was a "free ride" to salvation (indeed some non-believers "hitched a ride," but there are also non-believers who become close to the church and Christians because of this and wind up on the road to salvation; not to mention that this in itself reflects Jesus Christ's concern for the weak—therefore, it is most worthy of encouragement), but it is certainly not the case that philanthropists can therefore be "justified by good works," replacing the mechanism of salvation itself. The church's charity work is a telling of the classic story of Jesus Christ as "the way, the truth and the life," and therefore, it is a mechanism that rejects sanctifying the government yet can elevate the spirit of the political system and the political culture.

It is the Christian church—rather than government buildings and the buildings of political parties—that is the real place to place [one's] commitment. Christian democracy and democratic socialism place Christ Jesus' church within a social structure system with no connection to public welfare and charity, inevitably leading to society's further secularization and pluralization and causing the state (government) to take up heavy moral obligations beyond its ability to bear. Due to man's inherent sinful nature and the intrinsic nature of power to expand and [impose] comprehensive control and its instinctive tendency toward tyranny, when nationalistic passions are aroused by state governance-induced financial crises and by the common occurrence of crises over national sovereignty, the previously potent mechanisms of separation of powers and checks and balances will very easily become ineffective, putting in jeopardy the polycentric order within the boundaries of nation-state sovereignty; this is the unavoidable "road to serfdom." This logic was more or less the reason for the failure of the Weimar Constitution and the rise of Nazi Germany.

In other words, like Weber, Christian democracy makes the same mistake about people-oriented moral decisiveness, especially in placing moral decisiveness at a level similar to that of the operations of state power, which is a temptation beyond man's inherent ability to overcome. As the Lord's Prayer says:

> Our Father in heaven, hallowed be your name,
> your kingdom come, your will be done,
> on earth as it is in heaven.
> Give us today our daily bread,
> And forgive us our debts,
> as we also have forgiven our debtors.
> And lead us not into temptation,
> but deliver us from the evil one,
>
> for yours is the kingdom and the power and the glory forever.
> Amen. (Matthew 6:9-13)

Temptations of a political nature are unavoidable to non-Christians; the same is true for Christians as well.

IV. Which Legal System Best Fits the Market Economy System: the political principle of justice monism based on faith and the rule of law

Discussions about legal tradition must include mention of the concept of "legal system." As a concept used in comparative jurisprudence to categorize different types of law, it refers to the totality of a certain kind of legal system that has the same or similar elements, such as tradition, principle, system, characteristics, etc. A legal system usually covers a number of countries or regions, but sometimes different regions in one country may adopt different legal systems. There is no absolute criterion to categorize legal systems. Based on different research needs, a legal system may be divided into different subcategories. For example, British law and American law are two different subcategories of the common law system. The Anglo-American legal system and Europe's continental legal system are generally considered the world's two most important and influential legal systems. Nevertheless, there has been increasing interaction between these two major legal systems and they are becoming increasingly integrated.

The Anglo-American legal system is also called the common law system. It includes Britain and its former or current colonies (dependant territories and members of the British Commonwealth), such as Canada, Australia, New Zealand, Singapore, Malaysia, India, and Pakistan. The common law system began to take shape beginning in the 12th and 13th centuries, following the conquest of Normandy by England's King William I in 1066 A.D. To reinforce judicial jurisdiction, the royal court dispatched itinerant judges who traveled from town to town to try cases. There were many legal problems in the country but no codified legal standards, so judges could only base their rulings on folk customs, habits, moral concepts, and common sense, the most important of which, naturally, was Biblical teachings. Over time, the case law grew, and because judges customarily would respect and follow the principles of the rulings of earlier judges (especially judges of a higher level court), these precedents after several centuries became the law of the land. After printing became commonplace, more lawyers made records of many important precedent-setting cases and printed them for publication. Whenever new lawyers took on new cases, they would review the relevant case law for reference and judges would explain and analyze in detail their rationale for adjudicating and ruling on a case. By about the 15th century, these "laws" that had been "discovered" by judges rather than enacted by a legislative body had gradually established themselves. That's why common law is also called unwritten law. The common law system attaches great value to social norms, but due to a diversity of moral interpretations and the

59

unimaginable variability of ethnic traditions over several thousand years, it is difficult for the common law system to take root in a China that emphasizes "the rule of man."

The law of equity is also a legal concept that originated in England. Most courts try cases based on common law. However, because common law attaches great importance to procedure, many cases cannot get a fair ruling simply because of some failure to comply with relevant procedures, such as missing the deadline for an appeal. To address this problem, the Lord Chancellor of Britain set up another court to hear cases in a comparatively loose procedural process. Compared with common law, the law of equity emphasizes substantive justice more and adheres less rigidly to the principles of procedural justice. It used to be that common law cases and equity cases were heard in different courts. Once a case was lost in common law court, the plaintiff could apply to have the case heard in equity court. This lack of unity in the judiciary created massive problems. So Britain passed the Judicature Acts (1873-1875) to combine the courts of common law and equity. Equity was made superior to common law, and in any conflict between common law and equity, the law of equity prevails. In this respect, equity demonstrates respect for the will of people that is characteristic of judicial democracy.

The continental legal system was adopted mainly by countries on the European Continent and countries under their influence. Its historical origin was mainly the law of the ancient Roman Empire. In Medieval times, Roman law became important again on the European Continent. One after another in the 18th century, many European Continent countries promulgated numerous legal codes, trying to set out detailed standards for various branches of law. Unlike common law, continental law is also called statutory law, European law and Roman law. It has its own strengths, such as certainty of legal provisions, so common law began to gradually absorb the form and the strengths of continental law and developed into a hybrid legal system. Due to their historical legacies, some regions, such as Scotland in the United Kingdom, Louisiana in the United States, Quebec in Canada, and South Africa, have characteristics of both common law and continental law. Louisiana, which used to be a French colony, gradually adopted common law for criminal cases after it became part of the United States for the sake of judicial uniformity and to protect human rights. The European Court of Justice, as the only court that transcends national sovereignty and borders and has direct legal jurisdiction, has to face the longstanding contradictions between common law and continental law and carefully reconcile them.

Common law attaches great importance to case law and precedent and comparatively less importance to statutory laws. This is both an opportunity and a challenge. The opportunity is that it gives legal professionals more [room] to be pro-active, while the challenge is that it might give to legal professionals functions that exceed their moral character and abilities. To restrict and moderate legal professionals, a system must be established to safeguard the serious nature, continuity and efficacy of [previously] decided cases. The law cannot take shape if judges do whatever they please. Courts in the common law system all follow some self-imposed regulations: the lower court must follow the precedent of the higher court; although judges at the same level try cases independently, unless there is a very good reason, they must brainstorm together and uphold the case law, which is more "convincing." Court decisions are themselves part of the nation's body of law. Since the requirements for judges in the common law system are completely in line with the requirements for lawyers in private practice, when appointments are made, many judges are selected from among successful lawyers with years of experience in private practice. The opposite is the case in countries having a continental law system, which regards the judges' main function as interpreting and applying laws and regulations and which have comparatively lower standards for their judges and without much expectation of the "experience" and "moral character" of legal professionals. It could be said that judges and lawyers in the common law system are natural "jurists" compared with legal professionals in the continental law system. Which is why Tocqueville, in his book *On Democracy in America*, praised legal professionals in America as "jurists" with the "spirit of jurists." This is the significance of the community of legal professionals in the common law system. It can be said that without the community of legal professionals rooted in divine faith, there would be no effectively and soundly functioning common law system, nor would there be the commitment to and improvement of polycentric order and its monistic justice in the political and social realms.

Generally speaking, in the transformative process of modernization, common law countries are much more stable than continental law countries. The two major common law nations of Britain and the United States were among the first wave of democratic countries to date. Although the two countries experienced various forms of civil wars, they have never experienced major setbacks in their governmental system. By contrast, countries that adopted the continental law system, whether that be Germany, France, Japan, or Russia, Portugal or Spain, all went through a return to traditional dictatorship at some point. The motive of all these countries when they first adopted the continental law system was to maintain the dictatorship and reinforce centralized power, not to promote freedom and democracy. Such was the case in France in the Napoleonic Era, Germany in the Bismarck Era, Japan during the Meiji Restoration, and China in the Late Qing Dynasty and early Republican era, for instance. The basic reason that continental law countries stick with the system after their transition is that historically they have always been continental law countries, which reflects the tendency to stick to old ways in institutional transition.

Compared with common law, continental law is more dependent on lawmakers having more foresight than other people. However, the intellect of lawmakers and their ability to foresee is ultimately limited because, as we all know, all life forms are limited and mankind is universally sinful by nature. It's hard to imagine that there are many people who can successfully foresee what will happen hundreds of years into the future. A person's life span is just a few decades, but the establishment of a nation and ethnic group and of the law and a system cannot happen in a brief historical moment. Therefore, deriving the law from customs and tradition is far superior to lawmakers making the law. With the development of the commodity economy, market information has become ever-changing, far beyond lawmakers' ability to foresee; in this way, the superiority of the common law system over the continental law system is manifest. For a long time, common law was the main system used by the international community in areas such as ocean voyages and import and export. In particular, the rise of modern finance and the birth of several world financial centers in civilization to date reflect the superiority of the common law system even more. Modern finance deals with such massive wealth and requires such expertise that the security of strong and effective rule of law becomes even more necessary. This means that a nation's legal system must be able to change readily with the nation's financial developments. Common law obviously is more capable of this kind of adaptation.

Fairness and justice are the foundation and core principles of modern finance and the securities market; to implement these principles and promote the healthy development of finance and securities exchange, the finance and securities industry in common law countries applies the principle of "presumption of guilt" in securities regulation." In 1720, due to a lack of regulation of the stock market, institutional investors manipulated stock prices and insider trading was rampant, ultimately leading to the collapse of Britain's stock market. Insider trading was also one of the reasons for the collapse of the U.S. stock market in 1929. Because of this, the U.S. government set up the Securities and Exchange Commission. At the same time, in order to have effective regulation and to prevent damage to the securities market from insider trading, the U.S. government applied the "presumption of guilt" [principle] to securities traders. Because capital is regulated by the logic of justice, all of the world's financial centers to date were birthed in common law countries and regions, such as New York, London, Hong Kong and Singapore. Likewise, the Sherman Antitrust Act, which was enacted for the purpose of constraining capital, is a principle used in the common law nation of the United States to promote justice: The Act laid a solid foundation for anti-trust laws and remains to this day the United States' basic anti-trust principle, yet it does not provide a clear explanation for what is considered a monopolistic act or what activities limit trade, leaving a great deal of room for judicial interpretation, and such judicial interpretation is profoundly influenced by the economic context.

More importantly, the success of common law is not so much the success of the common law system as it is the success of the Christian tradition in these countries and of the rule of law tradition of these small communities. Nations that adopted the common law system were usually very different from nations that adopted the continental law system in terms of the circumstances of the people and the political culture. Even so, even among common law nations, differences in the circumstances of the people can still result in a loss of efficacy of laws and regulations and difficulties in establishing rule of law. In *The Old Regime and the Revolution*, Tocqueville sharply criticized his own country, while in *On Democracy in America*, he passionately praised the United States. People generally attribute the two different development models to the adoption of different legal systems. However, "Mexico, which is not less fortunately situated than the Anglo-American Union, has adopted the same laws, but is unable to accustom itself to the government of democracy."[13]

The way that common law facilitated economic development in Britain and the United States inspires us in areas far beyond reforming the judicial system. The "feasibility" of systems and procedures is predicated upon their being definite, easy to comprehend and not open to manipulation, and not upon anti-transcendent pluralism nor confusion-inducing skepticism. A life from which decisions are lacking does not exist. Rule of law without decision-making is [mere] fantasy. Therefore, a successful judicial system must at a minimum encompass monism on multiple levels.

The first is in the sociological sense: a country must choose a political system and a judicial system that fit with the circumstances and customs of her people. Such consistency is conducive to the formation of a solid culture of rule of law in society. Nothing would be better than that the various small communities in the country are all guided by the rule of law and justice. A strong government often poses a threat to the rule of law; small communities here can provide the best possible material benefit to ordinary people, thereby reducing the gap between rich and poor which creates the need in society for and dependence on an almighty government.

---

[13] Tocqueville (France), *On Democracy in America*. Translated by Dong Guoliang. Commercial Press, 1988, p. 357.

Second, judicial justice should be made the bottom line for decisions that involve national sovereignty, and any political power outside the jurisdiction of the law should never be allowed to operate, such as substituting law-making and executive [rule] for judicial decisions. Legislation must reflect universal love, while the judiciary must reflect the principle of universal justice in independent and fair ways.

Third, the laws and regulations of this nation must be internally consistent, not contradictory in form and logic, nor turning into a variety of standards, which would put those who abide by the law at a loss and force them to knowingly become lawbreakers in order to survive while law enforcement agents follow the law of the jungle and do as they please. If the law changes with people and events or is enforced selectively, underprivileged social groups will inevitably be caught up in legal interpretations that favor them the least. This is the basic principle discussed in the well-known "eight ways to fail to make law" in the history of legal system.

Fourth, this nation's rules of judicial operation must be defined and consistent. Except for applying—with restraint—the presumption of guilt to certain privileged social groups (such as the government, officials, and powerful economic organizations), and applying the presumption of innocence to the general public, in particular to underprivileged social groups, a principle of procedural justice that fully guarantees the freedom and the rights of ordinary people, especially underprivileged individuals, [should] eventually be established.

Because of the Enlightenment and the influence of Oriental culture on the West, the great significance of the aforementioned four levels of consistency and hierarchy of the Christian faith and Western legal tradition to an understanding of civilization and governance of a nation appears to be fading in today's world of global economic integration and age of the civilization of increasingly diversified powerful economic entities. The result is, the world today is seen as an indivisible "global village"; politically, culturally, and judicially, and especially with regard to core values, the "global village" is nowhere near to achieving the heights that its admirers would like it to achieve. Even if every nation were to make "protection of human rights" a fundamental principle, the standards that different nations have for human rights still are not the same. Therefore, the result has been that the former unbreakable relationship between faith-based values and market choice is being regarded more and more as irrelevant due to the "eastward spread of Western learning."

Nonetheless, if we agree that the political and sociological phenomena displayed in the table on the following pages is factual, then we should acknowledge that nearly all the countries once governed by member parties of the Socialists International had a Catholic, Anglican or Lutheran religious background, and that, at a minimum, these countries at the same time all had influential politically active Christian democratic parties, and that, in fact, the socialist parties and the Christian democratic parties took turns governing these countries; that once the participation and counterbalance of conservative parties were removed from these countries, Hayek's fear will immediately become a reality because of Hayek's "anti-socialism." In addition, we will also acknowledge that the three-way interaction of government, businesses and society is civilization's normal state and the way to protect against violations of personal freedom and social autonomy. Government controls [the use of] force, the economy controls wealth, and society tends to be the weakling. Social autonomy can be safeguarded only by small communities bound together by traditional values that unremittingly transcend the interests principle that is common among secularized rights defenders. The only possibility of establishing a constitutional democracy rule-of-law society is by checks and balances on the government and market and through society's own power (such as collective protests) to maintain the relative balance of government, market and society.

Table: Major nations and their forms of government, legal systems, religion, welfare systems (whether socialist parties are in power), and status as a world financial center (Some statistics were taken from the Wikipedia entries of the specific country, Feb. 16, 2010))

Nation	Political system	Legal system	Religion	Welfare system	World financial center (by city)	Notes
USA	Presidential system, federal constitutional democracy	Common Law (except for Louisiana, which follows Continental Law but is gradually switching to Common Law	Mainly Protestant (which laid the foundation for the nation's political culture), Catholic	Community welfare system, business insurance system, no tradition of socialism	New York	Vast land, sparsely populated, rich in natural resources, no powerful neighboring states
France	Semi-presidential system; semi-representative democracy	Continental Law	Mainly Catholic	Welfare state; had been governed by the Socialist Party		During transition period, political system was repeatedly shaken up; was occupied during WW II
Germany	Parliamentary republic; representative democracy	Continental Law	mainly Lutheran & Catholic	Welfare state; had been governed by the Social Democratic Party		Previously governed by the Nazi regime; was divided into East Germany and West Germany
Italy	Parliamentary republic; representative democracy	Continental Law	Mainly Catholic	Welfare state		Had been governed by a Fascist regime

Britain	Constitutional monarchy; representative democracy	Mainly Common Law system (Scotland has distinctive characteristics of a Continental Law system and a mixed law system	Anglican, a Protestant denomination, is the official religion	Welfare state; had been governed by the Labor Party	London	An island nation; comparatively few invasions by foreign countries
Canada	Constitutional monarchy; representative democracy	Mainly Common Law (Quebec has a Continental Law system)	Mainly Protestant	Welfare state		Vast land; sparsely populated; rich in natural resources; shares land border only with the US
Australia	Constitutional monarchy, representative democracy	Common Law	Mainly Protestant	Welfare state; had been governed by the Labor Party		Became independent in 1986
Switzerland	Directorial system, direct democracy	Continental Law	Equally Protestant and Catholic	Welfare state		A long-standing "neutral state"
Austria	Semi-presidential system, representative democracy	Continental Law	Mainly Catholic	Welfare state; had been governed by the Social Democratic Party		Defeated in WW II

Norway	Constitutional monarchy; representative democracy; one-house parliamentary system	Continental Law	Lutheranism is the state religion	Welfare state; had been governed by the Labor Party		
Sweden	Constitutional monarchy; representative democracy	Continental Law	Lutheranism was the state religion until 2000	Welfare state; had been governed by the Social Democratic Party		
Finland	Constitutional monarchy; representative democracy	Continental Law	Mainly Lutheran	Welfare state; had been governed by the Social Democratic Party		Invaded by the Soviet Union during World War II, was part of the war's "Eastern Front"
Holland	Constitutional monarchy; representative democracy	Continental Law	Catholic in the South and Protestant in the North	Welfare state; had been governed by the Socialist Party		Occupied during WWII
Belgium	Constitutional monarchy; Cabinet collective responsibility	Continental Law	Mainly Catholic	Welfare state; governed by the Socialist Party		Occupied during WW II
Poland	Representative democracy	Continental Law	Catholic			Occupied during WW II

Japan	Constitutional monarchy; representative democracy	Continental Law	Mainly Shinto	Welfare state; Communist Party stopped governing long ago		Defeated in WW II; "Peace Constitution"; a democratic state defended by the U.S. Armed Force
Spain	Constitutional monarchy; representative democracy	Continental Law	Mainly Catholic	Had been governed by the Socialist Workers' Party		A "Third-Wave Democracy" country
Portugal	Constitutional monarchy; representative democracy system	Continental Law	Mainly Catholic	Had been governed by the Socialist Party		A "Third-Wave Democracy" country
Russia	Semi-presidential system	Continental Law	Mainly Eastern Orthodox	Union of Social-Democrats		Long plagued by the Stalin model; a victor in World War II
South Korea	Constitutionally a presidential system; in reality, a semi-presidential system	Continental Law	20% Christian, 10% Catholics, 20% Buddhists; more characteristic of a Christian culture			Previously a colony of Japan; a democratic country defended by U.S. troops

India	Representative democracy	Common Law	Mainly Hindu	Some states are governed by the Communist Party and have not become part of the territory of the "dictatorial regime"	A British colony for more than 300 years; facing pervasive internal ethnic & religious conflicts
Brazil	Presidential system	Continental Law	Mainly Catholic		Longtime military rule; "Latin Americanized"
Argentina	Presidential system	Continental Law	Mainly Catholic		Longtime military rule; "Latin Americanized"
Singapore	Semi-presidential system, representative democracy	Common Law	Mainly Buddhist; Christianity is also influential	Governed by the People's Action Party; authoritarian-style rule of law strictly enforced Singapore	Put forth the concept of "East Asian values"; generally considered an authoritarian state

Market economy, social justice, judicial justice and Christian tradition appear to be totally unrelated. However, the jurisprudence conclusion of "regulation of capital" derived from Christian justice monism points out that economic liberalism is essentially tyrannical and, coupled with the institutional fulfillment of judicial justice, helped to create world financial centers in common law countries, thereby achieving globalization and integration of the world economy. The participation of the Christian church in social justice and public welfare, whether in countries where Lutheranism is the state religion or in communities deeply impacted by Calvinism, all [became] a solid foundation for effectively curbing capital-labor conflicts and avoiding the "road to serfdom." The great significance to constitutional politics of "Christian justice monism" based on Christian faith and the Western legal tradition is profoundly evident when compared with the secular version of justice monism that idolizes institutions.

Christian Constitutionalism and Theories of Human Nature

Man De (Baosheng Guo)

Politics is unique to human society. It is the various activities, knowledge and institutional arrangements for handling interpersonal relations. People are the basis of politics. As English political theorist Graham Wallas said in *Human Nature in Politics*, "The only form of study which a political thinker of one or two hundred years ago would now note as missing is any attempt to deal with politics in its relation to the nature of man. The thinkers of the past, from Plato to Bentham and Mill, had each his own view of human nature, and they made those views the basis of their speculations on government." [1] The fundamental difference among political theories is in how they view human nature, especially their conclusions about man's moral nature and their assessment of man's capacity to reason. Is human nature good or bad? Can human nature achieve perfection through man's own efforts? Is man's capacity to reason finite or infinite? In the absence of reason, are all the problems of human society impossible to solve? Everyone expects a nation's rulers or ruling class to be all-good, all-wise, and almighty, but how can the absolute nature of rulers be

---

[1] See *Human Nature in Politics*. (British) Graham Wallas. The Commercial Press. Tr. Zhu Zengwen, 1995. A Collection of World Famous Academic Works Translated into Chinese

consistently guaranteed? The differing answers to these questions form the foundation of different political theories.

The political phenomena related to theories of human nature are easy to recognize: the theory that human nature is intrinsically good and that man can achieve "perfection" and "holiness" through moral cultivation without institutional checks and balances never leads to constitutionalism—this doctrine can only result in the "kingly way," "kingcraft," and "dictatorship" in which the head of state or ruling class enjoys unlimited power; believing that all men are intrinsically evil and that those holding power, in particular, are more inclined to evil, and that the evilness of human nature cannot be eradicated through man's own striving to be moral, will naturally lead to limitations, restraints and institutional checks and balances being placed on those who hold power.

As for man's reason, the idea that reason can solve all social problems and that reason can grasp the absolute law governing human history, that is, the historicism criticized by Karl Popper[2] and the idea that reason can construct a perfect society, that is, the constructive rationalism proposed by F. A. Hayek, without doubt form the conceptual basis for a planned economy and communism; this over-estimation of reason in human nature undoubtedly runs counter to the constitutionalist ideal. Whereas, the notion, held by the likes of Hayek, that man possesses only bounded rationality, or that held by Kant and others that the "thing-in-itself is unknowable" and that finite humanity cannot grasp the infinite, absolute and ultimate knowledge, will never cause rulers to place themselves above all and dictate all things, but rather will make people more humble and obedient to the law. As the Bible says in Proverbs 1:7,"The fear of the Lord is the beginning of knowledge." Man can do nothing but fear when facing the eternal Truth (God). Any act by any political leader or group that usurps God's authority or deifies oneself is bound to lead to dictatorship and totalitarianism.

---

[2] See *The Poverty of Historicism*, by Karl Popper. Huaxia Press. Tr. Du Ruji & Qiu Renzong, 1987.

Clearly, the theory of human nature, i.e. deciding what man's moral nature and capacity to reason are, and the theory and practice of constitutionalism are closely linked. Man's utter moral depravity, his powerlessness to attain salvation and perfection through his own efforts, the limits of his reason and knowledge, in short, the exposition of man's "sin," is what moves the Christian theory of human nature beyond the theories of other faith traditions, naturally becoming the foundation for forming the theory of constitutionalism, whereas the explanations of "bounded rationality," "man's limitations," and "the darkness of unconsciousness"[3] proposed by liberals are no more than academic expositions of the Christian concept of "sin."

The Christian view of man's moral nature is not simply that human nature is evil. Looked at as a whole, [this view] divides human nature into three stages. In the beginning, man was created good and perfect, but then, because of separation from God, man fell into sin. [Because of] salvation in Jesus, Christians after they accept Jesus as savior are called righteous (the Chinese character 义 is translated as "righteousness" or "justice" in English; it means to be without sin). However, this is just passively being reckoned by God as free of sin (Justice: judged by God and deemed a sinless and righteous person), but in essence, the sin nature still exists. The third stage is when the believer dies and goes to Heaven or at the time of Jesus' Second Coming. Only then is complete sanctification and perfection achieved. Of the three stages, neither the initial stage nor the future are of the now, and in the current stage, man both in reality and historically is sinful.

Likewise, Christianity holds a very pessimistic view of man's capacity for reason. In God's view, man both historically and in reality is "blind" and "deaf." "You will be ever hearing but never understanding; you will be ever seeing but never perceiving." (Matthew 13:14) The knowledge that mankind has acquired is no more than "the elemental spiritual forces of this world" (Colossians 2:8), and man's attempts to achieve absolute truth and knowledge of God is as futile and as destined to fail as was the construction of "Babel"(that is, the "tower to

---

[3] See *Consciousness of Darkness and Democratic Tradition* by Zhang Hao. Xinxing Press. 2006.

the heavens" in Genesis 11). As 1 Corinthians 1:21 says, "For since in the wisdom of God the world through its wisdom did not know him, God was pleased through the foolishness of what was preached to save those who believe."

If God had not taken the initiative to reveal His Word, the Bible, and had not taken the initiative to reveal Himself by becoming flesh (John 1:18), mankind would not know God—the absolute truth, absolute goodness and absolute beauty. Revelation is an absolute object taking the initiative to display [itself] to a subject, while knowledge is the subject, which is man, taking hold of the absolute object. The latter is futile because only through revelation is it possible for mankind to be in contact with the absolute.

Compared with the theory held by the Chinese legalists Han Fei and Li Si and by Machiavelli that human nature is evil, Christianity's view of man's evil nature is more comprehensive because both [Machiavelli and the Chinese philosophy of legalism] placed more emphasis on the evil nature of the ruled while the rulers all seemed to be great, honorable and right—since "the end justifies the means." In *The Prince*, Machiavelli said, "Therefore a wise lord cannot, nor ought he to, keep faith when such observance may be turned against him, and when the reasons that caused him to pledge it exist no longer. If men were entirely good this precept would not hold, but because they are bad, and will not keep faith with you, you too are not bound to observe it with them."[4]

Clearly, the Machiavellianists view of man's evil nature was selective, with the rulers being good by nature while the ruled are evil by nature. This would never lead to constitutionalism, but rather to totalitarianism. In contrast, the Bible says in Romans 3:10-12, "As it is written: 'There is no one righteous, not even one; there is no one who understands; there is no one who seeks God. All have turned away, they have together become worthless; there is no one who does good, not even one.'" Not only the ruled, but also kings, emperors, archbishops, and

---

[4] See *The Prince*, by Machiavelli. Tr. by Pan Handian. Commercial Press. 1985.

popes, are all sinners, none is righteous. "Power corrupts and absolute power corrupts absolutely." (So said Lord Acton, an English Catholic.) The Christian view of human nature became the theoretical basis for imposing restrictions on the power held by those in authority.

Not only that, in expounding upon man's sin, man's evil nature and the limits of man's reason, Christianity more than any other political theory or religion (Confucianism, Buddhism, etc. all speak of man's sin) brings into play the ultimate in human language, emphasizing to an incomparable degree that man's sin is the cornerstone of Christian doctrine and theology. It also offers the earliest and most powerful footnote to mankind's theory of constitutionalism. For example, it was precisely the Puritans' doctrines and tenets in the *Westminster Confession of Faith* that paved the way for the basis of the theory of human nature behind the "constitutional monarchy" that was established nearly 40 years later by the Glorious Revolution of 1688 and was much admired by the Chinese intellectual community: civil war in England broke out in 1642 and for several years the army of Charles I, representing the Church of England, fought the Puritan troops representing Protestantism, finally ending in 1649 with the beheading of Charles I. As the war drew to a close, the members of Parliament, the majority of whom were Puritans, met in Westminster Abbey and established theological principles for the ideological foundation of the new political system. Of those in attendance, 121 were ministers, 30 were members of the House, and eight were representatives of Scotland. The *Westminster Confession of Faith* was completed in December 1646. This creed was for Parliament and for the citizens of the entire nation, and without doubt became the theological foundation of English constitutionalism, providing the theoretical premise for the view of human nature and for the contract theory behind the constitutional monarchy, separation of powers, representative government and other English institutional arrangements. For example:

Chapter VI (Of the Fall of Man, of Sin, and the Punishment thereof), of the *Westminster Confession of Faith* says in Article II, "By this sin they fell from their original righteousness and communion, with God, and so

77

became dead in sin, and wholly defiled in all the parts and faculties of soul and body." Article IV says, "From this original corruption, whereby we are utterly indisposed, disabled, and made opposite to all good, and wholly inclined to all evil, do proceed all actual transgressions." Article V says, "This corruption of nature, during this life, does remain in those that are regenerated; and although it be, through Christ, pardoned, and mortified; yet both itself, and all the motions thereof, are truly and properly sin."

Chapter 19 (Of the Law of God), Article VI says, "discovering also the sinful pollutions of their nature, hearts and lives; so as, examining themselves thereby, they may come to further conviction of, humiliation for, and hatred against sin, together with a clearer sight of the need they have of Christ, and the perfection of His obedience."[5]

Not only are all sinful, but even those redeemed by Jesus Christ still have the "corrupt nature" and still need [to use] the law to examine themselves. The theory of human nature in the *Westminster Confession of Faith* had a profound impact on the English church and England's political realm. It influenced the English political system immediately upon its promulgation and right up to the time of the official establishment of a constitutional monarchy by the Glorious Revolution.

We will now look at the influence of the Christian theory of human nature on the concept of constitutionalism from three perspectives: Biblical text, Christian doctrine and theology, and the history of theological thought.

Unlike the people in China's historical and classical texts, no one in the Bible, except Jesus, was perfect, and all were flawed; for example, Moses, David, Peter, Paul, etc. This is because the emphasis of the Bible is on God rather than man, and praise is given to God, not man; through man's depravity, God's glory is highlighted. Whereas in China's classical texts, the emphasis is on man, and every saint and wise ruler is great, glorious and correct; most history books do not

---

[5] See *Ecumenical Creeds and Reformed Confessions and Catechisms.* Tr. Zhao Zhonghui, etc. Reformation Translation Fellowship P.C., Taipei. 1993

record their flaws because historians wanted to set them up as idols for people to model themselves after. In the Bible, the sin and depravity that accompanies man is clear to see, shocking people from beginning to end.

The Bible opens with the first man and woman, Adam and Eve, disobeying God's command, eating the forbidden fruit and falling into sin. (Genesis 3) Their two sons, the second generation of the human race, committed fratricide over making offerings [to God]. (Genesis 4) In the time of Noah, human hearts became so depraved that "the earth was corrupt in God's sight and was full of violence. God saw how corrupt the earth had become, for all the people on earth had corrupted their ways."(Genesis 6:11-12) After the baptism of the Flood, mankind became rebellious again and began to build the Tower of Babel "so that we may make a name for ourselves." (Genesis 11:4) Even Abraham, who was appointed by God to be the Father of All Nations, lied and said his wife was his sister to [protect] his own personal safety. (Genesis 12)

The great leader Moses who brought the Israelites out of Egypt, though nearly perfect, disobeyed God's instructions and struck a rock, and he was punished by not being allowed to enter the Promised Land of Canaan in his lifetime. (Numbers 20) As for David, the most accomplished, glorious and correct king of Israel, after attaining success and recognition and bringing peace to the nation, actually committed adultery with a married woman and murdered her husband, and all these crimes were meticulously recorded in the Bible. (2 Samuel 11) The kings and the people of Israel after David became more rebellious. The people worshipped idols and were sexually immoral and defiled, the government was corrupt and trampled on justice, which eventually resulted in the nation being divided and to multiple conquests by foreign invaders. This is how the Bible portrays human nature, full of wickedness and desperately in need of God's redemption. Of the kings and political leaders in the Old Testament, not a one was an all-knowing, all-powerful and all-good saint. They were all sinners and needed systems, laws (The Ten Commandments) and God to restrain and [impose] checks and balances on them.

In the Bible, in the New Testament, the Jews were so sinful that John the Baptist made this appeal, "Repent, for the kingdom of heaven is at hand." (Matthew 3:2) The two most revered saints in the New Testament, Peter and Paul, were exemplary figures, and Peter was even recognized as the first pope by the Roman Catholic Church. The Bible, however, shows no mercy in exposing their flaws. When Jesus Christ was about to be crucified, Peter disowned him three times and denied that he was a disciple of Jesus. This was a lie. (John 18). Later, in the days of the early church, Peter acted hypocritically out of deference to the elders of the church in Jerusalem. (Galatians 2:13) The Apostle Paul, the wisest and most able of the apostles, always referred to himself as "the worst of sinners" (1 Timothy 1:15), and admitted that he "was given a thorn in my flesh" (2 Corinthians 12:7), which became a physical defect that could not be removed.

To sum up, all the leaders and heroes in the Bible had a deep-seated sinful nature, and they themselves often were keenly aware of their sin. Generation after generation of Christians and people in the West reading the Bible have been "infected" by this awareness of sin, knowing intuitively that they need to constantly repent and confess their sins, that no one in this world is perfect, and that the sinful nature of those with authority and power needs to be monitored and restrained all the more. This is what constitutes the basis of the theory of human nature for constitutionalism rather than that of monarchical rule or dictatorship.

In Christian doctrine and theology, doctrines about man's nature and redemption are most closely related to the theories of Christian constitutionalism, so this will be the focal point of our analysis. The utter depravity of man's nature after the Fall and the theory of salvation through God's grace alone, which is fundamentally different from Confucianism's becoming a sage and Buddhism's attaining enlightenment through one's own efforts, and is also fundamentally different from [the teaching in] Judaism and other religions that man is saved through religious practices, put more emphasis on the theory that man is evil by nature, thus bringing even closer the relationship between Christianity and constitutionalism.

The Bible teaches that man was created by God using dust and his spirit. "Then the Lord God formed a man from the dust of the ground and breathed into his nostrils the breath of life, and the man became a living being." (Genesis 2:7) The dust became the flesh man. "All come from dust, and to dust all return." (Ecclesiastes 3:20) The flesh is also what makes man vulnerable to the temptations of the Devil, an angel who vainly tried to become God and after he fell became the Devil. Human nature, which originally was good, started to forsake God because of the Devil's temptations After being punished by God, [man] was ever after separated from the eternal truth, goodness and beauty—God—and fell into sin, from which he could not deliver himself. This was the original sin committed by Adam, just as Romans 6:23 says, "For the wages of sin is death." Since Adam represented the entire human race, all generations of the human race he represented shoulder [the blame], so that "just as man is destined to die once, and after that to face judgment." (Hebrews 9:27) That is also why upright conduct became distorted (Genesis 4:5, 8), purity became filthy (Genesis 19:31, 38), knowledge became ignorance (Genesis 11:4), and man seemed to have completely lost the image of God. (Genesis 6:5, 11-12)

Sin—moral depravity, limited and shallow knowledge, and being powerless to save oneself—is the essence of **man's** nature. The Bible says, "The heart is deceitful above all things and beyond cure. Who can understand it?" (Jeremiah 17:9) "Surely I was sinful at birth, sinful from the time my mother conceived me." (Psalms 51:5) This is the reality of human nature. It applies to everyone, whether emperor, king, president or [Communist Party] general-secretary. Even Christians who have been redeemed by Jesus Christ are just sinners covered by grace who have simply put on the "robe of righteousness" given by Jesus Christ but who actually still have a sinful nature. Due to the existence of the flesh, the bodies of believers are not yet redeemed. (Romans 7:23-24 says: "but I see another law at work in me, waging war against the law of my mind and making me a prisoner of the law of sin at work within me. What a wretched man I am! Who will rescue me from this body that is subject to death?") Therefore, this sinful nature still exists in Christians, and Christians also need to be constrained and supervised.

Because of its emphasis on man's moral corruption and limited knowledge, the Christian theory of salvation—how man can have eternal life, be one with the God of perfect truth, perfect goodness and perfect beauty, be free from sin and be with God or achieve "the unity of Heaven and man"—is typical of the theory that salvation comes through God's grace alone. This "only by God's grace" theory [says] that man contributes nothing to salvation. Man's salvation, that is, being with God, is entirely an act of God alone. Man's path to attaining salvation through his own conscience, good works, knowledge, law, penance or even his faith (rather than being moved by the Holy Spirit to make Jesus the object of his faith) has been completely blocked. Man cannot contribute even 0.001% to his salvation; man's attainment of salvation is 100% the work of God. Ephesians 2:8-9 says, "For it is by grace you have been saved, through faith—and this is not from yourselves, it is the gift of God—not by works, so that no one can boast."

Galatians 2:16 says, "...know that a person is not justified by the works of the law, but by faith in Jesus Christ. So we, too, have put our faith in Christ Jesus that we may be justified by faith in Christ and not by the works of the law, because by the works of the law no one will be justified." The law is about man's actions. Nullifying the role of the law in salvation is to also nullify the role of man. Such teachings about the theory of salvation emphasize once more man's limitations, powerlessness and moral corruption, and emphasize once more how unique and precious is God's grace. This is "predestination," the most attractive and penetrating of the Christian theory of salvation, about which we will elaborate later.

In stark contrast to the theory of salvation by God's grace alone are traditional Chinese philosophy and beliefs, as well as Marxism. Though they all address the evil of man, they only scratch the surface; moreover, not all men are evil, some have the potential to become sages, attain Buddhahood, and become masters of history.

Confucianism believes that it is entirely possible for man to become a sage on his own because man is innately good and simply became defiled by the world; and man can remove this defilement and become a sage simply through self-cultivation, knowledge and meditation and other means. Thus the saying, "Men at their birth are basically good." Mencius went further, saying, "Everyone can be [a sage] like Yao and Shun", and that "man is inclined to good as water is inclined to flow downhill." Mencius believed that man is born with "sprouts of virtue" by which man can become moral and become a sage.[6] Obviously, the Confucian view that man is inclined toward virtue, especially the view of the king's potential for virtue, is diametrically opposed to the Christian theory that man's nature is evil.

On [the question of] the nature of man, the Confucian Xunzi held the man-is-evil theory, but with regard to the heart, he held the theory of sage kings, that is, "A man in the street can become a Yu (a sage king)." In the *Xunzi* chapter "Bugou" or "Nothing Indecorous," he said, "If with truthfulness of mind he upholds the principle of humanity, it will be given form. Having been given form, it becomes intelligible. Having become intelligible, it can produce transmutation. If with truthfulness of mind he behaves with justice, it will accord with natural order." "Heaven and Earth give birth to the gentleman, and the gentleman provides the organizing principle for Heaven and Earth. The gentleman is the triadic partner of Heaven and Earth, the summation of the myriad of things, and the father and mother of the people." Clearly, by "observing the virtue of benevolence" and through other ethical means, the gentleman can become a sage king or even God, taking part in all things in Heaven and Earth.

This kind of self-confidence in or wild arrogance of man also showed up in late Confucianism. For example, prominent neo-Confucian scholar Zhu Xi proposed a comprehensive way of "cultivating oneself, **harmonizing homes, governing the country and controlling the world with justice**" and achieving "inner sage and outer sovereign," and systemized that way—predicated upon man's innate goodness—to

---

[6] See *Consciousness of Darkness and Democratic Tradition* by Zhang Hao. Xinxing Press. 2006.

achieve salvation, eternity, and the unity of Heaven and man. Master Wang Yangming, the leading figure in the Neo-Confucian School of Mind, held that "the heart-mind being principle, nothing exists beyond the heart-mind," attributing the ultimate existence of the universe to one's own heart-mind or consciousness. This already is a radical form of thinking of the human self as the source of nature and the universe itself, but another prominent thinker, Lu Jiuyuan, believed that "the universe is my mind and my mind is the universe" and said, " Looking up, I can climb the constellation Saggitarius; Rolling over, I lean upon the North Star; Looking around the universe, there is none like me." This is the n-th degree of anthropocentrism and the arrogance of man.

Mainstream Buddhist ideas also exalt man, convinced that man is not thoroughly corrupt but rather is possessed of Buddhahood potential, and that it is entirely possible for man to attain Buddhahood through personal efforts, such as spiritual cultivation, enlightenment, meditation, penance, charity, incantations, and religious rituals. Mahayana Buddhism emphasizes Buddha-nature and Dharmakaya, which is equivalent to nirvana. Both are rooted in the individual's inner nature, that is, that man has the potential to achieve Buddhahood. By "bringing forth" the mind, one can bring this potential into play, demonstrating the Buddha-nature, and achieve Buddhahood. As is written in the Buddhist sutras, "Living beings have Buddha-nature. I am Buddha and Buddha is me," and "Buddha is in my heart; by purifying my heart and seeking enlightenment, the Buddha-nature will show and I will achieve Buddhahood." Hui-neng, the sixth Patriarch of Zen Buddhism, used Confucian ideas to Sinicize Buddhism. As Hui-neng said, "At the time of a single enlightened thought, all living beings can be seen as being Buddha" and "The Tree of Perfect Wisdom [Bodhi Tree] is originally no tree. Nor has the bright mirror any frame. Buddha-nature is forever clear and pure. Where is there any dust? " It was this stanza that Hui-neng wrote that earned him his prominent status in the history of Zen Buddhism, because it expresses to the extreme the belief that man's nature is good, man is God, and man can become God through his own efforts.

Marxism's view of human nature is very optimistic. It asserts that man, by relying on his ability to reason, can grasp the laws of history and the universe. It proclaims that socialism will inevitably replace capitalism in human history and that the oppressed proletariat class in capitalist societies will be the creators of human history and of a new world. The proletariat has already discovered the law governing the universe and human history (i.e. dialectical materialism and historical materialism), discovered that the final outcome for capitalist society is to become extinct (i.e. political economy), and also discovered the way for man to reach the kingdom of freedom (i.e. scientific socialism). The proletariat will dictate human history, save mankind and bring them into the "new heavens and the new earth", i.e. communist society. The proletariat has been deified and become mankind's messiah and savior of the world. Mao Zedong, the representative of Marxism in China, once said, "Why should you obey God rather than obey yourself? You are God. Is there any God other than yourself?" and "The six hundred million of this divine land are all [sage-kings like] Yao and Shun." Without exception, these all reveal man's wild arrogance in wanting to become God. The pernicious influence of Marxism is the deification of man, making certain leaders God, and turning a certain social class and its pioneers into the messiah.

To sum up, Christianity, unlike other religions, completely rejects man's role in its theory of salvation (similar to the "unity of Heaven and man," "becoming a Buddha immediately," etc.) limiting man's [potential for] perfection, man's arrogance, and man's utter lawlessness, thus laying a solid foundation of the view of human nature for mankind's correct political arrangements and institutions. Constitutionalism, rather than dictatorship, deservedly and as a matter of course became the system of choice in regions where Christian culture was mainstream.

As for the history of Christian theology and thought, whether it was the Apostle Paul, Augustine, Aquinas, Martin Luther, or John Calvin, all produced brilliant theological expositions on man's evil nature and the checks and balances it requires, profoundly influencing the history of ethics and political thought in the West. The Five Points of Calvinism, in particular, is intimately tied to the constitutionalist value system.

The Apostle Paul, under the inspiration of the Holy Spirit, penned many books of the New Testament. One theme of Pauline theology is opposition to legalism. Simply put, legalism is salvation through man's religious practice and religious tenets. Paul pointed out that salvation is solely through "justification by faith"(Romans 1:17) and by God's predestination before the foundation of the world (Romans 9:11), and that it simply was never dependent on observing the Sabbath, circumcision, keeping dietary rules and other Jewish laws, nor through man's good works because man's good works and merits and virtues are nothing more than tattered rags in God's eyes (Isaiah 64:6: all our righteous acts are like filthy rags). This utmost emphasis on God's grace and man's corrupt nature and his powerlessness resulted in the complete separation of Christianity from Judaism, and Christianity began to influence the social culture of Europe.

As Christianity began to go mainstream in the West, the great theologian Augustine gave many brilliant discourses on man's evil nature and on checks and balances on kings. He staunchly maintained that man's nature was so corrupted by Adam's Fall that man was utterly unable on his own to follow the law or receive the Gospel. Sinners must have God's grace in order to believe and to be saved, but God's grace is only given to those predestined before God created the world to receive eternal life. The act of faith comes not from "the free will of sinners," but rather from the grace of God, and that grace is only for the elect.[7] In *The City of God Against the Pagans*, Augustine pointed out, "...other sins do not alter human nature as it was altered by the transgression of those first human beings, so that on account of it this nature is subject to the great corruption we feel and see, and to death, and is distracted and tossed with so many furious and contending emotions, and is certainly far different from what it was before sin, even though it were then lodged in an animal body."[8]

---

[7] See *The Five Points of Calvinism*, p. 20. Reformation Translation Fellowship P.C., Taipei.

[8] *The City of God Against the Pagans*, p. 207. Tr. Wu Fei. Joint Publishing Co. 2008 (quote in English taken from *City of God*, Book 14 Chapter 12, electronic version by New Advent Inc., 1997 accessed at

Man's evil nature caused societies and states, which are made up of men, to be corrupt and warped. Were it not for the Fall by man's first ancestors, the state would be completely unnecessary. "...not man over man, but man over the beasts. And hence the righteous men in primitive times were made shepherds of cattle rather than kings of men, God intending thus to teach us what the relative position of the creatures is... "[9] It's clear that the state is nothing more than a tool that God had no alternative but to set up so as to deal with man's evil nature. Because earthly states are corrupt and twisted, they are inferior in status to the state in heaven, i.e. the "city of God." And on earth, the representative of this "city of God" is the church. Augustine elevated the Catholic Church to unprecedented heights, making it possible for it to start constraining the secular powers of the world. This meant that Christian individuals had two identities: [religious] followers and subjects [of a ruler]. Since the heavenly kingdom is above the earthly kingdom, then the identity of the [religious] follower was also higher than his identity as a subject, and reverence for and obedience to God take absolute priority while loyalty and obedience to kings are secondary.

The dichotomy Augustine presented in *The City of God Against the Pagans* of the heavenly city and the earthly city also precipitated the dualism and confrontation in Western history between the church and state, pope and monarch, believers and subjects, and religious freedom and political oppression; this no doubt provided the duality in the constitutional democracy of the West of a social structure of checks and balances.

Thomas Aquinas, the great Medieval synthesizer of Christian theology, stuck to the man-is-evil theory, and also believed that human society would inevitably fall into tyranny because of man's sin nature, that the ideal situation was that rulers would obey God, but that it was always

---

http://www.unilibrary.com/ebooks/Saint%20Augustine%20-%20City%20of%20God.pdf; April 26, 2014)
[9] *The City of God Against the Pagans*, p. 150. Tr. Wu Fei. Shanghai Joint Publishing Co. 2008.

possible to have God-defying tyrants. "Therefore men hide from tyrants as from cruel beasts, and it seems that to be subject to a tyrant is the same thing as to lie prostrate beneath a raging beast."[10] When faced with a tyrant, men ought to cry out to God for help. Aquinas believed, "Should no human aid whatsoever against a tyrant be forthcoming, recourse must be had to God, the King of all, who is a helper in due time in tribulation. For it lies in his power to turn the cruel heart of the tyrant to mildness. According to Solomon: 'The heart of the king is in the hand of the Lord, withersoever He will He shall turn it.'" (Proverbs 21:1) [11] In the meantime, people have the right to disobey. "...for the tyrant lays himself open to such treatment by his failure to discharge the duties of his office, and in consequence his subjects are no longer bound by their oath to him."[12]

Martin Luther, who launched and championed the Reformation, reaffirmed the doctrine of "justification by faith," because in late Medieval times the Catholic Church ignored man's evil nature and limitations, exalted man's religious practices, and made salvation contingent on good works, merit, and even indulgences. The emphasis on "justification by faith" in actuality emphasized man's powerlessness to achieve salvation and emphasizes that it is God's work alone. Luther believed, "Besides the historical Cross, the preached Gospel and the faith in sinner's heart, nothing is necessary for salvation. No need for additional redemption can increase any layer of the salvation. The righteousness of Christian belongs to Christ so the righteousness is given and from outside."[13] Here, with *sole fide* [by faith alone], Luther nullified legalism and told people that it is by faith and the grace of God alone that sinners are forgiven and the righteousness of Christ is imputed to sinners.

---

[10] *Thomas Aquinas Selected Political Writings.* Tr. Ma Qinghuai, .pp. 52, 53. Commercial Press. 1982.

[11] Refer to the article "The evilness of human nature and freedom and Constitutionalism"

[12] *Thomas Aquinas Selected Political Writings.* Tr. Ma Qinghuai, pp. 59, 60. Commercial Press. 1982 (Quote in English is from Aquinas' *On Princely Government*, chapter VI).

[13] *The Story of Christian Theology*, p. 422. Peking University Press.

In Luther's theory of *sola gratia* [by grace alone], he emphasized that salvation is a free gift from a merciful God; mankind is totally powerless when it comes to salvation. Luther called any method that does not rely on the supernatural gifts of grace and faith but rather seeks to discover God's ways through human reason and action the "theology of glory." The theology of glory is centered around human virtues and reason; it overestimates man's powers and abilities and is the fountainhead of all rationalism and humanism. In contrast, Luther's theology of the cross proclaims man's complete dependence upon God, aside from God's revelation of Himself, man is incapable of understanding anything about God. The shift from the theology of glory to the theology of the cross actually reaffirmed the Christian theory that man is evil by nature and has limited capacity for reason.

Calvinism, a Christian theological system composed of a wide range of beliefs, is the name given to the beliefs of the famous French reformer and theologian John Calvin and his faithful followers. Theologian J. I. Packer said that the five points of Calvinism were the most valuable tool for summarizing Calvinism. [14] The five points (TULIP) of Calvinism refer to:

> 1. Total depravity or total inability: because of the Fall of Adam and Eve, man cannot, using his own abilities, do any spiritual good works.
>
> 2. Unconditional election: God's election of sinners is unconditional. His selection based not on a person's ethical or moral merit, nor on foreseen faith in that person.
>
> 3. Limited atonement: Jesus died only for the elect, not for everyone in the world.
>
> 4. Irresistible grace: Mankind cannot resist God's salvation. Human factors cannot interfere with God's saving grace and man cannot resist it.

---

[14] *The Five Points of Calvinism,* p. 34. Reformation Translation Fellowship P.C., Taipei

> 5. Perseverance of the saints: Those who are saved cannot lose their salvation. God preserves the elect.

The first letter of the first word of each of the five points spell out the word "TULIP." With great logical cohesiveness, TULIP begins with man's sin and ends with God's sovereignty. Once the basic cognition of man's utter depravity is declared and confessed, the other points are easy to comprehend and fall easily into place. What the five points show of the Calvinist view of salvation is that it is absolutely by God's grace alone. This absolute-ness deeply roots the concept of the utter depravity of man in people's hearts—relying on man's reason, morality, willpower, spiritual cultivation or any religious rites or anything else is of no value to one's salvation. And an individual's personal situation also has nothing whatsoever to do with his election. The only source of salvation is in God exercising his sovereignty.

Calvinism had an enormous influence on the world in contemporary and modern times, but this fact is not well known to the academic community of China. At the beginning of Weber's classic work of unprecedented historical importance, i.e. the *Protestant Ethics and the Spirit of Capitalism*, is this statement, "Calvinism was the faith over which the great political and cultural struggles of the sixteenth and seventeenth centuries were fought in the most highly developed countries, the Netherlands, England, and France." And what the faith of Calvinism refers to is predestination.[15] Indeed, different theological views eventually lead to different political views, different economic views and different political and economic practices. We can see that the TULIP predestination doctrine makes people thoroughly understand man's limitations and evil nature and, when they are designing ecclesiastical and governmental institutions, without exception it is premised on the assumption of [people being] "scoundrels"; various institutional arrangements are set up to guard against and monitor people's "scoundrel nature," especially those with power or status. It laid the foundation for equal and free ecclesiastical systems, constitutionalism, and the rule of law. Without exception, this is the

---

[15] Max Weber, *The Protestant Ethic and the Spirit of Capitalism* (electronic version)

basic theoretical basis for separation of the three powers, multi-party competition, the media's watchdog role and other democratic systems and basic institutions. Wherever Calvinism spread, it profoundly altered people's thoughts and ideas and the nation's political system. The great theologian and evangelist Charles H. Spurgeon once said with great feeling, "Taking these things [Calvinism] to be the standard of my faith, I see the land of the ancients peopled with my brethren; I behold multitudes who confess the same as I do, and acknowledge that this is the religion of God's own church."[16]

In this paper, we examined the Christian view of human nature and its influence on the concept of constitutionalism from three angles: Biblical text, Christian doctrine and theology, and the history of theological thought. We ought to sense that there is not another religious faith or ideological system that puts as much emphasis on man's sin—moral corruption, limited capacity for reason, inability to save oneself—as Christianity does, nor any other religious doctrine that takes man's sin as the logical starting point of a system of theology and insight into society. With such a theory of human nature, a balance of power, supervision of power and restriction of power are inevitable when put into practice in society.

We Chinese people all need to understand: man is not God, nor can man through any human effort ever become God. Residing within man himself are multitudinous kinds of sin nature and finiteness, and man, especially those with power, must be subject to adequate supervision and constraints. Moreover, man's sinful nature cannot be eradicated through one's own moral cultivation; it can only be changed through repentance of sin and trust in the true God, so man must fear God, abide by the rule of law, restrain evil, and do everything possible in the economy and politics to use institutions to check and balance man's sin nature. This undoubtedly constitutes the basis for the theory of human nature in constitutionalism.

---

[16] *The Five Points of Calvinism*, p. 15. Reformation Translation Fellowship P.C., Taipei. Original quote in English from *Spurgeon's Sovereign Grace Sermons*, Still Waters Revival Books, p. 170, accessed athttp://www.swrb.com/newslett/actualNLs/spurgeon-quotes.htm on June 1, 2014

July-December 2013 Vol. 9, No. 2

The Advance of Civilization: the deepening growth of Christianity in China

By Mark Chuanhang Shan

The history of mankind can be regarded as a process in which God has been constantly teaching mankind and gradually elevating human civilization. Once it comes into being, this kind of civilization is just like the sun and the spring rains: It is universal grace that God's children and everyone on earth can all enjoy. How and what God taught mankind are all recorded in the Bible; they are also reflected in the history of the Judeo-Christian civilization.

The growth in China of the church of Jesus Christ and of Christianity is at the point today of urgently needing to enter into a maturation and solidification stage of **a deepening of the faith**. Deepening of the faith refers to the need of the church and of Christian individuals to profoundly and widely put into practice in their personal lives, in the family, in the church and in society those truths that come straight from the Bible as well as the knowledge of how to apply those truths by extension. One of the results of doing this is that society and civilization will be influenced and transformed.

For individual Christians, this deepening of the faith is mainly seen in a deliberate transformation of psychological patterns. For churches, it is mainly in beginning to deliberately influence and transform society and culture. Only in this way can individual Christians and the Christian church grow up and mature, to become a city on a hill and the light for society and to inevitably create **a system for Christian civilization in the Chinese context**. Then, using the structure of this new civilization as a vehicle, continue within [the church] to save lost souls and transform human hearts and social morality, while reaching out to engage in cross-cultural missions, expanding God's kingdom, impacting the civilizations of other ethnic groups, and bringing glory to the holy name of Jesus Christ.

This is an exciting and spectacular new chapter in the history of Christianity worldwide and in the history of the church in China, when Christians and the church are deliberately establishing a Christian civilization in Chinese society.

I. The Old Testament and Jewish Civilization

What is civilization? Simply put, I think civilization is the degree by which human beings take the initiative to turn away from evil, ignorance and damnation while drawing close to truth and gaining freedom; that is, it is the process of constant improvements in ethics and morals, objective knowledge and philosophical thinking, as well as getting closer to God's expectations. Therefore, civilization is not static, but rather it is the ever-growing life of the individual, family and society, similar to a form of art. Civilization begins in man's heart and soul, reaches man's mind and is expressed in man's words and actions.

The most ideal form of social civilization ought to include **two key cultural elements: a divine culture founded on Biblically based faith and a human culture based on reason, logic, and metaphysics**. The former is God's revelatory teachings to man's hearts and souls while the latter is the responsibility of man's creative mind. When the two work together, they produce the most vibrant and promising ecosystem for civilization. This kind of civilization is an important characteristic that sets man apart from the animals and is a beautiful expression of man bearing the image of God.

By looking at the Bible's Old Testament records of early man and the development of the Jewish civilization and its essence, we can gain a profound understanding of and learn from the principles of the formation of an ideal civilization and the four components of such a civilization: Biblical divine faith (God's sovereignty), a code of ethics (human rights), constitutionalism (management), and man's freedom (art).

1. The civilization of early man

The origin of human civilization is recorded in the Bible. From the book of Genesis, we know that God created the heavens and the earth in five days, and on the sixth day, he created mankind and gave them the ability and responsibility to create civilization. The two Bible passages below contain a wealth of information and truths: civilization is a human affair and is based on the family and on society as a body; God attaches great importance to man's level of civilization, and therefore, he constantly provides instruction to help man.

> And God said, Let us make man in our image, after our likeness: and let them have dominion over the fish of the sea, and over the fowl of the air, and over the cattle, and over all the earth, and over every creeping thing that creepeth upon the earth. So God created man in his own image, in the image of God created he him; male and female created he them. And God blessed them, and God said unto them, Be fruitful, and multiply, and replenish the earth, and subdue it: and have dominion over the fish of the sea, and over the fowl of the air, and over every living thing that moveth upon the earth. (Genesis 1:26-28)

> And the LORD God formed man of the dust of the ground, and breathed into his nostrils the breath of life; and man became a living soul. And the LORD God planted a garden

eastward in Eden; and there he put the man whom he had formed. And out of the ground made the LORD God to grow every tree that is pleasant to the sight, and good for food; the tree of life also in the midst of the garden, and the tree of knowledge of good and evil. And a river went out of Eden to water the garden; and from thence it was parted, and became into four heads. The name of the first is Pison: that is it which compasseth the whole land of Havilah, where there is gold; And the gold of that land is good: there is bdellium and the onyx stone. And the name of the second river is Gihon: the same is it that compasseth the whole land of Ethiopia. And the name of the third river is Hiddekel: that is it which goeth toward the east of Assyria. And the fourth river is Euphrates. And the LORD God took the man, and put him into the garden of Eden to dress it and to keep it. And the LORD God commanded the man, saying, Of every tree of the garden thou mayest freely eat: But of the tree of the knowledge of good and evil, thou shalt not eat of it: for in the day that thou eatest thereof thou shalt surely die. And the LORD God said, It is not good that the man should be alone; I will make him an help meet for him. And out of the ground the LORD God formed every beast of the field, and every fowl of the air; and brought them unto Adam to see what he would call them: and whatsoever Adam called every living creature, that was the name thereof. And Adam gave names to all cattle, and to the fowl of the air, and to every beast of the field; but for Adam there was not found an help meet for him. And the LORD God caused a deep sleep to fall upon Adam, and he slept: and he took one of his ribs, and closed up the flesh instead thereof; And the rib, which the LORD God had taken from man, made he a woman, and brought her unto the man. And Adam said, This is now bone of my bones, and flesh of my flesh: she shall be called Woman, because she was taken out of Man. Therefore shall a man leave his father and his mother, and shall cleave unto his wife: and they shall be one flesh. And they were both naked, the man and his wife, and were not ashamed. (Genesis 2:7-25)

From the above verses we know, **first, that mankind bears the image of God and that he is a living soul; this is the essential**

characteristic that sets man apart from the animals. How then are "the image of God" and "the breath of life" specifically manifested in mankind? This is a challenging theological question because it falls into the category of revealed truths; without specific revelation from God, it is beyond the scope of human thinking. I hold that the image of God is symbolic of human civilization in its original form. Moreover, man's ability to create is an expression of the image of God. To create does not refer to the making of material objects, because everything made by human hands is nothing more than an imitation of God's creation. Man's ability to create civilization—this is the closest thing to the creation of "something out of nothing"—is a component of being of the image of God. Civilization comes from "the breath of life" God gave to man and is revealed through human nature.

Second, the first step in mankind's creation of civilization was to establish dominion and give names. Establishing dominion is related to politics and law, while giving names is related to art and literature. Establishing dominion and art and literature are objective indicators of civilization. The more advanced the civilization, the more developed its art and literature (aesthetics), and the more advanced are the skills of ruling and managing. Civilization can fulfill people's psychological and spiritual needs—needs that were endowed by God at the time of creation. The responsibility of establishing dominion was an authority bestowed by God, and it operates mainly through the mind. Animals cannot form societies, only man can. This is mainly because man is able to establish dominion and give names. Societies are not formed simply by group living or shared interests, but rather by complex interpersonal relationships within a framework of ethics and law that, having been granted authority, carry out the responsibility of establishing dominion and the giving of names. If you observe people's speech, you will notice that most of what people say are evaluative, such as "what something is , what something is not, " "how something should be, how something should not be," etc., etc. This stems from an awareness of establishing dominion and giving names.

Third, divine law and ethics are the cornerstones of civilization. God put Adam in dominion over the Garden of Eden and at the same time gave him this commandment, "You are free to eat from any tree in the garden; but you must not eat from the tree of the knowledge of good and evil, for when you eat from it you will certainly die." God's command was both ethics and law; its intent was to restrict man's authority to establish dominion, so that there would be no arbitrary law-breaking and recklessness, because man is not the master of those over whom he has dominion. However, Adam and Eve disobeyed God's command and ate the forbidden fruit, and they not only abused the authority to establish dominions but [their actions] also resulted in Satan's successful spreading of the sinful nature to mankind and destroying the first human civilization, which was launched by God in the Garden of Eden. So pure and advanced was this first civilization that God was present with mankind and spoke to them face to face. After that, God exiled Adam and Eve into a lowly civilization, which was further corrupted by sin and became so wild that Cain, Adam's first-born son, murdered his own brother Abel.

Exercising self-restraint according to God's ethics and law is a necessary prerequisite for higher forms of human civilization. Freedom within a civilization is a safety zone within the framework of ethics and law; it is emancipation and peace and safety that has been bestowed by truth. The higher a society's form of civilization, the stronger the self-restraint of the people and the more easily they comply with the law, ethics and morality. Because Adam and Eve did not attach importance to self-restraint or failed to exercise enough self-restraint, they made a fatal mistake that resulted in the most serious of consequences. In Chapter 3 of Genesis, God's judgment of Adam and Eve for their sin has such key words as "pains," "painful labor... all the days of your life," and "the sweat of your brow," demonstrating that the essence of human civilization after the Fall is one of hopelessness. Then, "the Lord God made garments of skin for Adam and his wife and clothed them," marking the beginning of the lessons God would teach man about civilization. Just like the lessons parents give to rebellious children, it was out of everlasting and long-suffering love.

Fourth, marriage, family and children. The family is the basic unit of society. God said, "It is not good for the man to be alone. I will make a helper suitable for him." Whereupon, God instituted the first marriage, the first couple and the first family. The family is the basic unit of society and two families are enough to form a society. God also had the family "be fruitful and increase in number; fill the earth and subdue it..." And thus did society formally come into being. Marriage is the distinctive mark of human civilization and the union of a man and a women is even more unique, setting them apart from all other creatures. That God created only one woman, Eve, to be Adam's spouse and helpmate, and that the natural birth ratio of male and female is always roughly equal demonstrates that God's original intention was that the institution of marriage be between one man and one woman. Therefore, monogamy (one man and one woman) is the highest form of the civilization of marriage and family and the expression of man's success in being accountable to God by adhering to ethics and morals in exercising self-restraint.

2. The Old Testament civilization of the Israelites

The book of Exodus in the Bible recounts how the process of forming a civilization by the people of Israel occurred under God's personal instruction and supervision. By making **divine and truthful faith the core, [adopting] laws on the ethics of human responsibility and [setting up] a rule of law-constitutional management system,** the human civilization of the Israelites advanced quickly and their society developed day by day.

The Old Testament clearly shows that whenever mankind becomes ethically and morally depraved, when human nature becomes corrupt, when there is rebellion against divinity, civilization is degraded or lost. It can even ultimately result in God's destruction of mankind. For example, in Noah's time, before God used the flood to destroy the human race, "every inclination of the thoughts of the human heart was only evil all the time," (Genesis 6:5) "Now the earth was corrupt in God's sight and was full of violence," (Genesis 6:11) even to the point that "the Lord regretted that he had made human beings on the earth, and his heart was deeply troubled." (Genesis 6:6) After Noah's time,

God destroyed Sodom and Gomorrah because the sin of the people in these two cities also was "grievous" in the sight of the Lord

The Israelites suffered the bondage of slavery in Egypt for 400 long years and their social civilization hit rock bottom. However, after God led them out of Egypt and into the land of Canaan, within just two generations, God had educated and trained them into a great civilized nation. This is an invaluable case study on civilization. The way God educated the Israelites was mainly in the following three aspects.

First, establish a divine faith that is holy and true. Beginning with Abraham, God started to cultivate and establish a divine faith among the Jewish patriarchs. By the time of Moses, reaffirmation and strengthening of this divine faith had reached a historic high. God first revealed himself to Moses in the burning bush, then he performed many great miracles through Moses. These miracles straightforwardly affirmed and solidified the Israelites' divine faith—the fountainhead of civilization.

God performed 12 historically unprecedented miracles to punish the Egyptians and delivered the Israelites out of bondage under the Egyptian regime, bestowing upon them human rights, dignity and freedom. At the same time, this gave the Israelites a foundation of historical facts for their divine faith and also produced a sense of awe. "The fear of the Lord is the beginning of wisdom." And wisdom nourishes civilization. When miracles occur, man—out of pride in human nature—is likely to forget or deny them. So, God instituted Passover, an annual celebration for the Israelites to commemorate their witnessing with their own eyes the great miracle God performed to deliver them out of slavery. At the same time, a centuries-old prophecy was hidden in the Passover feast that was ultimately completely fulfilled in Jesus, thus providing mutual confirmation of the divine origin and meaning of Passover. Furthermore, after leaving Egypt, the Israelites wandered in the wilderness for 40 years, during which time undeniable miracles, including manna falling from the heavens, continued to solidify and deepen their divine faith.

God revealed himself to mankind through miracles in order to stimulate their divine faith, elevate goodness in human nature and justice in society, and in this way advance human civilization. Human civilization must have the fountainhead of truth and divinity, otherwise it is bound to be contaminated and corrupted by sin, and even become completely depraved, leading to the degradation or even loss of civilization. God chose the Israelites in Old Testament times because they were the direct descendants of Adam and Eve and Abraham and Sarah, and therefore they represented the entire human race. It was also how God kept his promise to Abraham and the covenant he made with him.

Second, the law endows rights and responsibilities. After the triumphant exodus from Egypt, God issued the law through Moses. These laws also included provisions about ethics and morality, thus effectively safeguarding the healthy growth of civilization. After the Israelites experienced the great benefits of going from slavery to being freed men, God enacted through Moses the Ten Commandments (Exodus 20: 1-17) and corresponding detailed regulations.

The Ten Commandments are constitutional in nature, consisting of two parts. The first four commandments address how man ought to treat God, i.e. the responsibilities associated with divine faith and also God's **divine rights** before the human race. The next six commandments address how mankind ought to treat one another, i.e. the responsibilities associated with human ethics and also basic **human rights.** The interaction between the responsibilities of divine faith based on God's truths (also divine rights) and the responsibilities of human ethics (also human rights) directly created the Jewish civilization, while at the same time enriching the essence of human civilization in general and elevating the level of civilization.

After issuing the Ten Commandments, God began to issue detailed laws and regulations. The first was on how to build an altar for making offerings to God, meaning that responsibility to divinity takes precedence. Codes on how to treat one another followed, the first of which was how to treat those of the lowest status in society, the slaves.

Following that, God issued a large number of detailed laws and regulations mainly divided into these two categories: responsibility to God and responsibility to other people. Of these, the laws in Leviticus mainly address specifics on how to fulfill one's obligations towards God, the aim of which was making people holy. Then in Deuteronomy, the focus was fulfilling one's rights and responsibilities in relation to others (including one's neighbor), the aim of which was making people just. Of course, these two books also have some overlap in the two categories of divine responsibility and human responsibility. For example, Deuteronomy also has content that emphasizes divine responsibility, in particular Deuteronomy 4:24, which says, "For the Lord your God is a consuming God, a jealous God." (See also Hebrews 12:29) (Adapted from the author's *Divinity and Humanity: The Burning Bush*.)

Only upon the foundation of truth-based divine faith can responsibility and rights be fully advanced, thereby elevating social civilization. By communicating to the people through Moses, by reinstating the Abrahamic Covenant, and after enacting laws prescribing the dual responsibility of divine faith and human ethics, God quickly elevated the Jewish people from slaves to a civilized ethnic group, made them more prosperous and strong, and prepared them to receive the greater blessings—of establishing a nation, impacting other nations, and bringing glory to God's holy name—that were in store for them in the land of Canaan.

Third, rule of law and constitutionalism guarantee social justice. Once God issued the law, he began to strictly enforce it. In the process of enforcing the law, God showed the Israelites that the individual cannot be separated from the community; one person's breach of law can bring consequences for the whole community. At the same time, although Moses was the one through whom the law was given, he and the other top leaders of the Jewish people, be they political, religious or military, all had to abide by the same law as the people. This is why even the most prestigious political leaders, like Moses and King David, were still punished when they disobeyed the law. Moses even lost the glorious right to enter Canaan. At the same time, the dual authority of the political leader (king) and the religious leader (prophet) of the Jewish people formed a political management model of two separate powers that check and balance each other. This was an early primitive model of civilization with constitutionalism and the rule of law, which was directly bestowed by God upon humanity, with God himself providing practical guidance to mankind.

Because they had broken the law, the whole generation of Israelites that left Egypt lost the right to enter Canaan. Only after that generation had all passed away after 40 years of wandering in the wilderness did the new generation enter Canaan, and they did so under a new leadership. After the entry, God implemented an intensive educational policy of a series of strict laws and code of ethics to educate the Israelites, so that all the Israelites, from the leaders to the commoners, would all—out of great reverence for God—strictly abide by the law and the code of ethics, hold fast to their identity as God's children, and fulfill their dual responsibilities to God and to mankind, the result of which was that the entire nation of the Israelites was holy in God's eyes, divine rights were honored, human rights were protected, and justice was manifested in society. Thus, the Jewish civilization as a whole took a great leap forward and the Israelites received abundant blessings from God both spiritually and materially.

At times, this harsh thunderclap-like enforcement of the law not only struck fear in the hearts of the Israelites but also even caused them to lose heart. For example, when King David transported God's Ark of the Covenant, he ignored the rule that only the Levites, as God's appointed priests, were qualified to touch sacred vessels, and he had non-Levites do the moving. And tragedy struck. "When they came to the threshing floor of Nakon, Uzzah reached out and took hold of the ark of God, because the oxen stumbled. The Lord's anger burned against Uzzah because of his irreverent act; therefore God struck him down, and he died there beside the ark of God. ... David was afraid of the Lord that day and said, 'How can the ark of the Lord ever come to me?' He was not willing to take the ark of the Lord to be with him in the City of David. Instead, he took it to the house of Obed-Edom the Gittite. (2 Samuel 6:6-7, 9) At this early stage in the operation of this system of constitutionalism and the rule of law, even David was not accustomed to it and lost heart. However, he soon figured out where the problem lay and had the Levites move the ark in strict accordance with God's law and regulations. The ark arrived at its destination safely and God therefore richly blessed David. (1 Chronicles 15) Even God's chosen and anointed king David had to submit to God's law: Therein lies the essence inherent to constitutionalism. (Adapted from the author's *Divinity and Humanity: The Burning Bush*.)

It was precisely due to the strictness of constitutionalism and the rule of law that the Israelites rose quickly from a slave culture to becoming a highly civilized, powerful and prosperous people and nation. Approximately 250 years passed from the Israelites' conquest of Canaan under the leadership of Joshua to the reign of King Solomon; in that time Israel became the nation with the most advanced civilization, its fame so widespread that envoys and rulers of foreign nations came to pay tribute. According to 1 Kings 10:23-25, "King Solomon was greater in riches and wisdom than all the other kings of the earth. The whole world sought audience with Solomon to hear the wisdom God had put in his heart. Year after year, everyone who came brought a gift—articles of silver and gold, robes, weapons and spices, and horses and mules." What was most amazing was that even Pharaoh, the king of the ancient civilization of Egypt and formerly the slave master of the Israelites, gave his daughter to Solomon in marriage. (1 Kings 3:1) During King Solomon's reign, the Jewish civilization was characterized by holiness, justice, wisdom, prosperity, affluence and military strength. The name of the Lord was greatly glorified.

The decline of the Israelite civilization: A civilization can be established in the space of a single generation; it can also be lost in the space of a single generation. The foundation of the Israelite civilization was divine faith. The decline of the civilization also began with faith. 1 King 11:4, 9-10 recorded the beginning and the cause of the civilization's decline: "As Solomon grew old, his wives turned his heart after other gods, and his heart was not fully devoted to the Lord his God, as the heart of David his father had been... The Lord became angry with Solomon because his heart had turned away from the Lord, the God of Israel, who had appeared to him twice. Although he had forbidden Solomon to follow other gods, Solomon did not keep the Lord's command."

The forsaking of faith and the corruption of man's heart resulted in the decline of civilization, and the empire began to collapse from within. Eventually, Israel split internally and became two nations. Then, because of its weakened national strength, foreign enemies began to invade, causing no end to wars and chaos. None of the successive kings of the two nations was as remarkable as David and Solomon, although God never stopped sending prophets to the rebellious kings to warn them mainly about these two subjects: **social justice and the sanctity of faith.** Israel's political civilization continued to be preserved by the political model of separation of power between king and prophet, but it was beyond repair because the kings and the people had turned away from divine faith and fallen short in human ethics. As the representatives of human culture, the kings always wanted to possess freedom and power independent of divine faith while the prophets, representing divine faith, tried to subordinate the king's power and the people's freedom to God's ethical framework.

When the civilization flourished under the reigns of David, Solomon and others, human culture and divine faith functioned in mutual harmony; hence, civilization was highly developed. But in the times that followed, the two clashed and constrained each other, resulting in the decline of civilization. Nevertheless, those kings who valued divine faith received blessings from God, and so civilization was safeguarded; when the opposite happened, the nation suffered. This happened time and again, but the general trend was toward national destruction—the situation was beyond the point of help. In addition to condemning the kings, God also sent prophets to condemn the sins of the people. Be it kings or ordinary people, they were all the same in terms of their sinful nature (the only difference was in the opportunity to act on it) and they all needed to submit to God's ethical restraints. In that respect, the democratic system predicated on the "infallibility of the people" advocated by the political liberals in the West today is both naïve and absurd, and cannot stand up to the test of time or [real life] practice.

According to 2 Kings 22:1-2, God was pleased with Josiah, the king of Judah who ascended the throne 300 years after Solomon, because "he did what was right in the eyes of the Lord and followed completely the ways of his father David, not turning aside to the right or to the left." In the eighteenth year of his reign, King Josiah ordered the temple to be repaired, and thus discovered the key to civilization left by his ancestors, i.e. The Book of the Law. According to 2 Kings 23:1-3, "Then the king called together all the elders of Judah and Jerusalem. He went up to the temple of the Lord with the people of Judah, the inhabitants of Jerusalem, the priests and the prophets—all the people from the least to the greatest. He read in their hearing all the words of the Book of the Covenant, which had been found in the temple of the Lord. The king stood by the pillar and renewed the covenant in the presence of the Lord—to follow the Lord and keep his commands, statutes and decrees with all his heart and all his soul, thus confirming the words of the covenant written in this book. Then all the people pledged themselves to the covenant." Following that, King Josiah went about tearing down idols, outlawing pagan beliefs, and restoring truth-based divine faith. Holiness was beginning to be restored in politics and the culture.

What an admirable and awe-inspiring picture this was: the king and the people making a covenant with God, restoring the holy and truth-based divine faith and abiding by God's law and ethics. Therein lies the secret to the success of the Jewish civilization, which is also the basic idea behind constitutionalism and a civil society. Regrettably, this happy scene did not last long, as is recorded in 2 Kings 23:25, "Neither before nor after Josiah was there a king like him who turned to the Lord as he did—with all his heart and with all his soul and with all his strength, in accordance with all the Law of Moses." Therefore, desolation was doomed. In the lives of individual Christians, we also are like this, ignorant of how many opportunities we have missed to glorify God and receive his blessings.

Brief Summary

The Bible's Old Testament can be regarded as a textbook on human civilization. God plays the role of an advisor in the history of human civilization. Take the Jewish civilization for example. God began by helping the Israelites establish a holy divine faith in individuals and the community, then issued a code of ethics to establish the cultural concepts of divine rights, human rights, responsibility and freedom. After that, the social mechanisms of the rule of law and constitutionalism were established through the separation of church and state. Finally, emphasis was placed on holiness and justice in society. This was the developmental process and the basic elements of the Jewish civilization.

The main components of the Jewish civilization recorded in the Old Testament were divine faith, ethics and morality, and the rule of law and constitutionalism. That the Jewish civilization also borrowed from the advanced culture of Egypt, such as technology, art, etc. cannot be ignored. Moses was educated as a child in the royal courts of Egypt and grew up to be a member of the elite of Egyptian civilization. Naturally, he brought into the Jewish community some elements of Egyptian social civilization. Likewise, in New Testament times, Christian civilization not only inherited the Jewish civilization as it developed but also absorbed Greco-Roman logic, reason, and philosophy as well as their derivative science and political models— which were [based] purely [on] human knowledge—and in this way pushed human civilization to new heights.

The strictness of the rule of law put fear in the hearts of both king and commoner, but this was not God's ultimate intent. God wanted people to obey the law of their own volition and to naturally and gladly submit in their hearts to God's code of ethics. This was what God sought to accomplish in Old Testament times when he taught mankind (who were represented by the Jewish people). In other words, human civilization is derived from the self-restraint man exercises over his sinful nature, and the most ideal principle for this kind of self-restraint is the ethical and legal principles God gave to man—divine rights and human rights—and the most effective restraint comes from being faithful to the responsibilities of divine faith in God. The more elevated this kind of self-restraint is, the more elevated the civilization. Self-restraint exercised at the deepest level is the restraining one's own heart and mind. The great tree of civilization sprouts from the heart and soul. (See "Transforming the Chinese Christian's Heart-Mind" in the author's *Christianity in China—From the Heart into Society*)

II. Euro-American Christian Civilization

Jesus Christ came into this world and ushered in the New Testament era. This historical event became a watershed in the history of human civilization: God came into this world and became man, and the Holy Spirit from then on dwells in the hearts of believers and bestows on them a divine nature and the status of God's children, and in doing so, significantly elevates human civilization. On the basis of the Old Testament's strict code of ethics and law, the New Testament asked people to act from the love in their hearts, not out of fear of the law and punishment. The motivation and acts of love naturally perfected the purpose of the law, just as Jesus said, "Do not think that I have come to abolish the Law or the Prophets; I have not come to abolish them but to fulfill them." (Matthew 5:17) After the lengthy divine education during Old Testament times on the rule of law, human civilization had reached the point of being able to receive the lofty New Testament teachings on ethics.

The Christian Euro-American civilization of the West can be seen as representative of man's New Testament civilization and also the pinnacle of human civilization, which to date has been unsurpassed. The development of Christian civilization has many similarities with the development in Old Testament times of Jewish civilization; it also incorporated secular Greco-Roman civilization. My observations, experience and research have led me to the conclusion that the brilliance of modern Western civilization is the great achievement resulting from the coming together of secular Roman-Athenian civilization and Judeo-Christian civilization. This coming together, however, was not voluntary but rather was the result of nearly 2000 years of competition, struggle and mutual containment, the main arena and battlefield of which was church-state relations. The essence of Greco-Roman civilization was a humanity-oriented secular culture with reason and law at its core, while the essence of the Judeo-Christian civilization is a divinity-oriented faith culture with law and ethics at its core. Ethics as a moral philosophical system shows why man needs and observes moral principles, and ethics provides standards for morality, while the ideology of faith provides the standards for ethics. (Adapted from the author's *Christianity and Civil Society in China*.)

1. Plato borrows from the Mosaic Law

The third century philosopher Clement of Alexandria believed that the Greek political views represented by Plato, in particular with regard to legislation, were influenced by Moses. Politics is [about] control and is concerned with people; therefore, it creates the need for the role and duty of a king. The king uses the law to govern and knows how to rule a willing populace. Plato held that politics included the law and political correctness, and the latter includes political vision and harmonious political order. On the one hand, the ruler needs to adjust himself to adapt to the ruled; on the other hand, the ruled need to submit to the ruler. Moses' management approach emphatically demonstrated this. Plato was also influenced by the teachings of Moses in his belief that law is predicated upon a person being born while politics is based on assembly and consent. (Excerpted from "Dual Identity and Dual Mission" in the author's *Christianity in China–From the Heart into Society*)

The concept of God suddenly emerged not just in Plato's political views, but also in his philosophical views, after he was thoroughly disillusioned with Greek politics and returned to Athens following a 10-year study tour in the Middle East and West Asia; his concept of God obviously came from the image of God in Genesis: the Creator of the heavens and the earth. This was not just a coincidence or speculation, because Moses' Books of the Law (the first five books of the Bible) circulated widely throughout the cultures of Egypt and western Asia at that time, especially when the exiled Jews returned and had finished rebuilding the Temple. The Bible in Acts 15:21 also testifies that this was the case, at least in the regions where the Jews lived, "For the law of Moses has been preached in every city from the earliest times and is read in the synagogues on every Sabbath."

Plato's student Aristotle developed "metaphysics" on the basis of this foundation and eventually synthesized the numerous schools of the Greek philosophical tradition into a clear-cut system of human reason and thought within a loose divine framework. Greek philosophy marked the highest level of achievement in terms of mankind's search for truth and it surpassed all the other civilizations except the divine civilization of the Jewish people. Nonetheless, it still was nothing more than generalized human truths, because people can only apprehend concepts and knowledge of God through God's special revelation. After Plato studied the view on God, the world and the rule of law in Moses' Books of the Law, he was able to propel Greek philosophical civilization to a new height, just as divine civilization elevated human civilization in ancient times: "The Nephilim were on the earth in those days—and also afterward—when the sons of God went to the daughters of humans and had children by them. They were the heroes of old, men of renown." (Genesis 6:4)

2. The victory of the early church in the Roman Empire: the establishment of divine faith

It was in the larger historical and civilizational context of Greek philosophy and Roman politics entering a stage of maturity and as the Roman Empire conquered Israel and other nations, resulting in the Hellenization of these regions, that Jesus Christ was born in Bethlehem, launching the great New Testament era and setting human civilization on its path to a historic high through divine education. Because Greek philosophy and Roman politics, representing the highest standard of civilization created by man, had received a little illumination from the light of truth in the ideas borrowed from Moses' Books of the Law, the minds and hearts of the people at that time were prepared to receive the perfect truth of Jesus Christ, especially through the narrative style of the Gospel of John.

In addition to its intellectual environment of philosophy and political culture, the Roman Empire's unparalleled territorial expansion, advanced transportation, thriving trade, and social stability guaranteed by a strong military reached levels of glory unmatched in the history of mankind; this was indisputably of most benefit to the spread of the Gospel. Upon this foundation, the mighty work of the Holy Spirit, as recorded in the Book of Acts in the Bible, rapidly spread the Gospel from the Jews to other ethnic groups and regions. The Church of Antioch, as the first non-Jewish church, sent out the first Christian missionary, i.e. the Apostle Paul, who brought the Gospel even to the capital city of the Roman Empire through three missionary trips. In spite of this, Christianity from the very beginning endured the joint efforts of conservative religious Jews and Roman political power to strangle it. Beginning with the crucifixion of Jesus, his disciples were unceasingly persecuted, with wave after wave of large numbers of men and women emerging to martyr themselves for the faith.

Before the Roman Empire granted religious toleration to Christianity, i.e. before the 313 B.C. promulgation of The Edict of Milan, and despite brutal persecution, Christianity still managed to exert an important influence on Roman civilization. The Christians living under the rule of the Roman Empire developed many tenacious characteristics of Christian ethics and culture which were in striking contrast to Greco-Roman ethics and culture. For example, the Roman culture revered the male physique and male prowess, which was why newborn male babies who did not appear to be strong would be abandoned in the wilderness. Christians however refused to abandon their children regardless of their physical condition (see the *Epistle of Mathetes to Diognetus* by Justin Martyr in the 2nd century A.D.). Furthermore, although polygamy was practiced in most parts of the world at that time, Christians adamantly adhered to monogamy. In respecting the rights of women and children, Christians went far beyond the Greco-Roman civilization, which was at the time the world's most advanced civilization. This was not a level of civilization attained by man through his own efforts, but rather, it came from the bright light and the elevated sense of civilization that were given to Christians through the revealed truths of divine faith and responsibility as well as a powerful spiritual motivation to fulfill the dual responsibility of divinity and humanity.

As an aside, even in regions beyond the Roman Empire, even as far away as ancient Persia (today's Iran), the Caspian Sea and regions near Central Asia, the Christian faith shone like a beacon in the local culture, far surpassing the local civilization that man developed on his own. Christianity's reach extended so far east that people were amazed, according to the *Book of the Laws of the Lands* by the Christian Bardaisan (154-222, who later was condemned as a heretic) of Edessa Kingdom, which was located on the border of the Roman and Persian empires and was variously allied with each empire at different times. In his book, he described how the Christian communities there and to the east held to faith-based ethics and customs that put them at odds with the local culture. He said, "Our brothers from Parthia do not marry two wives; Jewish Christians are not circumcised, our sisters from Gilan and Kushan do not associate with foreigners; those from Persia do not marry their daughters; those from Media do not abandon their dead, nor do they give them to the dogs to eat, nor do they bury the dying while still alive, Christians from Edessa do not kill their wives or sisters who commit adultery, and those from Hatra do not stone thieves."

After Christianity became the official religion of the Roman Empire, it injected elements of truth and divine faith into Greco-Roman culture. The church grew by leaps and bounds, and doctrine and the institution of the church began to mature. In 476 A.D., the central part of the Roman Empire, including its capital city, was defeated and occupied by barbarian tribes from Northern Europe, bringing the Western Roman Empire to an end. In the following 500 years, it was only through the church's successful civilizing influence on these barbarian tribes combined with the Eastern Roman-Greek culture of Eastern Europe that the prototype of a new Western civilization with the Christian faith at its core was shaped, and eventually, through the Reformation launched by Martin Luther in Western Europe, this civilization—with its organic integration of divinity and humanity—was propelled to new heights. This process was similar to the Exodus model, i.e. starting with those on civilization's lowest rung, the slaves and barbarians, who accept divine faith, a code of ethics, and the constitutional separation of power of church and state, and achieving unprecedented progress and advancement in their civilization, both spiritually and materially.

Why, then, did the powerful Roman Empire that had existed for eight centuries collapse just one century after Christianity was made the official religion? This is why many people at the time blamed Christianity, saying it had weakened the culture and thus caused the decline of the Roman Empire. The great theologian Augustine witnessed the fall of the Western Roman Empire and, motivated by the desire to defend Christianity, wrote the great book *City of God* to show that kingdoms of the world are not eternal and their decline is inevitable, while the City of God transcends history and time as well as national borders and is eternal. Augustine's arguments are convincing. In other words, it is not a nation but mankind that the Christian faith and Christian civilization serve. It is a civilization of divine faith, with mankind at the center and Jesus Christ as Lord. Its central mission is to love God and love people. Patriotism is a product of human civilization; it advocates making one's country the object of one's highest allegiance, and therefore it has legal and "noble" reasons for trampling on the human rights and peace of other nations.

Christianity did not cause the decline of the Roman Empire. On the one hand, the military victory over settled people by barbaric nomadic tribes armed with bows and arrows and with fast horses could be regarded as the cause. Prior to the invention of fire power, this scenario played out in many regions throughout the history of world civilization; the Orient and China were no exception. On the other hand, what needs to be examined is, "How did the fall of the Western Roman Empire impact Christianity?"

In the hostile environment of the collapse of the Western Roman Empire and the devastation left by the barbarians, the church of Jesus Christ stood tall and firm. Monasteries preserved and copied a great number of books and classical works, thereby aiding the survival of the knowledge of Western civilization. Moreover, on the ruins of war, the church began to share the Gospel with these pagan barbarian tribes. Five hundred years later, all the countries in Europe founded by barbarian invaders had embraced Christianity and, having been tamed by the church and the truth of the Gospel, these countries became civilized societies and built emerging nations, including, in chronological order, France (496 A.D.), Ireland (561 A.D.), Northern Europe and Russia (around 1000 A.D.), etc. (Excerpted from the author's *Divinity and Humanity: The Burning Bush.*)

In other words, God's wisdom is higher than human knowledge. The fall of the Western Roman Empire gave the barbarian tribes an opportunity to enter into the Christian cultural environment, receive the Christian faith, and create a brand new Western civilization. The Eastern Roman Empire preserved Greco-Roman culture, but the Christian faith and social civilization in general did not experience considerable development because of the limitedness and restrictiveness of the traditional culture. After converting to Christianity, the Western countries emerging in the regions of the former Western Roman Empire were reshaped and refined by divine faith, and since they were free of the baggage of [Roman] cultural traditions, Christianity grew rapidly in these countries. Later, it was only by way of the Crusades that Western Europe came into contact with the secular humanistic civilization of the Eastern Roman Empire (which resulted in the Renaissance). The combination of the two gradually formed an ideal model of a new civilization, enabling Western civilization to begin to take the lead in the history of world civilizations.

3. The Civilization of the Middle Ages: the taming and transforming of human nature by divine ethics

The description "the darkness of the Middle Ages" is a criticism that came from the anti-Christian Western humanist camp. In fact, the medieval Christian church's profound control over and influence on society was an important reason for the invading barbarian nomadic tribes being transformed into civilized Europeans. It is fair to say that were it not for the refining fire of divine ethics in the Middle Ages, the ensuing brilliance of European civilization would never have occurred. Christianity's mistakes in the Middles Ages were mainly the theological error of using divine ethics to suppress man's freedoms and the errors committed by the hierarchy of the Catholic Church.

From a macro perspective, the first half of the millennium of the Middle Ages (beginning with the fall of the Western Roman Empire in 476 A.D.) was the process of civilizing barbarian tribes and establishing Christian nations, comparable to the Exodus of the Israelites. In the second 500 years of the Middles Ages, because of the integration of politics and divine faith, the strict enforcement of Christian laws and code of ethics in society was a necessary step in God's process of elevating human civilization, comparable to the Israelites' 40 years in the wilderness that refined their faith and ethics; this was also mainly accomplished through the model of integrating politics and divine faith while separating church and state.

The medieval church engaged in many corrupt practices, falling short of the glory of God. These included the buying and selling of the papacy, setting up religious courts to brutally execute heretics, selling indulgences, etc. As Augustine said, the City of God is invisible and everlasting. So too is the invisible church that is forged by the hearts of all saints united by the Holy Spirit and so also is the Kingdom of God which is made up of the invisible church, holy and without blemish. The problems of the visible church are never-ending, mainly because of man's sinful nature, particularly the mistakes of church leaders and theologians. The relationship between church and state in the Middle Ages, that is the relationship between king and pope, was patterned after the Old Testament's separation of powers. The power struggles between king and pope resulted in the waxing and waning of their respective positions, which was one of the prevailing themes of the Middle Ages.

In spite of the church's many mistakes, God never stopped growing and maturing his church, thereby continually transforming European civilization. In the Middle Ages, faith and ethics were made into laws, and through the imposition of harsh penalties, people were compelled into obedience. For these barbarian tribes that were newly converted to Christianity, it was through this system, in which all men, even the kings, had to submit to the authority of church and from which there was no escape, that they were compelled to practice Christianity's divine faith and human ethics in every aspect of life. This was also the pattern of the life journey and conversion of the prodigal son Augustine. Five hundred years of strict teachings and practical application raised people's moral standards and the quality of their personal spiritual lives to unprecedented heights; repentance and piety became social and cultural mores and a part of people's personal and spiritual life. This was the fruit of holiness, from which a solid social foundation for Christian civilization was laid and a cultural environment for traditional ethics was created, to embrace the comprehensive elevation of civilization in the third 500-year period after the Middle Ages.

In the second 500-year period, from 1096 A.D. to 1291 A.D., European kings and the pope jointly commissioned seven Crusades. In the process, Europe, which was very behind in terms of human civilization (art, architecture, science, technology, etc.), started to have contact with the traditional Greek culture of the Eastern Roman Empire, which opened people's eyes and captivated the social elites, including the pope. After the Crusades ended, Europe saw the rise of the Renaissance, beginning in the early 14th century and lasting into the 16th century; it's aim was to emulate traditional Roman civilization. "When the Renaissance spread to northern Europe, it sparked an academic movement. Not only that, but a large number of religious leaders also became scholars, not only studying ancient theological texts but also actively reflecting on the church's erroneous theological ideas of the time; this greatly promoted the healthy development of Christian theological ideas and laid a solid theoretical foundation for the advent and success of the Reformation," the author wrote in *Divinity and Humanity*.

The 200 years of the Renaissance was a process of developing human civilization on the basis of divine faith. Just as the Israelites learned human civilization from developed countries like Egypt, God began to guide the Europeans into a mature and healthy form of civilization. In fact, by late in the Crusades, the great theologian Thomas Aquinas had already annotated and developed Aristotle's metaphysics, which was the essence of the Greek philosophy, thereby elevating European civilization in the academic fields related to modes of thinking and philosophy. Therefore, the Renaissance was simply a process of comprehensive Greco-Romanization based on this foundation.

It would appear then that the development of European civilization was similar to that of the Jewish civilization: they dismantled and rebuilt their existing social civilization, first by establishing a strict divine faith (honoring God as the supreme sovereign), then constructing a code of ethics to renew the moral standards of the individual and society, and setting up the [governing] model of separation of power between king and pope, then learning from the advanced human civilization of other ethnic groups, and finally forming their own unique and glorious civilization. However, the problem the two civilizations had in common—and it was all because of man's sinful nature—was that after attaining a high level of civilization, people became arrogant, lusting after pleasures and striving for a sinful freedom constrained neither by God nor his ethics, which ultimately resulted in an abandonment of divine faith. As a result, civilization quickly degenerated and a ruinous end was doomed.

4. Anglo-American civilization in contemporary and modern times: the pinnacle of Western

The Reformation made it possible for Western Europe to begin to enter the land of Canaan. The focus of social culture shifted from pure divine godliness to the "priesthood of all believers" and "vocation as a calling" as a way of putting faith into practice in [real] life. Divinity and humanity both began to achieve a healthy balance in individuals' lives and in the social culture. The Renaissance had already resulted in diversity in the social culture; in particular, achievements in the arts had elevated the overall level of civilization. Except for Catholic groups, all of Europe was consumed with joy. The Reformation brought a breath of freedom that not only liberated ordinary Christians from the rigid rituals of faith but also brought a long sigh of relief to kings and nobility who were able to begin to enjoy the political freedom that came from the decline of Catholic power and the joy of the return of political power into Caesar's hands.

The correcting of false theology, doctrine and ecclesial institutions ushered in enormous changes not only in the church but in society as well. In the post-Reformation Enlightenment Movement, which began in the 17th century, Europeans' thinking and creative power erupted with unprecedented vitality, creating a new civilization as dazzling as fireworks. In the two centuries that followed, European society displayed amazing potential in an environment [created by] the balanced development of divinity and humanity; natural science, art, the economy, constitutional government and the military (the advantage of firearms) all experienced rapid and comprehensive development, hitting a pinnacle in the post-Roman Empire history of human civilization. Britain became the representative nucleus of these civilizations. Even though at the beginning of the 19th century the Enlightenment turned into a modernist ideological movement by way of academia and the political arena, becoming a force in Europe that openly opposed the Christian faith and Christian thinking, its healthy development still lasted for over 400 years, not slowing down until World War II.

These 400 glorious years resulted from the combining of the Roman and Greek traditions of secular human culture, especially science, technology, literature and arts, getting the space needed to develop, and were predicated on divine faith and Christian ethics guiding the management of political power and social culture. It was the good fruit that came from the union of the culture of a truth-based divine faith and the human culture of Grecian reason, logic and philosophy; at the same time, the important role played by constitutional governmental system should not be overlooked. Although the then-prevailing secular culture that emerged was anti-Christian, it operated as an undercurrent which did not grow into a force dominating society but perfectly made up for the deficiencies of the human culture in Europe. This was a predestined coincidence.

Furthermore, since the mid-17th century, in addition to European civilization, Western civilization also yielded the amazing bloom of American civilization. The developmental process and model of American civilization was very similar to the process that Jewish civilization went through under Moses' leadership. Therefore, this civilization also yielded great fruits and, on the foundation of European civilization, attained new heights and reached a new peak in the history of human civilization. In 1620 A.D., a group of Puritans from England and some other regions departed from Europe (Egypt) where they had been persecuted, boarded the *Mayflower*, and, arriving at what is now northeastern United States, disembarked at Plymouth, formally entering into the Promised Land of Canaan.

Before they disembarked, the passengers of this ship agreed as a group to sign "The Mayflower Compact," the first political contract in U.S. history, which says:

> In the name of God, Amen. We, whose names are underwritten, the loyal subjects of our dread Sovereign Lord, King James, by the grace of God, of Great Britain, France and Ireland king, defender of the faith, etc. having undertaken, for the glory of God, and advancement of the Christian faith, and honor of our king and country, a voyage to plant the first colony in the Northern parts of Virginia, doe by these presents solemnly and mutually in the presence of God and one of another, covenant and combine ourselves together into a civil body politick, for our better ordering and preservation, and furtherance of the ends aforesaid; and by

virtue hereof to enact, constitute, and frame such just and equal laws, ordinances, acts, constitutions and offices, from time to time, as shall be thought most meet and convenient for the general good of the Colonies unto which we promise all due submission and obedience. In witness whereof we have hereunder subscribed our names at Cape-Cod the 11. of November, in the year of the reign of our sovereign lord, King James, of England, France and Ireland, the eighteenth, and of Scotland the fifty-fourth. Anno Dom. 1620.

At least three components of the ecosystem for an ideal civilization are included in this pact: First, [the phrases] "in the name of God" and "advancement of the Christian faith" laid the foundation for divine faith. Second, the Christian faith also includes Christian ethics, as well as "just and equal laws, ordinances, acts, constitutions and offices." Third, they confirmed the constitutional [form of] governance and citizens' rights [in the statement] "doe by these presents solemnly and mutually in the presence of God and one of another, covenant and combine ourselves together into a civil body politick."

The Mayflower Compact clearly defined these three components of an ideal civilization, and it was signed corporately. This was the direction that American civilization followed in its development. As for civilization's fourth element, i.e. the development of literature and art, it occurred as a matter of course under the [positive] conditions created by the first three components. This compact was more significant to the formation of American civilization than was the Declaration of Independence, which focused on political and citizenship rights. The Declaration of Independence is more representative of Roman politics-Greek culture rather than the divine faith of Christianity. Therefore, the Mayflower Compact and the Declaration of Independence constitute the two elements of the ecosystem for an ideal civilization: **the culture of divine faith based on Christianity and the human culture based on the model of reason, logic and philosophical thinking.**

In the 300 years following, American civilization developed rapidly and after the Revolutionary and the Civil wars, the civilization began to mature, and the United States emerged at the beginning of the 20th century as a superpower civilization. In the 20th century, American civilization brought about globalization, thus exerting a decisive influence on the whole world, touching upon every aspect of human civilization: the Christian faith, science and technology, politics, the economy, military affairs, literature and art, sports, etc. American civilization is not only the pinnacle of Christian civilization but also the highest level of human civilization so far.

In chapter 15 of his famous work, *Democracy in America*, the French political theorist Alexis de Tocqueville (1805-1859) profoundly expounded on the indispensableness of Christianity to American civil society, and he called for government to abide by Christian ethics. Of the role of Christian faith in American civil society, he said,

> In the United States, on the seventh day of every week, the trading and working life of the nation seems suspended; all noises cease; a deep tranquility, say rather the solemn calm of meditation, succeeds the turmoil of the week, and the soul resumes possession and contemplation of itself.

> Upon this day the marts of traffic are deserted; every member of the community, accompanied by his children, goes to church, where he listens to strange language which would seem unsuited to his ear. He is told of the countless evils caused by pride and covetousness: he is reminded of the necessity of checking his desires, of the finer pleasures which belong to virtue alone, and of the true happiness which attends it.

> On his return home, he does not turn to the ledgers of his calling, but he opens the book of Holy Scripture; there he meets with sublime or affecting descriptions of the greatness and goodness of the Creator, of the infinite magnificence of

the handiwork of God, of the lofty destinies of man, of his duties, and of his immortal privileges.

Thus it is that the American at times steals an hour from himself; and laying aside for a while the petty passions which agitate his life, and the ephemeral interests which engross it, he strays at once into an ideal world, where all is great, eternal, and pure.

I have endeavored to point out in another part of this work the causes to which the maintenance of the political institutions of the Americans is attributable; and religion appeared to be one of the most prominent amongst them. I am now treating of the Americans in an individual capacity, and I again observe that religion is not less useful to each citizen than to the whole State.

The Americans show, by their practice, that they feel the high necessity of imparting morality to democratic communities by means of religion. What they think of themselves in this respect is a truth of which every democratic nation ought to be thoroughly persuaded.

Regrettably, the West's secular liberalist ideology, whose main theme is to resist Christianity and which began during the Renaissance and grew and developed during the Enlightenment and the Modernist movements, gradually matured after World War II. In the post-modernist era (the1960s and 1970s), it ultimately gained complete control of European society and culture, becoming the prelude to European civilization going astray and inevitably declining. The same force, coming from Europe but about 50 years later, also has gradually penetrated American society and culture, and as it did in Europe, it took over the field of higher education, winning a decisive victory at the beginning of the 21st century. Now, highly confident, it has begun a comprehensive destruction of the great American civilization.

5. The decline of contemporary Euro-American civilization: the loss of divine faith and divine ethics

After Martin Luther's Reformation, European civilization developed rapidly upon the foundation of the Renaissance and within the healthy socio-cultural environment of divine faith, divine ethics and human freedom, and because of the Enlightenment, it developed further and was heading to a peak. However, just as Jesus Christ said in Matthew 13:24-24, "'The kingdom of heaven is like a man who sowed good seed in his field. But while everyone was sleeping, his enemy came and sowed weeds among the wheat, and went away. When the wheat sprouted and formed heads, then the weeds also appeared.'" In these circumstances of social and cultural upheaval, the Enlightenment which began in the 17th century, harbored a secular anti-Christian undercurrent which slowly gathered momentum in Europe and gradually began to rage. This force represented Roman secular democratic politics and the Greek philosophy of naturalism (atheism and deism). Greek philosophy, in particular, after being absorbed and incorporated into Augustinian theology and reduced to being its maiden for over 1000 years, finally took advantage of the rift within Christianity, the fanning of the flames of the Reformation by the king's political forces, and the discontent of the people long suppressed by religious laws, and grabbed the historical opportunity to begin to advocate for the liberation of man, thus covering up its plans for rebellion. Finally, in the early 19th century, it became the ideological trend of modernism.

Thereupon, the two great anti-Christian ideologies of this undercurrent, with the support and encouragement of the two banners of modernism—Darwin's theory of natural evolution and the scientific materialism of atheism—finally "reached the inner sanctum" and become a socio-cultural trend. The former presented itself as science and the latter employed methods of political philosophy. The two world wars of the 20th century were a watershed of modern Western civilization, and in the 1960s, it entered into the postmodernist era, i.e. the contemporary era. That's when Western civilization began its decline from the pinnacle of its glory; this happened because the frontlines of science, education, and political philosophy have been taken over by anti-Christian liberalism. Now, at the beginning of the 21st century, the corrupt decline of Western civilization has begun to surface, like the tip of the iceberg. Of course, Western civilization is declining only in comparison with when it was at its prime; compared with the civilizations of the rest of the world, it is still far ahead.

In *Divinity and Humanity*, this author analyzed the problem of modernism this way:

> The birth of modernism was mainly the result of the French Revolution and Napoleon's military expansion, which caused Europe to become skeptical of the ideological civilization of the Enlightenment and to start looking for new propositions. At the same time, the emergence of Darwin's theory of evolution was a banner marking the formation of the modernist ideological movement. The modernist ideological movement has two main branches: atheistic scientific materialism and the Christian liberalist thinking born of the influence of atheistic scientific materialism. The former emphasizes the non-existence of divinity and "the sure victory of man over nature"; the latter emphasizes the autonomy of humanity apart from divinity. The Enlightenment essentially gave a big boost in advancing Christianity's human civilization, and it continued to emphasize truth and certainty within the divine framework and the indispensability of the Christian ethical system, and therefore it falls into the category of realism illuminated by divinity. The modernist ideological movement, however, is a great rebellion by humanistic civilization against divine civilization. Although it still emphasizes the concept of truth, it abandoned Christian ethics and established an ethical system on the principle of human (and sinful) freedom. Due to its great confidence in man, it believes that man can become good without relying on divinity, and that a society without divinity can be more ideal and civilized; therefore, it is human idealism that is

blind and naïve. It was on the basis of this ideology that Marx and others developed the ideals of communism.

The main source of the confidence of modernist ideology is the development of modern science and secular philosophy, in particular, Darwin's theory of natural evolution, which posed a great challenge to the Christian theory of creation and swept over academia, becoming a new faith religion from which a new ideological system was derived. Today, science has advanced to the stage of genetic studies, yet many scientists still believe in the theory of evolution. What is most ironic is that the teaching of the theory of evolution that in the West begins in elementary school is no different from the brainwashing education of communist countries. In Europe, after less than a century of the development of the atheistic materialistic ideology with the theory of evolution at its core, the two world wars that shocked all mankind broke out, completely destroying the high confidence man had placed on the autonomy of human nature and on [the concept of] man as master of his own fate.

The outbreak of World War I was but a warning to Europe's arrogant and blind humanity that had deviated from the path of divinity, but, European society actually drifted even further away from the right path. The outbreak of World War II was inevitable, and Germany, Italy and Asia's Japan played evil roles. Japan was the only non-European disciple of the modernist civilization. The impact of the wave of modernism on North America was more superficial and slower because the Puritans who founded and influenced American civilization placed a high value on divinity and it was solid and strong. The growth of modernist and post-modernist civilization in Europe has always been one step ahead of that in North America.

Darwin's theory of natural evolution destroyed Europe's Christian culture of truth-based divine faith, and the modernist ideology destroyed the authority of the Christian code of ethics; thus was the ground prepared for Europe's civilizational decline. After World War II, having learned the lesson of the consequences of racism—though refusing to acknowledge the influence of the theory of natural evolution on racism—the [European] people put into practice the policy of political liberalism (not Christian ethics, although superficially similar; liberalism in essence is anti-truth). Liberal thought holds the view that racial equality is based on civilized feelings of secular noble [virtues] and that mankind is by nature virtuous and therefore is capable of solving its own problems. Christian ethics, however, is based on revealed truths from God and believes that everyone created by God is equal, but emphasizes that everyone has a sinful nature and that mankind is not capable of saving itself.

Great attention must be paid [to the fact] that the most influential product of modernism—communism, the crystallization of Darwin's theory of natural evolution and atheistic scientific materialism—is the main force opposing Christianity and corrupting European civilization. "A spectre is haunting Europe—the spectre of communism," Marx said, setting in motion in the last century the worldwide communist movement of totalitarianism that enslaved approximately one-third of mankind to violence and poverty and trampled mankind's basic dignity. After the Cold War, people applauded the chain-reaction collapse of communist regimes, but by ignoring the essence of communism, the result has been the revival of the specter of communism seizing the opportunity and striking back, this time in the disguise of political liberalism, and it is achieving a great victory by way of peaceful evolution.

The essence of communism is not totalitarianism and a planned economy; these are simply methods of governance used by communist regimes once they are in power. Rather, the nature of communism lies in its political, social and philosophical ideals, [which are]: inequitable distribution in society is caused by the pursuit of profits by capitalists; the rich and the elites are the cause of all the problems of the poor; ordinary people, not the social elites, are the ones who create history;

violent methods are necessary to achieve the equitable distribution of social resources.

The communist movement of the 20th century was rooted in these false, grand and hollow ideals, especially hostility toward the rich, which successfully fanned people's sinful nature to covet material things and power. This resulted in the success of revolutionary movements and the destruction of the elites in society, and ushered in an era of communist regimes. In the spiritual realm, communism gives free reign to man's sin nature by providing the pretext of lofty excuses to [engage in] moral hypocrisy and evil politics, and the disastrous consequences of its unrestrained and reckless evil acts are therefore inevitable. So, people quickly realized that the slogans of the communist revolution were just empty talk, because people were even poorer than before, society was even more unfair, and politics even more corrupt. Because of the systematic destruction of the elite class, the productivity and operational efficiency of all of society plummeted. Moreover, a new elite group came to the fore from among the people, whose abilities fell far short of the previous noble elites that it had destroyed but who nonetheless surpassed them in their desire and greed for power and wealth. Its vicious tyranny over the people reached historically unprecedented heights. As a result, communist regimes birthed from violent revolutions soon collapsed or were on their last legs because of their own dysfunction and opposition from the people.

What was surprising was that the communist movement did not perish because of this, but rather through a process of peaceful evolution has continued on in Europe and the United States. Since the 1960s, liberalism and anti-Christian secular forces have worked together, gradually and systematically conducting brainwash-style education on the people through the educational system and mass media, so that the public unconsciously accepts the fundamental ideals of communism. Since violent revolution has been universally condemned, advocates of communist ideals have called for using the vote in the democratic system to engage in subversion, then [they] make new laws and use violent methods that they have legalized to carry out equitable distribution of social resources, trampling on the principle of fairness in the free market of "more work, more pay" while encouraging the thieving and parasitic culture of "reaping without sowing." This is how the peaceful evolution of communism is at work in Europe and the United States today, and it is destroying in every domain the ecology for civilization founded on such Western Christian ideals as "godliness, justice and love."

In *Christianity and Civil Society in China*, this author uses church-state relations to expound on the principles behind the corruption of Western civilization by anti-Christian ideological trends and its consequences.

The political philosophy and the constitutional system of government upon which the United States was founded, including its Declaration of Independence, were borrowed almost lock-stock-and-barrel from the theoretical system of the great English Christian scholar John Locke. Everything related to the constitutional system of government, separation of church and state, citizenship rights, and religious toleration, etc., all came out of the Christian theological proposition that "all men are created equal" by God. The main drafter of the Declaration of Independence, Thomas Jefferson, who was a deistic Unitarian, an outstanding representative of the Roman civilization and the third U.S. president, trimmed Locke's original model, ignored his theories on economic property, and used words like "God" and "self-evident" to "trick" the good-hearted Puritans. This resulted in ambiguity and a lack of clarity from the very beginning as to the extent of the separation of church and state in the American system. In Jefferson's view of the Bible and in his deist beliefs, the "God" he refers to is actually the God in Aristotle's metaphysical philosophy. This was a clever, sneaky conceptual substitution. Among Jefferson's contemporaries, it appears that only John Adams, a representative of Christian civilization who later became Jefferson's political rival, saw something fishy. Adams, who served as the first U.S. vice president and second president, clearly stated, "Our constitution was made only for a moral and religious people. It is wholly inadequate to the government of any other." At the time, this reference to "religious people" meant Christians. The U.S. model of church-state relations is the most advanced system in the history of Western civilization and in world civilization, but there is still room for improvement.

Furthermore, when the Western constitutional government paradigm was first created, its purpose was primarily to limit abuse of power by monarch and government and to protect citizens' rights. But Christian theology regards both king and commoner as sinners and both in need of restrictions; before God, all men are equal, and victims are not necessarily righteous. It took Western civilization 300 years to finally limit the power of monarch and government, only to discover to its surprise that the rights of the people also need to be restricted, especially in situations when the interests of nations (or ethnic groups) clash. The false premise of the theorists of the all-powerful democracy is that the people and the majority are always right. But in reality, this is not necessarily the case. Through violent revolution and the democratic system, the people can abuse the right to participate in politics, unite to form a "Korah and his party" (see the Bible, Numbers 16) to satisfy their lust for power and their sinful nature. Examples of this are the French Revolution with its slogans of patriotism and the pursuit of freedom and equality; fascism in World War II Germany and Japan that worshipped racial patriotism; communist tyranny in the Soviet Union, Eastern Europe, China and North Korea; democratic tyranny in some countries today after the Middle East's Arab Spring; and the collective corruption in some African countries of constitutional citizenship-democratic governments. That's why the post-World War II founding of the United Nations and the international laws and conventions drawn up and enacted since then were all intended to protect human rights, a concept that goes beyond the rights of a citizen of a country—and also a very Christian concept. In reality, though, achieving compliance with international laws is difficult because when theocratic and monarchial power have been eliminated, the state becomes deified by patriotism, and citizens become deified by the democratic system and they become the supreme authority. This is yet another bizarre cycle.

Modernism's anti-Christian secular atheist belief and ideology has persisted in the West. On the coattails of the philosophy of skepticism and existentialism (its trademark slogan: God is dead), it ran roughshod through the entire 20th century, peaked in the West in the 1960s and 1970s, and then entered into the postmodernist-relativist era. Today, it has already won a great victory in Europe and is marching towards the United States. The characteristics of this era are: people no longer believe in the existence of absolute truth, or do not even believe that truth exists, because everything is relative; they declare loudly that the diametric of beauty and ugliness and good and evil has vanished, even believing in the non-existence of evil; psychology, psychiatry and brain science explain and make conclusions about all human behavioral phenomenon; pluralism is blindly worshipped by both the elites and the common people. This terrible, ignorant philosophical Zeitgeist has swept over academia, politics and other public spheres of society, becoming an idol of political correctness that cannot be challenged. But the evil and terrorizing gunshots that rang out on the island of Utoya, Norway, in 2011 and in the U.S. town of Newtown in 2012 were a sign that postmodernism in the West is already bankrupt.

When the Europeans abandoned the Christian faith and its ethical culture and, having already separated government and church, took another step towards an absolute separation of church and state, i.e. politics and Christianity, and secularization of education, they deified the people and country, or deified the European Union. In post-1960s

Europe, anti-Christian secular and liberal forces facilitated the immigration of large groups of non-Christian foreigners by advocating and practicing religious and cultural pluralism and engrafting this belief and ideology into public education. This experiment, however, has failed. In just a few decades, Islamic social forces started to rise up in Britain, France and other countries, leading to the dismantling of the singular dominating structure of traditional European civilization. In particular, the forceful promotion of Islamic ethics and religious law by Muslim communities and the rapid growth of the Muslim population have created a powerful challenge to the "universal values" (such as monogamy and gender equality) in the belief system and ideology of European secular liberalism. Though they may be reluctant to admit it, Europe's elites and common people ought to begin to see that even the secular anti-Christian values of Western society bore the marks of baptism by Christian culture; hence, they are not "universal values" that are recognized by non-Christian cultures and ideologies. In light of this, the September 11 tragedy in the United States and the challenges posed by Muslim communities to European civilization in Britain, France and Germany are signs that pluralism in the West is already bankrupt.

Clearly, secular postmodernism-relativism and pluralism (multiculturalism) based on a diversity of faith traditions have quietly become the platform for overthrowing the West's established singular dominating culture through shifting demographics and the democratic system, and is therefore a process that is neither static nor balanced. The ideal of a world order of religious multiculturalism can be realized only through the peaceful co-existence of different nations, but the conflict resulting from the cross-border expansion of religious civilizations and from the paramount importance placed on national interests makes it difficult to establish this order for the long term and (or) in large areas.

Today, as Christian communities are seriously shrinking and as post-modernism and a multicultural faith culture rises in Western society, anti-Christian secularism and liberalism have gained an advantage through democratic methods and, through the gradual enactment of new laws, are moving towards openly opposing and suppressing the lawful influence of Christian faith and culture on society. This reality will also lead to a slight majority of citizens having control over the slight minority of citizens, and even to the imposition of a faith ideology that does not sit well with the conscience of the slight minority. Furthermore, this will happen through political correctness in the social culture and by the noble means of the rule of law, carrying off constitutional government to Rome and kidnapping democracy and bringing it to Athens.

Encouragingly, some truth-seeking scholars have started to abandon postmodernism and to reflect on the dilemma of faith-based pluralism (pluralistic civilization) and the malfunction and embarrassment of a democratic system based on this kind of cultural environment.

Brief Summary

The decline of Western civilization is a foregone conclusion if no action is taken to pull it back from the brink. Europe will become part of the Islamic world and, through the strategy of peaceful evolution, the dream of Islam occupying Europe that Islamic Arabs have held since the 8th century but failed to realize through bloody wars of knives and swords will finally be fulfilled. In the near future, Europe may go through the model of social change that South Africa and Zimbabwe went through and repeat their same mistakes. And the United States may be reduced to a quasi-communist nation in the wake of the surge of immigrants from backward countries and the government's continually expanded welfare spending, falling into the political, social and economic model of present-day Latin America.

The root cause of the decline of Western civilization and of its shameful moral and ethical behavior is not necessarily the might of anti-Christian forces but rather the domino effect of the corruption of a series of elements that are essential to civilization. It started with the decline of divine faith, which was caused by the decline of the church and theology, which was caused by the decline of elite churches, which was caused by shrinking numbers of Christian elites, which was caused by the mistakes of theologians and church leaders. The decline of divine faith led to the decline of ethics and morality, which then led to problems emerging in the law and the legal system. Finally, the constitutional system of government became a tool of the covert dictatorship of the slight majority of the population to engage in lawful violence. Furthermore, although there have been ever-changing and epoch-making advances in science and technology, Europe and the United States today have not experienced any historic breakthroughs in literature and art for a long time.

In modern Western history, elite churches have been society's most important positive force and the creator of civilized Christian groups. From those who brought Britain's constitutional government into being to the leaders of the Revolutionary War and the Civil War in the United States, those who played decisive leadership roles were all Christian elites and elite churches. Nevertheless, today's churches in general have also accepted communist ideas and neglect or even reject the important role of Christian elites, striving to make Christians with five silver talents and Christians with one silver talent do the same work and play the same role. The problem is: how shall the Christians with five talents give an account when they stand before the Lord?

III. Churches and Christians are creating a new civilization in China

To this day, the Chinese people still have great difficulty grasping the meaning of civilization, so it is hard to prove whether this highly intelligent ethnic group has sufficient ideas, wisdom and ethics and morals to successfully manage a society. Traditional Chinese civilization was a hodge-podge of low-grade, ignorant and demonic cultures such as Confucianism, Buddhism and Daoism. Food and sex remain of the core of Chinese civilization, which is an **anthropoid** civilization or characteristic of advanced animals. Added to which is the fact that the Chinese people to this day have kept up the practice of eating placenta, so Chinese civilization has not yet left barbaric customs behind. Regrettably, as with many ethnic groups at the low end of civilization, the Chinese people also lack clear self-awareness, unaware that they are light years behind advanced civilizations and possessing a false self-confidence.

Many Chinese people believe that the components of an advanced civilization are: economic success, a fair social system, higher education, popularization of science and knowledge, diligent work and high IQ. However, in the past three decades, despite the great investments that have been made in these areas and the successes that have been achieved in some aspects, the overall level of civilization of Chinese society has actually regressed. Consequently, people blame all the problems on China's unfair social system and on government corruption. While these are certainly important factors, they are still not the decisive ones.

A conspicuous mark of advanced civilizations is the importance attached to self-criticism and being open to criticism from others. The exact opposite is the case in low civilizations, which do not allow criticism from others and blame others for all of one's own problems. Advanced civilizations place greater emphasis on loving people, especially loving fellow citizens of one's own country, while low civilizations emphasize loving one's country [patriotism] yet cruelly treat the citizens of one's own country. Counterfeit products, including poisonous infant milk powder; piracy, the highest form of which is copycat culture; and a thriving sex industry, etc., etc., these are all diseases of the civilization and a direct consequence of cutting corners because of animal-like greed.

What is civilization? Let's use an analogy: the difference between fresh flowers and fake flowers is whether or not the flowers have life; life represents civilization.

Without holy divine faith and its ethics, humans relying on human nature, their own conscience and their minds can at most achieve the level of civilization that Augustine described as "happiness by sharing a common good." However, it is when there is a clash of interests between individuals, between groups and between nations that the quality and level [of advancement] of a civilization are evident. The ideal form of advanced civilization can be called an "olive civilization" while low civilization is a "thorn civilization." (See the author's *Christianity and Civil Society in China*.)

From now on, Chinese Christians should make use of their own strengths to deliberately participate in facilitating the birth of a new civilization in family and society. The key elements for the development of Christian civilization in China include: **individuals establishing a Christian divine faith, popularizing Christian ethical culture in society, advancing human freedom in the family and society, transforming psychological patterns and modes of thinking, and establishing constitutional government and rule of law to guarantee citizens' rights; and Christians holding fast to their dual identity and faithfully fulfilling their dual mission.**

1. Establish Christian divine faith in personal lives

To advance civilization overall for the individual, family and society, the Chinese people need to establish in their personal lives a Christian divine faith based on the Bible. The establishment of this kind of faith and its maturation [process] does not occur in isolation but rather in connection with church life. The church is the platform for creating a new civilization in China and Christians are the workers on this platform, engaging society via the **bridge of ethics** and fulfilling their dual responsibility of advancing God's kingdom and social civilization.

As soon as more than 30% of the Chinese people are Christians, the soil for the growth of a new civilization will be ready. When there are this many Christians, church revival will be inevitable, and church revival is the hallmark of the victory and expansion of God's kingdom on earth. Spiritually, church revival serves the purpose of purifying and transforming society, storing up power for righteousness, and further sustaining and improving the quality of individual faith.

In this process, importance needs to be attached to establishing groups of Christian elites and elite churches. The first step is setting up elite fellowships, which could be either a loosely structured circle of Christian friends bound together by social backgrounds and personal friendships, or a formal church fellowship. Then, when membership in these groups of Christian elites is sufficient, it is time to establish elite churches with a specific focus. In large cities like Beijing and Shanghai, elite churches have already emerged, an important sign that churches and the faith of individuals are becoming mature.

Elite Christian groups represent the highest level of civilization in society and are qualified for the roles of leading and planning; therefore, their strength is in creating a new civilization for society. Because they have been indoctrinated with and brainwashed by elite-hating communist ideas, the Chinese people today regard the common people as the creators of history—even the elites themselves hold this view. The correct interpretation ought to be that, only when they have submitted to the leadership of Christian elites can the Chinese people change and create history and enjoy the beautiful fruits of civilization. Without the leadership of Christian elites, the public is blind; this is true even for the Christian public. At the same time, the elites cannot carry out their plans without the support, cooperation and compliance of the public. Be aware that non-Christian elites often exploit, extort and deceive the public, which makes them intellectual elites, not elites of civilization.

Establishing a personal faith and becoming mature in it is inseparable from church and community life. At the same time, emphasis needs to be placed on the practice of personal faith in family life. The family is the basic unit of society. Beautiful Christian civilization can first be realized in the family and need not wait for civilization to be realized at the societal level. Elite Christian families must first achieve Christian civilization, otherwise there is no evidence of their status as Christian elites. Christians elites also need to actively proclaim the Gospel among social elites, turn people's hearts back to Christ and exert an influence on both the church and society.

Elites are a social group in a relative sense. Each social class, culture and ethnic group has its own group of elites. Therefore, elites are widespread throughout society, not a small group at the pinnacle. An awareness of [the role of] the elite [among the people] is civilization's major driving force, and a social culture that values elites is one that follows biblical teachings. In the Old Testament, God focused on choosing elites to accomplish great historical tasks. In the New Testament, God chose both grassroots people and elites because Christianity was not just for the Israelites but rather was for people of all social classes from all nations and all ethnicities. So, God tasked the elites with the missions meant for elites and ordinary people with the missions meant for ordinary people, just as different parts of the body work together to glorify the holy name of Jesus Christ. As a representative of the Christian elite, Paul accomplished the greatest mission, which included writing one-third of the New Testament and pioneering missionary work to the Gentiles. In the same way, God also used uneducated common people like Peter and John.

As 1 Corinthians 12 teaches, every part of the body is equally valuable and each has a unique responsibility. Though some are more honorable or better looking than others, each is of equal value and respectable. The eye must do the work of the eye, the hands and feet must do the work of the hands and feet. Likewise, in the church and society, some Christians have more honorable jobs and responsibilities, such as elite jobs, while others may have jobs and responsibilities not as dignified, such as grassroots jobs in society. Nevertheless, in Christ these jobs are equally important in terms of value and role. Both elites and grassroots commoners need to humble themselves and avoid criticizing and despising one another. It is also important, however, that elites not play the role of non-elites and that non-elites do not do the work meant for elites; otherwise, the "body" will become dysfunctional. This is precisely the problem with communist ideology and Western liberalism.

Chinese Christians should rise up and vie to be Jesus Christ's elite forces, fighting the good and victorious fight in this grand and historic spiritual warfare. As was stressed earlier, a person with one talent should not attempt to play the role meant for someone with five talents. Likewise, a person with five talents should not work a job that only requires one talent. Fulfilling one's responsibility according to one's call and talents from Jesus Christ is the way to live out one's faith so that it shines brightly and to maximum effectiveness. The development of Christianity is a responsibility entrusted to ordinary believers while the transformation of social civilization through Christian faith is a responsibility entrusted to Christians elites. The remarkable development of the church in China is the great achievement of the Christian faith movement at the grassroots level. Because of it, the church as the platform for the creation of Christian civilization has been put in place, but of the Christian elites not even a shadow has yet been sighted.

2. Popularizing the culture of Christian ethics in society

For individuals, Christian ethics is the rational principle behind the acknowledgement and repentance of sin that leads to the cleansing and transforming of one's life by the Holy Spirit. For society, Christian ethics is the public moral standard that purges society of the sin nature and purifies social civilization. A young pastor of a house church in China made this profound analysis of sin and civilization in an email to me:

> I suddenly realized that eliminating evil is a very complicated task and comes with a high price. I have now taken another look at the preference in the Chinese churches for the "sacred/secular divide" and see it as an idol-worshipping mentality that expects to reach one's destination in just a single step. Believers are very happy to make the

claim that "I'm a new creation," but lack the zeal for "ongoing transformation." The sin nature is intertwined into man's life and it is inevitable that it will be intertwined into the culture as well. If the weeds are not pulled out, the wheat will be damaged. Transforming the sin nature in secular culture is like pulling the sin nature out of the lives of Christians. Seen in this light, the advancement of civilization should be an upward spiral. This way, God's redemption is fulfilled simultaneously for the individual and for human civilization as a whole.

It is not possible that all members of a society will accept the Christian faith, but a society must have a unifying ethical system or it will fall into chaos. It has been proven in the 2000 years of the history of human civilization that Christian ethics is the most ideal for personal, familial and social ethics. Christian civilization does not necessarily have to be built on the foundation of the conversion of all. When the majority (70%) of the people in society become Christians, Christian ethics can be deepened and popularized and can take root in society. In other words, a person does not have to accept the Christian faith but ought to accept Christian ethics. The popularization of Christian ethics does not need to be done by force because people find them easy to accept due to the good works of Christians and the popularization today of universal values (the secular version of Christian ethics), and there is no other loftier ethics that can compare with it. For example, no one can argue against the Christian ethic of "love your neighbor as yourself"; as Jesus taught, "Do to others what you would have them do to you." The superiority of Christian ethics is a main reason the Chinese people in general have a positive view of Christianity.

Christian ethics includes respect for divine rights and protection of human rights. With regard to human rights, the overarching principle is the advancement of justice and loving others as oneself in one's personal moral standards and society's moral code. Christianity also emphasizes the virtue of hard work, illustrating principles like "wages are an obligation to the one who works" (Romans 4:4) and "the one who is unwilling to work shall not eat" (2 Thessalonians 3:10).

Interestingly, not all social cultures and civilizations put the same emphasis on the virtue and practice of hard work. Every civilization is ultimately carried out by the concrete work of the people. Therefore, among the early American settlers, the principle of creating wealth through hard work as a way of practicing the faith was strongly advocated by John Wesley, which greatly advanced the development of America's early material civilization. The slogan of John Wesley that influenced the early Christian social culture of the United States was: gain all you can, save all you can, and give all you can.

The work ethic of Christians is to glorify the name of Jesus, assume the responsibility of providing for one's family, and help those in financial need. Material civilization is the indispensable foundation for social civilization, so work and paying taxes is the duty of every citizen. The more advanced the civilization of a community, the more importance people in this community attach to hard work, and they consider it shameful to rely on social welfare and government aid to live. A society composed of such communities is bound to become affluent under the rule of law. Paul teaches that each one should carry his own load, and on top of that, to carry each other's burdens. This is a sensible principle.

Just as is the case with political systems, ethical culture can be either a positive force for civilization or a negative force. The Chinese people are hardworking, but because the cost of an ethical culture and [a good] political system are too high, the material civilization of the Chinese people is still among the worst in the world, as is the spiritual civilization. Popularizing Christian ethics can improve the cultural environment, and that will eventually change the irrational social system too. In addition to the overarching principles of justice and love, hard work is also an important virtue.

Furthermore, ethics in the family and marriage are also extremely important. Monogamy is a Christian ethic and it is widely accepted in today's world, having advanced mankind's overall civilization. However, monogamy is a fruit of Christian civilization; people will reject monogamy if their civilization does not reach a certain level. In

Chinese society today, monogamy has been mandated by law and practiced in society for over 60 years, but the Chinese people, from high-ranking government officials to grassroots commoners, will still practice the traditional marital culture of "polygamy (one husband and multiple wives)" whenever they have the chance or the resources to do so. Civilization can be likened to the precious necklace worn by a beautiful woman; when the necklace is placed around the neck of a pig, civilization is lost. Therefore, civilization is a form of art.

The Christian faith and Greco-Romanesque rational thinking are the co-carriers of Western civilization. Only when divine rights are held in reverence can human rights be protected and rational thinking be creative. Many people have the mistaken idea that it is democratic systems, constitutional governments, civil societies, and science and technology that are the carriers of Western civilization—[in fact] they are tools—and that they lead to respect for and protection of human rights and the development of and stability and prosperity in society. However, after the colonial nations of Africa gained independence one after another and the European colonialists handed political power to the locals, in spite of the fact that they had inherited the rule of law and constitutional democracy, the level of social civilization in these nations fell dramatically, rule of law fell apart, and economic performance plummeted. How is this to be explained? Zimbabwe and South Africa are two typical examples. Despite having astronomical wealth from selling from their bottomless oil reserves, the civilization of countries in the Middle East remains at a level where polygamy is practiced and science, technology and education are also extremely backward. Yet, many Latin American countries where the ratio of Christians in the population is very high also lag far behind the United States and Canada in terms of advanced civilization even though their natural resources and social institutions do not differ much [from their northern neighbors]. This is mainly due to the lack of a rational mode of thinking and its practical application, which has resulted in poor management and low efficiency. The solution is popularization among the general public of modern higher education, which was influenced by Greco-Roman rational civilization. In China, despite great advances in higher education, science and technology and the economy, and despite the gradual popularization of a rational mode of thinking, people's quality of life is still very poor and the serious absence of ethics and morality has resulted in a serious proliferation of evil throughout society. Even in the most developed Asian countries and regions, such as Japan, Taiwan Singapore and Hong Kong, that have adopted the full package of Western democracy, constitutional government, and economic and educational systems, the level of civilization still lags far behind that of Western countries. South Korea is an interesting case because its traditional culture represented by Confucius and Mencius hemmed in the functionality of Christian ethics and the traditional Buddhist way of thinking hampered the rational and logical mode of thinking, all of which led to Christian civilization being squeezed by the thorns of traditional culture.

So, an advanced civilization is not just a simple system or a technique that can be copied; its core is the ethics of the Christian faith and the Greco-Romanesque rational and logical mode of thinking. You cannot have just one or the other. Be aware that as Christian civilization grows, heresy and cults masquerading as the Christian faith are heinous spiritual viruses and chronic mental illnesses that are very dangerous and need to be resolutely resisted and mercilessly wiped out.

Christians in Chinese society promote Christianity's ethical culture mainly by setting an example in their social circles, church communities and personal relationships. In addition, churches and Christians should also establish communities of Christian culture in their residential areas and invisible and unstructured church communities, transplanting Christian ethics into these communities and cultivating a new community culture.

3. Promoting human freedom in the family and society

Even though everyone in Europe during the Middle Ages was a Christian, there were no breakthroughs in the development of civilization. After the Renaissance started, and especially after Martin Luther's Reformation, the conflicts between Catholic and Protestant church forces created a small bit of empty space in which people discovered the paradise of human freedom. However, sin nature also seized the opportunity and grew in this space and eventually went to the extreme of resisting the divine nature.

The key to Christian civilization lies in the balance between the divine nature and human nature as a person lives out his faith after repenting and being born again in Christ. In *Divinity and Humanity*, this author analyzes and elaborates on the premise of the divine nature, the importance of the free and healthy development of human nature, and the principle of the balance between divine nature and human nature.

The development of human civilization is the process by which the Bible and its divine civilization continuously transforms and elevates human civilization. Human history is the process in which God continuously educates mankind and elevates human civilization. Through the revelations, nurturing, shaping and enriching of human nature by the divine nature, human civilization is continuously elevated through individuals, families, society and ethnic groups, giving full play to the potential of human nature that God created, becoming light and salt, driving out the dark power of evil, and glorifying God's holy name.

Divine nature is like fire and sunlight. At an appropriate distance, it can provide human nature with wonderful warm support, but too close and human nature will be parched and even baked dry. Theology and doctrine and faith practices ought to set aside sufficient space for human nature to bask in the sunshine of divine nature, which is the only way to foster human nature's bearing of fruit, growth and glorifying of the divine nature.

Christians need to be aware that it is beautiful human nature that is to be offered up on the altar as an aromatic offering, pleasing to God. Why did God say that he delighted in mercy and not offerings? Jesus taught that before a person brings his offering to God, he should seek peace with his brothers. God attaches such great importance to human nature, but too many people focus only on pursuing divine nature and, as a result, they neglect and even suppress human nature. Another extreme, which is due to the influence of secular culture, is that Christians do not have confidence in the divine nature they possess and, as a result, they ignore or even abandon their divine nature, which leads to the depletion of their human nature and disappoints God and earns his condemnation.

Because of the influence of Confucianism and Buddhism, family culture in Chinese families in general suppresses human nature, is overly serious and insufficiently lively, especially in the education and discipline of children. Because promotion to the next grade [in school] is the only measurement of children's success, the childrearing [approach] of Chinese parents is mainly focused on achieving high grades and high intelligence, which stifles the [all-]important vitality of the heart and creativity of the mind. Civilization is the crystallization of beautiful hearts and creative minds, not the fruit of the simple acquisition of knowledge and accumulation of high intelligence. The key factor in the creation and advancement of civilization, other than the true divine faith and its ethics, is human wisdom, which has almost nothing to do with intelligence.

The level of civilization is influenced by two factors: the holy, truth-based divine faith and the culture of rational, logical and dialectical thinking. Specifically, the two factors are the Christian faith and Greco-Roman culture. Civilization/culture varies in quality. Just as is the case with nations, there are developing civilizations/cultures and developed civilizations/cultures. Human civilization, based on Western/European-American civilization, still has much room for improvement.

The lack of wisdom can be compensated for after Christian faith and ethics are established. The Bible says in Proverbs 9:10, "The fear of the Lord is the beginning of wisdom, and knowledge of the Holy One is understanding." It is a very important beginning, after which is the need to attach great importance to human freedom. The main expressions of a human nature that is free are psychological freedom and the freedom to choose a mode of thinking. A Christian can popularize human freedom in society only once he has successfully put it into practice in the family. Some Calvinists are of the view that the Christian faith should occupy all of society, but this is actually an incorrect theological view. In order to preserve human freedom, there must be room for secular culture in society; otherwise society will regress back to the Medieval model. However, the space for secular culture must be subordinate to the framework of Christian ethics and should not be a minor player stealing the show; otherwise, man's sin nature will use the excuse of freedom to rebel, break God's commands and reach for the forbidden fruit, resulting in punishment from God and the bitter fruit of a fallen human civilization.

4. Transforming hearts and modes of thinking

In "Transforming the Chinese Christian's Heart-Mind," this author elaborates on the principle and methods of transformation. A person's sin nature can be eradicated at the root and suppressed through a heart transformation.   The main problems with the psychology of the character of the Chinese people are **cowardice** and **falsehood**, which can only be overcome by the faithfulness and love of Christians. The two main problems with the Chinese people's psychological behavior are **emotions controlling the mind** and **psychological parasitism**, which can be overcome and transformed through the model of the heart submitting to and obeying the mind, aided by God's truth and the power of the Holy Spirit.

Below are excerpts from the beginning and end of "Transforming the Chinese Christian's Heart-Mind".

> Looking at the body of knowledge about psychology, it can be divided into two simple parts: **psychological personality** and **psychological behavior**.   Below, I examine the traditional psychological patterns in Chinese culture from these two perspectives and advocate the establishment—through Christian truth, ethics and the work of the Holy Spirit—of a psychological model that suits the life of a Christian.

After I became a Christian, by the grace of the Lord Jesus Christ, it was many years before I became aware of my wrong-headed psychological patterns. Then I set about changing and transforming my heart; it has been a slow and long journey, but one from which I have constantly benefited. I also grasped an important truth: **the true me is actually my heart (i.e. my psychology)**.

....

The Holy Spirit and Truth set us free, which is life being set free, the main expression of which is gaining and feeling the freedom of being psychologically strong and beautiful. In other words, the standard for whether a life is free is psychological freedom and well-being. With truth as the foundation, justice and love are the core of Christian psychological patterns. Justice and love are both the essential properties of psychology and psychology in action. The Holy Spirit endows us with everlasting love and eternal life, nurturing the essential properties of our psychology like a sweet spring. How broad and wide is our psychology, so broad and wide is our mind and our life.

For Christians, faith is the combined activity of the simultaneous processes in one's heart, soul and mind. Faith can also be seen as a process originating in the soul that systematically transforms and constructs psychological patterns and the mode of thinking. For Christians, faith is the process of growing in the life of Jesus Christ and his truths. 2 Corinthians 4:7 says, "But we have this treasure in jars of clay to show that this all-surpassing power is from God and not from us." The Holy Spirit is the treasure in the jars of clay (Christians) and the church is the body of Christ. That is to say, we have in the Holy Spirit a powerful support for our psychology, in Christ is our psychological fulcrum, while the church is our psychological rear guard. Through our faith, the Holy Spirit and the church help us complete our psychological transformation and reconstruction.

Christians need to deliberately examine and break their fixed psychological patterns (habits), accept the transforming [work of] the Holy Spirit and truth, and elevate their psychological state, allowing new wine to be poured into new wineskins. The "old self" often referred to by Christians can be understood to be old psychological patterns and the last stronghold of the power of evil in one's life. Therefore, Christians must have the resolve to crucify their old psychological patterns on the Cross and be resurrected in the truths of Jesus Christ and in the Holy Spirit, thus becoming a new creation. As Galatians 2:20 says, "I have been crucified with Christ and I no longer live, but Christ lives in me...."

A tombstone in the cemetery of Westminster Abby in London, Britain, reportedly has this inscription carved on it:

> When I was young and free and my imagination had no limits, I dreamed of changing the world. As I grew older and wiser, I discovered the world would not change, so I shortened my sights somewhat and decided to change only my country. But it, too, seemed immovable. As I grew in my twilight years, in one last desperate attempt, I settled for changing only my family, those closest to me, but alas, they would have none of it. And now as I lie on my deathbed, I suddenly realized: If I had only changed my self first, then by example I would have changed my family. From their inspiration and encouragement, I would then have been able to better my country and, who knows, I may have even changed my world.

The point I am trying to make is that, it is through changing our psychological patterns that we truly change ourselves, transform ourselves. Only by actively expanding our psychological patterns will there be corresponding growth in our life. With that as the basis, and as the number of Christians grows, healthy psychological patterns in the church community will gradually take shape, influencing the psychological patterns of the social culture to change and be transformed, and a healthy social psychology will finally be formed, which will elevate social civilization. The seed that grows into the great tree of human civilization germinates in human hearts.

More importantly, we are not blind nor ruled by emotions, but rather, we have a rational and spiritual basis for our faith, because 1 John 4:4 teaches us, "You, dear children, are from God and have overcome them, because the one who is in you is greater than the one who is in the world."

It is easy to bring the rational mode of thinking into play in scientific systems because logical deductions made at the micro-level in an established system of rational mode of thought still fall into the category of imitative thought. But when psychological patterns are irrational, it is hard to give play to a rational mode of thinking, and that is precisely where the problem lies in the lack of creative thinking in many Chinese intellectuals. In other words, a rational mode of thinking can only be brought into full play when there are complementary psychological patterns. Deliberately transforming one's psychological patterns can reduce the psychological cost in one's life as well as in one's work of the old psychological pattern as well as the cost of its resulting mode of thinking, gradually achieving psychological patterns that are pure, upright and free and a mode of thinking that is full of creativity.

5. Establishing constitutional government and the rule of law to protect citizens' rights

As mentioned earlier, the Bible's Old Testament provides a primitive and simple model of constitutional government with a separation of powers between **king and prophet,** and this model operated on the basis of a divine faith in God and obedience to ethical laws. The ethical codes God enacted through Moses were divided into two main parts: divine rights and human rights. Legal systems and the rule of law are the bridges connecting divine rights and human rights.

Only when people first safeguard divine rights can there be an awareness of and motivation for respecting human rights. This is also the case for a Christian civilization society; it must simultaneously respect divine rights and protect human rights, and through the rule of law ensure that Christian ethics dominate. Only in this way can the healthy functioning of society attain its maximum efficiency. In *Christianity and Civil Society in China*, this author expounds on civil society, constitutional government and the legal system originating from the divine culture of Christianity and being the fruits of Christian ethics and the workmanship of the politics of Christian elites. Today, China's churches and Christians have already advanced the development of constitutional government and civil society in China even if their actions were generally speaking unconscious. Below are some excerpts from the book.

> Christianity is promoting citizenship rights in China today primarily through invisible and unstructured church communities. Through the pastoral regions' culture based on "justice- and love-centered Christian ethics," churches and Christians are holding fast to their faith ideology and its application principles, not giving up meeting and worshiping together, popularizing the model of using the law to defend their rights, and influencing church and society. This model has pushed forward the development of civil society in China and facilitated the birth of a new form of church-state relations. To sum up, the model of a constitutional

citizenship society and church-state relations, an institutional cultural capital borrowed from the West, is being contextualized in China in a positive way through Christianity's "new culture movement," and it will avoid the situation that exists in the modern Western model of a civil society from which a code of ethics is absent.

Citizenship rights in modern Europe came into being and developed thanks to the 17th- and 18th- century labor movement among British industrial workers fighting for their rights as capitalism developed; this occurred mainly in Christian pastoral regions and was the product of the institutional relations model of the three major factors of "law, communities and political culture." Citizenship therefore is not a status but rather a constantly evolving instituted process (Margaret Somers, 1993).

Modern citizenship comes with three major rights (T. H. Marshall, 1964): civil rights (the right to work, legal rights, etc.), political rights (the right to vote and the right to stand for election, etc.) and social rights (the right to social welfare and the right to education, etc.). Chinese citizens are fighting for five major rights: the three just mentioned as well as birth rights and religious rights.

The development of Christianity in China, particularly that of the "invisible and unstructured church communities" that are growing and maturing non-stop, along with the Christian ethical culture of these communities and the current pseudo-constitutional legal infrastructure in China together have become the three major factors that are shaping and giving impetus to the development of Chinese citizenship rights and a constitutional citizenship society. The fight for religious rights (faith ideology rights) is being waged mainly in these two ways: refusing to give up meeting and worshipping together and using the law to defend one's rights.

Today, the rapid development and growth of China's invisible and unstructured Christian communities has already provided the needed Christian ethical component to promote the development of a civil society. So, the church legal rights defense movement, which was started to fight for citizens' religious rights, has—through invisible and unstructured church communities—along with the "pseudo-constitutional law infrastructure" and the "Christian ethics-based pastoral regions culture," pushed the substantive development of China's civil society forward. In the process, Christian ethics has bestowed upon China's Christian elite groups a brand-new perspective for understanding and exercising citizenship rights, and because of this, the elites have enough stature to criticize the state's violation of citizenship rights, thereby shaping a plain and simple pastoral regions political culture. This, however, also touches upon another theological and political philosophy issue which must be addressed, and that is, what kind of church-state relations is needed for Christianity's growth in China—that is, what kind of relationship between politics and religion (including the relationship between government and church)?

It is important to note that what this paper discusses is how China's actual situations have led to the development of a civil society. It is possible for countries with different cultural backgrounds to all develop civil societies in their own faith ideologies, though the performance of these civil societies will vary and they may even be unrecognizable. However, based on the principium that it was the environment of the West's Christian culture that gave rise to modern civil society, this borrowed social system model from which experiences can be drawn will, ideally, be contextualized in China through Christianity's new culture communities. This kind of civil society social capital remittance and positive contextualization could bring unexpected future dividends to China: the formation of harmonious church-state relations held together by Christian ethics (biblically based conservative ethics) and fixed in place by the constitution.

This model of church-state relations will correct the weaknesses of the modern Western system of constitutional citizenship and democratic society, i.e. a whole series of dilemmas resulting from the absence of ethics, because Christian ethics tell us that "...the entire law is fulfilled in keeping this one command: Love your neighbor as yourself" (Galatians 5:14). Jesus even taught, "But I tell you, love your enemies and pray for those who persecute you." (Matthew 5:44). This "citizen of the world" ethics system in which God and man (neighbor) rather than nationality, ethnicity and citizenship are the highest authorities to whom one is accountable can better resolve the dilemmas of justice, morality, citizenship rights, democracy, pluralistic faith-based civilization, nationalism, racism, ethnocentrism, world peace, ecological justice, etc. At the same time, a left wing and a right wing will still emerge within this system, i.e. a relatively conservative force and a relatively liberal force competing with and constraining one another.

Due to the indivisibility of political power and ideology, China's elites and populace will have the right in the future to choose, to adopt what they deem to be the correct faith ideology as China's founding principle. Christianity's influence on Chinese civil society and its ultimate triumph could lead Chinese society in the future to adopt Locke's contractualism, which is based on conservative Christian ethics (biblical ethics), and the constitutional government mode of American Puritanism, and in so doing, realizing the ideal of a contextualized model of civil society and merging the two to give rise to a new mode of church-state relations. This would be a limited pluralistic social structure that avoids the flaws in the present-day Western constitutional democracy system which esteems pluralism and lacks the order of a dominant faith, is based on the singular dominant order of Christian ethics as the guiding standard, esteems the rational culture of modern science, values the Western (Athenian) model of higher education, encourages secular culture and tolerates other religious faiths. This type of social structure founded in Christian ethics provides a sacred umbrella protecting the individual, and the society thus composed operates under the sacred dome of the superstructure (Peter Berger, 1967). This would be equivalent to taking another step from the historical foundation of America's traditional political culture, i.e. government and church remain separate but political philosophy and Christian ethics are integrated, thus becoming political power supported by Christian faith ideology. This characteristic feature of this kind of constitutional government culture is that the constitution has a clear and decisive place for divinity (the U.S. Declaration of Independence has only a blurry divinity and the place for divinity is therefore also blurry) and for humanity based upon the divinity. (The Ten Commandments in the Old Testament of the Bible is of revelatory and enlightening significance; please see the author's *Humanity and Divinity*.)

In short, not only can the borrowing of the Anglo-American cultural capital of the constitutional citizenship system that grew out of Christian faith and ethics, taking place upon the powerful platform of a contextualized and swiftly growing Christianity in China, resolve in both theory and practice the predicament of China's churches and Christian elites constantly having restrictions imposed upon them and being persecuted and promote the contextualization of citizenship rights and civil society in China, but it can also be a further step toward producing dividends in church-state relations: separation of church and state but the integration—through ethics—of politics and Christianity. Starting from today, this principle can be the guide for China's church and

Christians in their interactions with the government in deciding what to do and what not to do, rather than following the wrong-headed thought process of "should Christians be involved in politics?"

6. Christians faithfully fulfilling their dual mission

Neither the development of the church nor the development of social civilization can happen apart from Christians faithfully and conscientiously fulfilling their mission. Christians in China need to deliberately take on the dual mission of impacting the church and impacting society, as required by the dual identity of a Christian as a citizen of God's kingdom and citizen of society. The responsibility to impact the church involves evangelism, discipleship, church planting, developing theology, carrying out the Great Commission, and establishing mechanisms and models for Christian communities and Christian organizations. The responsibility to impact society involves politics, business, social culture, academics, education, etc.

Christians ought to be faithful servants. Below are excerpts from "Christians' Dual Identity and Dual Mission" in the author's *Christianity in China–From the Heart into Society*:

> The faith responsibilities and ethical responsibilities that the Bible teaches and explains define the Christian's ecclesiastical identity (as Christians) and social identity (as citizens). Because of the New Testament principle that responsibility determines identity, Christians ought to faithfully fulfill their dual responsibility and impact and transform the church by fulfilling their faith responsibilities and impact and transform society by fulfilling their ethical responsibilities. There are two ways to fulfill responsibility: individually and collectively.

> Christians in China ought to be God's faithful servants and use our God-given talents, remaining faithful to our dual identities as citizens of both the kingdom on earth and the

kingdom in heaven, and fulfilling the dual responsibility of faith and love (loving God and loving people) that God has entrusted to us. Through our faith and our good works, we ought to raise our responsibilities to a higher level, turning them into faith missions (church missions) and ethical missions (societal missions). This is the dual mission that Chinese Christians need to take up and to which they ought to give their utmost, so as to glorify God's holy name.

In the history of the church, church leaders and Christians have committed some serious mistakes, such as Christianity's suppression of human nature during the Middle Ages, the acceptance of slavery by many church leaders and Christians in America and Britain in the 17th to 19th centuries, the approval of many churches and Christians of Nazi Germany's massacre of the Jews in World War II, and post-World War II, the faith compromises made by the Orthodox Church in the Eastern European Communist countries and by China's "Three-Self" church system to communism's anti-Christ politics, etc. (See the author's *Beware of Patriotic Heresy in the Chinese Church.*) Still, in the midst of these historical mistakes, there were always some church leaders and Christians who stood up in opposition instead of blindly following; their secret was to hold fast to the principle of ethical responsibility of "loving your neighbor as yourself" in society.

To sum up, we can see that two reasons and approaches can explain why churches made the mistakes mentioned above and brought shame upon themselves. The first is an erroneous understanding of the relationship between church and state, which leads to arm-twisting either of the church by the government or vice versa. The second is a blurred boundary between divine faith and human culture, which leads to either faith suppressing culture or culture alienating faith. This paper makes clear that if church leaders and Christians abide by the principle of faithfully fulfilling their faith responsibilities and ethical responsibilities, not only can they achieve an organic harmony of their ecclesiastical identity as God's children and their social identity as citizens, but they can also to the greatest extent possible avoid the two types of mistakes mentioned above, the result of which is that in the midst of various political, social and cultural trends, they will not get lost, will stand firm and will glorify the holy name of Jesus Christ.

Through faith in Jesus Christ and by relying on the transforming power of the Holy Spirit, not only can change of a revolutionary nature be brought into an individual's life, but the church and Christian groups will also bring life-giving influence and transformation to society.. The result of this kind of influence and transformation is that a new social civilization will be created in China. By conscientiously living out their dual identity and [fulfilling] their dual responsibility, Christians will directly and profoundly influence the church and society, thereby bearing beautiful spiritual fruit in the church and beautiful cultural fruit in society. Without question, Christianity is and will continue to be a major force in the creation of a new Chinese civilization.

In other words, when Christians live out their dual identity by fulfilling their dual responsibility and glorify God's name, a new social civilization will be created. Not only that, Christians in China also need to actively participate in the transformation of social civilization and release the fullness of God's blessings that he bestows to all mankind through divine faith and ethics. When churches and Christians in China have succeeded in creating a brand new and beautiful civilization and a glorious society, and the whole world sees this, then the era for the Chinese church to comprehensively evangelize the rest of the world will have arrived.

To create a new Christian civilization in Chinese society, the efforts of individual Christians cannot be separated from the platform of the church, fellowship groups, the Christian community, etc. Individuals and groups should work together. The elevation of civilization in an individual Christian reaches a certain point above which further growth is difficult, this is because of the communal and social nature of civilization. So it is only be relying on Christian groups that the civilization of an individual can be further elevated. The group's opinions, views and standards can give the individual the psychological motivation to actively maintain an identity that matches the group. In other words, because this kind of identity gives rise to a mentality of being accountable to the group and because study and mutual accountability is an encouragement to the individual, the individual's self-discipline and motivation to seek life transformation is greatly enhanced. When the civilization of a group reaches a certain level, breakthroughs also become difficult. Some representative individuals in this group then need to enter a church or social group with a more advanced civilization (for example, coming to the United States) from where, through study or being influenced and nurtured, they will be able to bring back as cultural capital the essential properties, standards and models of an advanced civilization to their original group and turn them into new standards and a new direction for the civilization of their group.

Summary: Civilization's Spiritual Significance

Christianity needs to create a new civilization in China and make the leap from faith to creation. With that as the basis, it needs to further impact the course of the world's civilization just as all Christian civilizations in human history have done, bringing glory to the holy name of Jesus Christ.

The Christian faith, or the faith based on the whole Bible, is in itself a complete package of ultimate truths that elevate the civilization of mankind: with the Gospel at its core, it addresses the individual's life including the repentance and transformation of the soul, psyche and mind, civilizational institutions such as marriage, family, fellowship, church, etc., and the Christian's dual identity in the church and in society, being light and salt, and his impact on and transformation of church and society, etc. God educates mankind through revelatory truths so that mankind can keep on creating civilizations that are ever more advanced. Human civilization advances in an upward spiral, just like the process of growth of a Christian's personal life.

Be aware that only the truth-based divine faith founded on the Bible can maximally advance civilization. Not all truths can advance civilization and not all faiths have a positive effect on civilization. As "The Tablet Eulogizing the Propagation of the Illustrious Religion in China" [better known in English as the Nestorian Tablet] points out: "Now without divinity, truth cannot become expanded; without truth, divinity cannot become magnified; but with truth and divinity united as the two parts of a signet, the world becomes civilized and enlightened." What this means is that truth without divine nature has limited impact and divine nature without truth is not great; only when divine nature and truth are in harmony can there be civilization in the whole world under heaven. This is quite a profound principle about the interdependent relationships of faith, divine nature, truth and civilization.

The Christian faith cannot but have a good effect on individuals, family, church and society. This is not some kind of mechanical effect, but rather, it is like the sweet fruit from a tree growing by a stream. Such fruits are seen in the new and abundant life of the individual; in the family, in holy and romantic marriages; in churches, in the formation of a fiery divine culture; and in society, in producing a human civilization like clear waters from a spring. The key for Christianity to impact social civilization is the balance of divinity and humanity. Christians in China need to put into practice the truths of their faith, transform their psychological patterns and mode of thinking, exercise rigorous self-discipline, obey the ethics of the Bible, thereby changing the genes of traditional and modern culture. On the basis of the platforms of individuals, family and the church, we need to deliberately transform society and take up the mission of cultivating Christian civilization in the Chinese environment. Christians are to fulfill the dual mission of transforming church and society; this is a holy calling.

Furthermore, God has throughout history been ceaselessly enlightening and educating mankind through signs and wonders. But the more advanced the civilization of a Christian society, the fewer supernatural means God employs to directly intervene and connect. This is because the Christianity-driven continuous advancement of human civilization is powerful evidence of mankind using faith in God and God's truth to fight against and achieve victory over Satan's temptations and destruction; this is what God anticipated and takes joy in. Therefore, all God's signs and wonders can ultimately be regarded as designed to enhance human civilization. Looked at from this perspective, the [end times] millennium, as the end of the history of human civilization that, after the fall in the Garden of Eden, peaked as the result of a long process of divine education and human development, is reasonable and worthy of praise.

First draft completed on Friday, June 21, 2013; final draft completed on Wednesday, Sept. 11, 2013

- Zhuang Daohe, Zhejiang University

Visit ChinaAid's websites:

www.ChinaAid.org   and   www.MonitorChina.org

Conclusion of English version